**St. Louis Community
College**

**Forest Park
Florissant Valley
Meramec**

**Instructional Resources
St. Louis, Missouri**

Pasteur and
Modern Science

SCIENTIFIC REVOLUTIONARIES
A Biographical Series

Pasteur and Modern Science

René Dubos

New illustrated edition
Edited by Thomas D. Brock
Foreword by
Gerald L. Geison
Princeton University

Science Tech Publishers
Madison, WI

Springer-Verlag
Berlin Heidelberg New York
London Paris Tokyo

Library of Congress Cataloging-in-Publication Data

Dubos, René J. (René Jules), 1901-
  Pasteur and modern science / René Dubos ; foreword by Gerald L.
Geison. — New illustrated ed. / edited by Thomas D. Brock.
      p. cm. — (Scientific revolutionaries)
  Bibliography: p.
  Includes index.
  ISBN 0-910239-18-5
    1. Pasteur, Louis, 1822-1895. 2. Scientists—France—Biography.
I. Brock, Thomas D. II. Title. III. Series
Q143.P2D79 1988
509.2′4—dc19
  [B]   88-11608
                                                                   CIP

Originally published in the Science Study Series by Anchor Books,
Doubleday and Company, Garden City, New York.
Copyright © 1960 by Educational Services Incorporated.

Science Tech, Inc., 701 Ridge Street
Madison, Wisconsin 53705 U.S.A.

Sole distribution rights outside of the U.S.A., Canada, and Mexico
granted to Springer-Verlag Berlin Heidelberg New York London
Paris Tokyo.

ISBN 0-910239-18-5   Science Tech Publishers   Madison, WI
ISBN 3-540-50101-0   Springer-Verlag   Berlin Heidelberg New York

Editorial, design, and production: Thomas D. Brock
Interior art: Edward B. Phillips
Cover art: Kandis Elliot

Printed in the United States of America

10 9 8 7 6 5 4 3 2

Table of Contents

Figure List

Foreword

Almost forty years ago, in 1950, René Dubos published a superb full-scale biography of Pasteur under the title *Louis Pasteur: Free Lance of Science*. Ten years later, in 1960, Dubos distilled the essence of that larger book into *Pasteur and Modern Science*, which was originally published by the Anchor Books division of Doubleday and Company as part of its now-defunct Science Study Series. This series of textbooks and biographies, conceived in the wake of the launching of the Sputnik space satellite by the Soviet Union in 1957, was prepared under the direction of the Physical Science Study Committee of Educational Services Incorporated for an intended audience of students and their teachers.

Like other books in the series, *Pasteur and Modern Science* was out of print for several years. After Dubos's death, Doubleday and Company released the rights to his widow, who transferred them in turn to Science Tech Publishers. Their new edition differs somewhat from the original edition: more than 40 illustrations and tables have been added to Dubos's originally unillustrated book, as well as a new biographical sketch of Dubos, a glossary of technical terms, a chronological outline of Pasteur's career, and a brief list of suggestions for further reading. Finally, there is a new chapter, "Pasteur's Dilemma: The Road Not Taken" (Chapter 14), based on an article published in 1974 by Dubos, that briefly develops a theme originally introduced at the end of Chapter 13 in the 1960 edition. These changes enhance the book's accessibility, appeal, and pedagogic value, which had already won it a wide audience in its original edition.

The book's enduring appeal is a tribute both to its subject and to its author. Few scientists indeed have so captured the public imagination as Louis Pasteur, and fewer still have had such a dramatic effect on everyday life. Pasteur began his career in the relatively abstruse field of crystallography, but his close study of what he once called "the arid details of crystal form" soon led him to a major achievement of broad significance: the discovery of optical isomers—left- and right-handed crystals of the same chemical composition—in the tartrates, a group of organic compounds associated with wine making. With this discovery in 1848, Pasteur penetrated more deeply than anyone before him into the relationship between crystal form and chemical structure; at the age of 25, his great scientific career was already launched.

During the next decade Pasteur pursued his study of the relationship between optical activity and crystal form. One aspect of that research appealed to the grandiose streak in his nature. Noting the correlation between optical activity, asymmetric crystals, and life, Pasteur briefly and privately sought to produce asymmetric, optically active, "living" substances from symmetric, optically inactive, "dead" starting materials—in short, he tried to create "the immediate principles of life" artificially in the laboratory. In undertaking these bold experiments, Pasteur hoped to become the Galileo or Newton of biology. And though the experiments failed, Pasteur never entirely abandoned his belief in a "cosmic asymmetric force." Late in life, he wished he could return to those exciting days when he was trying to solve nothing less than the mystery of the relationship between asymmetry and life.

By then, however, Pasteur had long been occupied with more immediately practical matters, beginning with fermentation. The products of fermentation and putrefaction are often optically active, and Pasteur soon linked these processes with life in the form of "germs" or microscopic organisms. No one did more than he to establish the germ theory of fermentation. He especially sought to demonstrate that each decomposition process results from the biological activity of a specific microbe, so that, for example, the lactic "ferment" that produces sour milk differs from the microorganism (yeast) responsible for alcoholic fermentation. At the same time, Pasteur devoted close attention to industrial fermentations, proposing new methods for the manufacture of wine, vinegar, and eventually beer, and new techniques for preserving the desired products from spoilage or the "diseases" to which they were susceptible. These preventive measures, consisting basically of sterilization by heat and cold, were labeled "pasteurization" almost immediately. By 1900, they had been applied to a wide range of substances, including notably milk.

Pasteur's excursion into the study of fermentation brought him into two related arenas of debate: spontaneous generation and disease theory. Fermentation, putrefaction, and disease had long been seen as analogous processes, and any theory of one was likely to be extended to the others. When Pasteur arrived on the scene in 1857, the prevailing theory of fermentation was chemical, though some observers had noted the association between microorganisms and fermentation or disease. Even those who accepted this association, however, did not always agree about the nature of the relationship between microbes and these processes of decomposition. Some maintained that the microbes were actually *products* rather than *causes* of fermentation and disease—living products that had arisen not by biological reproduction from parents like themselves but by "spontaneous generation" from dead, decomposing materials. By thus raising doubts about the origin of microorganisms and trivializing their causative role, the doctrine of spontaneous generation posed a challenge to the germ theory of fermentation and disease. Despite the advice of friends and mentors to avoid the issue, which had political and religious overtones, Pasteur mounted a vigorous and largely successful campaign against the doctrine of spontaneous generation, ignoring all the while his own early efforts to create life experimentally from dead, optically inactive materials.

Pasteur was quick to note the implications for disease theory of his work on fermentation and spontaneous generation, but he was uncharacteristically cautious about moving directly into the medical domain. The first halting step, a study of silkworm diseases, came in 1865 at the urging of a French government concerned about the economic consequences of a devastating silkworm blight. Even after 1870, by which point he had solved the silkworm problem to his satisfaction, Pasteur hesitated to undertake his long-projected investigation of infectious diseases, citing the need for qualified research assistants and his own lack of medical training. Finally, in 1876, Pasteur did enter directly into veterinary and medical research, beginning with anthrax, another economically significant disease that primarily afflicted sheep.

Once Pasteur did take up the study of infectious diseases, he enjoyed swift and spectacular success. His contributions to our understanding of the etiology of anthrax were less important that those of his great German rival, Robert Koch, but Pasteur and his collaborators quickly developed vaccines against chicken cholera, anthrax itself, and swine erysipelas. In 1885, their efforts were crowned by a successful application of rabies vaccine to humans. Long a French national hero, Pasteur now became an international legend and a leading symbol of the humanitarian benefits of scientific research. The vaccine against rabies produced a flood of donations from around the world, and the resulting Institut Pasteur, inaugurated in November 1888, has loomed large ever since in the history of science and medicine.

Such a career has naturally attracted a host of biographers. Two of the earliest biographies remain two of the best. Within a year of the master's death, his collaborator Émile Duclaux published *Pasteur: Histoire d'un Esprit*, a brilliant scientific biography which, though it ostensibly ignores personal matters, also provides a revealing glimpse into Pasteur's personality and scientific *modus operandi*, including his "Olympian silence" about the direction of his research. In 1900 Pasteur's son-in-law, René Vallery-Radot, published a detailed two-volume study, *La vie de Pasteur*, which remains a standard source despite its often worshipful tone. A third crucial source from within the Pastorian circle is almost unknown: in the late 1930s, a half century after Pasteur's death, his nephew and sometime research assistant Adrien Loir published a series of anecdotal but highly illuminating essays in an obscure journal under the collective title *À l'Ombre de Pasteur* ("In the Shadow of Pasteur"). There have been several fine full-length biographies since, but the best of them is René Dubos's 1950 *Free Lance of Science*, which is in part an elegant synthesis of the works by Duclaux, Vallery-Radot, and Loir.

In Dubos, Pasteur found a modern biographer almost ideally suited to the task. A distinguished French-born microbiologist of broad culture and wide sympathies, Dubos had a deep appreciation for the power and enduring significance of Pasteur's scientific work. He was also well equipped to recognize its nuances and weaknesses. To the more personal dimensions of the biographer's task, Dubos brought his keen insight into the wellsprings of human action, behavior, and personality. He appreciated the full range of factors, motives, and fears that needed to be kept in mind, including his subject's health, which was, like Dubos's own, sometimes precarious. Dubos also displayed a lively interest in the philosophical, religious, and political dimensions of Pasteur's life and times. He had the advantage that he had grown up in French culture, but had then spent most of his adult life in the United States, at a tempering distance from the more institutionalized aspects of the Pastorian cult in France. Finally, Dubos brought to the task his hard-won gift of graceful expression, which allowed him to convey the excitement and significance of even the most technical aspects of Pasteur's work. All of these impressive qualifications did not go for naught. In very large part, Dubos succeeded admirably in the role of Pasteur's biographer.

Inevitably, Dubos emphasized parts of Pasteur's thought and work that were in keeping with his own intellectual predilections. In particular, he drew attention wherever possible to what may be called the environmental strain in Pasteur's microbiological thought. Dubos's own environmentalism can be traced to his training in agricultural economics in France and then in soil microbiology at Rutgers University in New Jersey. It found expression in his attitudes toward health and disease, and especially in his opposition to the tendency to equate disease simply with the presence of a pathogenic microorganism. Furthermore, despite his own major contributions to the development of antibiotics, Dubos predicted that drug-resistant microbial strains would evolve, and he recognized the role of individual constitution, nutrition, host resistance, and adaptation in health and disease. That position could only have been reinforced by his personal experience with tuberculosis, which took the life of his first wife in 1942 and also afflicted his second wife, Jean. Together he and Jean published in 1952 the prescient book *The White Plague: Tuberculosis, Man, and Society*, which presented some of the arguments and basic evidence for the now widely accepted view that nutrition and environmental conditions are leading determinants of health. Dubos developed this theme further in his influential *Mirage of Health* (1959) and *Man Adapting* (1965). Eventually, Dubos extended his environmentalism into a vision of the delicate interconnectedness of all living things that brought him fame as a sometimes unwitting guru of the ecology movement of the late 1960s.

Long before Dubos became famous for it, his environmentalism was evident in his treatment of Pasteur. In some elusive way, it informed his entire quest as biographer. Consider, for example, his attempt to articulate the sense in which Pasteur was both "Of His Time and Timeless" (pp. 150–151). There Dubos insists that "all scientists, like artists, naturally reflect the characteristics of the civilization and of the times in which they arise." And if the great ones, like Pasteur, do sometimes seem to escape their cultural conditions, they should not be seen as "aberrations in the natural sequence of cultural events." Rather, they constitute "peculiar mentalities through which emerge and become manifest social undercurrents that remain hidden to less perceptive minds." Some of them, including Pasteur and other popular scientific heroes, "succeed in converting their visions—which are really signs from the social and cultural subconscious—into messages and products meaningful and of immediate value to their fellow humans." By pointing to this link between peculiar individual "mentalities" and "signs from the social and cultural subconscious," Dubos extended his environmentalism into the realm of human intellect, its products, and their cultural reception.

More concretely, Dubos gave special attention to Pasteur's relatively neglected work on the silkworm diseases, *pébrine* and *flacherie*. Dubos was especially impressed that, in the case of *flacherie*, Pasteur resisted the temptation to embrace a simple microbial explanation and emphasized instead the constitutional and nutritional susceptibility of diseased worms. In the full-scale biography of 1950, Dubos wrote of Pasteur's study of silkworm diseases that he did not know a "more beautiful example of scientific investigation," and he describes it in this book (page 94) as "one of the most dramatic and spectacular feats of [Pasteur's] scientific life."

Similarly, Dubos reveled in Pasteur's experimental demonstration of how temperature could affect an organism's susceptibility to microbial disease. Pasteur induced anthrax in a hen, ordinarily resistant to the disease because of its high body temperature, simply by chilling it in an ice-water bath. For Dubos, this experiment was a spectacular vindication of the environmental approach to disease, and he did what he could to enlist Pasteur in the cause. Ultimately, however, even Dubos had to concede that he could not quite transform Pasteur into a "Dubosian" ecologist of disease. Perhaps, theoretically, Pasteur could have followed this path, as Dubos suggests. Perhaps it was in keeping with the internal logic of his research. Yet in the end, as Dubos admits in the very subtitle of the new Chapter

14 printed here, this ecological road was, for Pasteur, "the road not taken."

Apart from his environmentalism, Dubos gently intruded himself into the Pasteur story in another way. In the personal realm, too, Dubos's Pasteur is more Dubosian than he was in real life. True, they were alike in many respects. Both were French-born microbiologists, "pure" scientists, who turned to practical issues partly out of a desire to contribute to human welfare. Both had a romantic, almost poetic side to their nature. But Dubos and Pasteur were by no means identical in personality and character. In particular, the biographer was more idealistic, optimistic, and generous of spirit than his subject. Dubos managed to extend his generosity of spirit to Pasteur, even when he seemed puzzled by the latter's behavior. Dubos did not ignore, but he did tend to minimize the less appealing aspects of Pasteur's character and conduct, including his preoccupation with fame and money and his self-serving treatment of his rivals and sometimes even his collaborators. If Dubos was too shrewd to miss the clear evidence of such behavior, he was also too generous or perhaps too wise to make much of it.

There was, in fact, only one real defect in Dubos as Pasteur's biographer: his scholarship was occasionally careless, and his decision to omit footnotes makes it hard to identify the sources of his information and insights. However, much the same could be said of all the existing books on Pasteur. Today there is still no proper scholarly biography of him, but such a book will one day appear. When it does, it will benefit from the rich collection of surviving Pasteur manuscripts, the bulk of which are now available to scholars at the Bibliothèque Nationale in Paris. Research into those manuscripts, which include Pasteur's laboratory notebooks, has been underway for some time now, and some of the results are beginning to appear (see Further Reading). Yet even when all the results of this future scholarship reach the light of day, readers will still turn with profit to Dubos's biographical efforts. They will still want to read the concise and accessible introduction to Pasteur found in *Pasteur and Modern Science*. Indeed, one can say of this book somewhat the same thing that Dubos says at the book's end about the work of Pasteur: it retains its value despite inevitable defects in details and changes of perspective. In this centennial year of the Institut Pasteur in Paris, the reprinted edition is especially welcome. It should find a new and larger audience still.

Gerald L. Geison
Princeton, New Jersey

About the Author

René J. Dubos, the noted scientist and author, died in 1982 at the age of 81. Throughout his long and productive career, he wrote 33 books and over 300 laboratory research articles. Among his books are important technical works for the physician and scientist as well as numerous books for the general public. He was one of those rare individuals able to write not only for the scientist but for the student and layperson as well. He was awarded the Pulitzer Prize in 1969 for his book *So Human an Animal.*

Dr. Dubos was born in France and received his early education there. He earned his Ph.D. in 1927 from Rutgers University (New Jersey). Except for a two-year period as a professor at Harvard University, he spent all of his long and productive career at the Rockefeller Institute for Medical Research in New York City. Although his early training was in agriculture and soil microbiology, he made major contributions to antibiotics research and to the understanding of tuberculosis and other infectious diseases. He was also a pioneer in the important and burgeoning field of environmental medicine. His prominent role in studying social and environmental effects on health brought him very early into the mainstream of the environmental movement in the late 1960s. His highly publicized views that everything in life plays an interconnected part made him a dominant spokesperson for those disturbed about the effects of rapidly expanding technological civilization on human life. His eloquent skills in speaking and writing, coupled with his stature as a scientist, enabled him to bring the issues to the attention of an extensive public audience. His well-deserved fame in his final years was a result of his passionate involvement in serving as the "conscience of the environment." His human-centered views, considerate of both liberals and conservatives in the environmental movement, continue to influence public policy.

His French upbringing and his background as an agricultural and medical scholar make René Dubos an ideal person to explain Louis Pasteur and his work to a broad audience, and his skills are evident in *Pasteur and Modern Science*. In addition to this book, his other popular books include *The White Plague: Tuberculosis, Man, and Society* (with Jean Dubos), *Mirage of Health: Utopias, Progress, and Biological Change, The Dreams of Reason: Science and Utopias, Man Adapting, So Human an Animal, A God Within, The Wooing of Earth*, and *Celebrations of Life*.

René Dubos achieved worldwide fame as a microbiologist, experimental pathologist, author, lecturer, and environmentalist. Any one of these careers would have sufficed for most people, but he managed to combine them all. He was endowed with many intellectual talents, great sensitivity, originality, and rigorous self-discipline. His contagious enthusiasm for new ventures and his endless curiosity and wonder about life are especially well revealed in *Pasteur and Modern Science*, a book he originally wrote for students but which can now have a much wider audience.

Pasteur and
Modern Science

1

From Schoolboy
to Scientist

In every country, and in every civilized language, the word *pasteurization* is now part of the vocabulary, just as meaningful to the homemaker as it is to the food technologist and to the research bacteriologist. This, of course, represents only one of Louis Pasteur's titles to fame, for his name is associated with some of the largest theoretical concepts and most practical applications of modern science. Thus, biochemists still discuss the metabolic reaction known as the "Pasteur effect," and physicians know that Pasteur's experiments on vaccination constitute one of the landmarks in medical history.

Pasteur's spectacular discoveries are only one of the aspects of his life that have contributed to his immense and universal fame. Equally important is the fact that, in addition to being a great scientist, he was a crusader, concerned as passionately with the welfare of the human race as he was with the search for abstract truth—always ready to engage in public debates and, if need be, in painful struggles, until he had made the world share his convictions and act upon them. Among his

1

contemporaries there were some who contributed as much as he to scientific progress, but of him it was said, "He was the most perfect man who ever entered the kingdom of Science." To achieve mastery over nature through the use of Science became for him a holy mission—a cause to which he devoted himself with astounding success and with religious fervor. Having become a legendary character even in his own lifetime, he has remained ever since in the public mind the "White Knight of Science."

Many books have discussed the development of Pasteur's genius, the philosophical, historical, and social factors that determined the problems on which he worked and his attitude toward them, the intellectual mechanisms of his discoveries, and the emotional atmosphere enveloping them. In the present volume I shall consider some of these problems again, but from a different point of view. I shall emphasize here the relevance of Pasteur's work to certain aspects of modern science and social technology, and try to extrapolate his influence into the future. To do this, however, it will be necessary that we look into the past, for there cannot be any prospect, or even perspective, without retrospect.

Birth and Background

Louis Pasteur was born on December 27, 1822, in the small town of Dôle in the eastern part of France. His father had been a sergeant in Napoleon's armies and after returning to civilian life had opened a small tannery in his own house. The elder Pasteur was obviously a man of high ideals, concerned less with earthly riches than with the dignity of human life, and even if he could give his son little in a material way, this much at least he could pass along.

A few historical facts might help to place the year of Pasteur's birth in relation to other events in the world. In 1821, Napoleon had died in exile on the island rock of St. Helena. Between

Map of France. Those cities shown in bold-face are associated with Pasteur's life and work.

1818 and 1823 Brazil, Argentina, and Peru became independent; Mexico, Colombia, Venezuela, and Ecuador were proclaimed republics; the Monroe Doctrine was formulated; Beethoven's Ninth Symphony was composed. The new state of Liberia was founded, and Greece began to struggle for her freedom. Any historical account of the nineteenth century will mention various other political events that occurred in these five years. You will be hard put to find in the standard school histories of the last century more than one reference to science—namely, that in 1819 steam navigation began between Europe and America. Yet the same period had witnessed several extraordinary scientific events which attracted little attention at the time. In Copenhagen, Hans Christian Oersted had found that an electric current tended to twist a magnetic pole around it; and in Paris Ampère had developed further the theory of the interaction between currents and magnets, pointing out the potential use of the phenomenon for telegraphic transmission. In England the great experimenter Michael Faraday had showed that a wire carrying a current could be made to rotate around the pole of a magnet—thus making possible the electric motor.

I have mentioned all these apparently unrelated facts to bring out three points. The first is that Pasteur was born in very exciting times—fully as exciting as our own, both politically and scientifically. The second is that the most important events of the period were not those that attracted public attention. Oersted, Ampère, and Faraday certainly did not make the front page in the newspapers of their day, and few people were aware of their names or even of their existence. Yet, there is no doubt that their achievements did more to revolutionize the ways of life all over the world than did the contemporary political revolutions. Third, it is not without interest to reflect on the fact that Michael Faraday, who occupies in the physical sciences much the same place that Pasteur occupies in biochemistry, biology, and medicine, also was born in very humble circumstances. Both Pasteur and Faraday had many occasions to capitalize on their fame and to acquire wealth from the practical applications of their discoveries. Yet both resisted the temptation for the sake of higher values. It is worth noting that both of them received official recognition fairly early in life, a fact which shows that thoughtful men of the nineteenth century were already conscious of the social importance of science.

House in which Pasteur was born, in Dôle, France.

The house in Arbois where Pasteur grew up. His father's tannery was in the basement. After he had become famous, Pasteur spent his summers here. Pasteur's father died here in 1865.

A Schoolboy Shows Promise

The young Louis Pasteur lived the typical life of a French boy in humble small-town surroundings. He seems to have been a serious, well-behaved child, devoted to his family, perhaps a little pompous if we can judge from the sermonizing letters that he wrote to his sisters. There is no indication that he was an especially brilliant student in school, but certainly he was diligent, thorough in his studies, and determined to fulfill his father's ambition—or dream—that he should become some sort of a scholar. What kind of a scholar? No one around him knew exactly. It was enough for his family to imagine that Louis would be a professor of some sort, because there was great social distinction in those days in being a professor. In fact, Louis eventually reached the famous École Normale Supérieure in Paris, a school devoted to the training of college professors in literature, arts, and sciences. Although he displayed great promise as an artist, he elected to work in science.

The school records show that he did very well at the École Normale Supérieure. Let me here take a malicious pleasure in quoting what his professors had to say when he was graduated from the school. "Will make a good professor," was their official comment in the school records. Their judgment was right in the sense that Pasteur became an excellent teacher, thorough in preparation and effective in delivery. Yet it was not as a professor that he would be remembered, but as a man whose discoveries would contribute immensely to human welfare. At this point, let me quote another opinion expressed by teachers concerning a young man who also was to achieve immense fame. When Napoleon Bonaparte was graduated at the age of eighteen from the Brienne Military Academy, his teachers sent him off with the statement, "Will go far, if circumstances favor him"— a truly prophetic judgment!

Pasteur, however, would not need to be favored by circumstances. At every step in his life Pasteur chose to take his stand against the odds, often at the cost of immense struggles and sacrifices. Whatever the circumstances in which he had to work, he never submitted to them, but instead molded them to the demands of his imagination and his will.

Pasteur as Painter

Of Pasteur's school years I shall confine myself to a few aspects, selected because they reveal traits of character that contributed later to his effectiveness as a scientist. Very early in life Pasteur displayed great skill at drawing and painting. Portraits of his father and mother that he painted at the age of thirteen reveal forcefulness and mastery of style. No sign here of the free-wheeling art of modern children, but clearly a disciplined and successful effort to represent what his parents looked like physically, and what they stood for in the eyes of their fellow citizens. Until he was nineteen, he continued to draw portraits of the townspeople and of his school friends, and professional artists

A drawing made by Pasteur when he was 19 years old. This is of his school friend Charles Chappuis. Pasteur's inscription is under the drawing.

have testified to the technical excellence of these works. The Finnish artist Albert Edelfelt, who painted a famous portrait of Pasteur in his laboratory in 1887, expressed in a letter the following judgment on Pasteur as a painter: "Outside of science, painting is one of the few things that interest him. At the age of sixteen, he had intended to become a painter and amused himself making pastel drawings of his parents and of other citizens of Arbois; I have looked at these pastels very often. They are extremely good and drawn with energy, full of character, a little dry in color, but far superior to the usual work of young people who destine themselves to an artistic career. There is something of the great analyst in these portraits: they express absolute truth and uncommon willpower. I am certain that had M. Pasteur selected art instead of science, France would count today one more able painter."

Looking at Pasteur's painting, one perceives the power of observation and concentration which was such an important part of his scientific endowment, but one cannot help noticing also another fact which certainly tells something of his character and of the environment in which he lived—the dignity of the sitters, and the seriousness of their expression. Clearly the acquaintances of the Pasteur family were solid citizens and clearly also the young Pasteur regarded life as a very serious matter. There is not a single smile in the twenty-odd portraits by him that I have seen. Interestingly enough, only one of his own photographs shows a smiling face. It shows Pasteur in the company of a colleague who tried to convince him that beer should not be regarded as a problem in fermentation alone, but also as a source of good cheer.

There is still another point of interest about Pasteur as a portrait painter. He intended at one time to become a professional artist, but at the age of nineteen he stopped painting abruptly and forever, obviously having decided that nothing should compete with his scientific work. And, in fact, nothing ever did. Except for summer vacations that he always spent at his family home in the country, he never took time off from

Pasteur at the time he was a student at the École Normale Supérieure in Paris.

work, cultivating no hobby and having no known vice or even a weakness. He was probably the most dedicated servant that science ever had.

The Urge for Perfection

Admission to the École Normale Supérieure in Paris was by competitive examination, and in 1842, at the age of 20, Pasteur was declared admissible, sixteenth in rank. For anyone else this would have been a very satisfactory result, but not for him. In a gesture which is probably unique, or in any case extremely rare, he refused admission to the school and took up his studies again to prepare himself better. He competed again in 1843, was fifth in rank, and this time entered the school. The urge for perfection revealed by this detail was to remain one of the dominant traits of his scientific career.

At the École Normale, Pasteur specialized in the section of physics and chemistry, and it is in this field that he won his first laurels. This fact is worth noting because his early specialization did not deter him from moving shortly after into purely biological fields. What Pasteur gained in school was a strong theoretical background and, more importantly, an exacting intellectual discipline. On this broad and solid basis he built the structure that led him step by step from theoretical studies on the properties of crystals, through prophetic discoveries on respiration and fermentation, to the most practical problems of vaccination and public health. In the course of the following pages, I shall attempt to show how this theoretical knowledge and intellectual discipline were illustrated in Pasteur's scientific life. As you will see, he never shied away from the problems that chance, and the times, placed across his way—however remote they were from his past experience. Although trained as a chemist, he was willing to venture into purely biological fields because of his profound confidence that the experimental method, of which he was a master, was applicable to all types of inquiry, and that the specialized knowledge required for each particular question could be acquired by diligent effort.

As an introduction to the review of Pasteur's scientific achievements, let me quote from a famous speech that he delivered late in life—in 1882—on the occasion of his being received as a member of the august French Academy of Letters. Appearing before literary people, philosophers, and historians, he expressed with his usual forcefulness the reasons that made him a devotee of science. He pointed out that while the experimental method may never be able to solve completely the riddle of the universe, it can always answer an unambiguous yes or no to well-defined questions asked in unambiguous terms. Facing the skeptical philosopher Ernest Renan, who was receiving him at the Académie Francaise, he spoke of

> this marvelous experimental method, of which one can say, in truth, not that it is sufficient for every purpose, but that it rarely leads astray, and then only those who do not use it well. It eliminates certain facts, brings forth others, interrogates nature, compels it to reply and stops only when the mind is fully satisfied. The charm of our studies, the enchantment of science, is that, everywhere and always, we can give the justification of our principles and the proof of our discoveries.

2

A Student of Crystals

In 1847 Pasteur buckled down to research work for his doctor's degree at the École Normale Supérieure. He was then twenty-four and letters of the time to his boyhood friend Charles Chappuis leave no doubt that, even so early in his career, there was deep in his heart the secret desire to accomplish some great feat. The problem that was then in his mind, as we shall see later, was the very origin of life on earth. In point of fact, however, the selection of his research project was not determined by some genial inspiration, or even by a philosophical preoccupation with some deep problem. As is the case with most graduate students, his project certainly arose from discussions that went on at the École Normale among his schoolmates under the influence of teachers whom they respected. Problems of *crystallography* were then scientifically fashionable, and Pasteur showed no originality in electing to work on them for his doctor's thesis. But his originality began to become manifest as he went deeper into this field. His career illustrates well that what an individual achieves in life depends less upon the circumstances in which he has to function than upon what he brings to bear upon them. Napoleon meant something of this sort when he wrote in his diary, "No situation is good or bad in itself, everything depends upon what one makes out of it."

A Crystallographic Problem

In the science department at the École Normale, there was much interest in the problems of crystallography, and Gabriel Delafosse, one of his most respected teachers, had made significant observations revealing the existence in quartz crystals

Jean-Baptiste Biot (1774–1862), famous French chemist who had done pioneering work on the optical activity of substances and who strongly promoted Pasteur's career.

of right- and left-handed facets. It was also known at the time that quartz in the crystalline state can rotate the plane of polarized light. Jean Baptiste Biot, a celebrated French chemist who was to become one of Pasteur's scientific protectors, had shown furthermore that certain organic substances like sugar or tartaric acid can also rotate the plane of light but, in contrast to quartz, exhibit optical activity even in solution. All these facts were much discussed at the École Normale and it was under this influence that Pasteur began to work on the optical activity of crystals. He selected *tartaric acid* and *tartrates* as the object of his studies because a great deal was known about these substances, and also because they readily gave beautiful crystalline forms.

At precisely that time Jean Baptiste Biot presented before the Academy of Sciences in Paris a note in which the German chemist Eilhardt Mitscherlich described a very odd fact concerning the optical activity of tartrates. Mitscherlich pointed out that among the usual large crystals of tartaric acid always present in the "tartar" formed during the fermentation of wine, there were found occasionally smaller crystals, needlelike tufts,

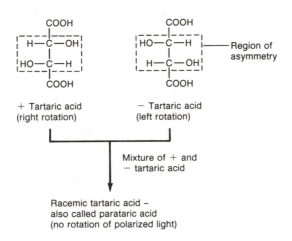

Chemical structures of the two forms of tartaric acid.

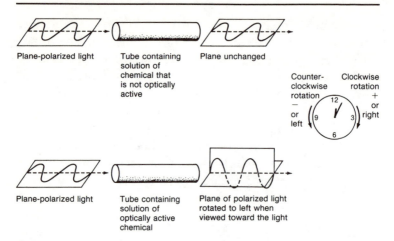

Plane-polarized light

Tube containing solution of chemical that is not optically active

Plane unchanged

Counter-clockwise rotation − or left

Clockwise rotation + or right

Plane-polarized light

Tube containing solution of optically active chemical

Plane of polarized light rotated to left when viewed toward the light

Substances which are optically active rotate polarized light. The instrument used to measure optical rotation is called a *polarimeter*.

which proved to be another form of tartaric acid. The latter form was called "paratartaric acid" or also "racemic" acid to recall its origin from the grape (*racemus* is the Latin for *grape*). According to Mitscherlich, these two forms of tartaric acids and their respective salts, the tartrates and paratartrates, had "the same chemical composition, the same crystal shape with the same angles, the same specific gravity, the same double refraction, and therefore the same angles between their optical axes. Their aqueous solutions have the same refraction. But the solution of the tartrate rotates the plane of polarization, while the paratratrate is inactive."

Pasteur immediately saw an incompatibility here. Could the two forms of tartaric acid behave differently toward polarized light and still, according to Mitscherlich's claim, be identical in every other particular? He was convinced that there *had* to be some chemical difference between the two substances, and he hoped that this difference would express itself in the shape of the crystals. It was the recognition of this incompatibility that provided him with the first well-defined problem on which to test his skill as an experimenter. By seizing on the occasion, he demonstrated one of the most fundamental characteristics of the gifted experimenter: the ability to recognize an important problem, and to formulate it in terms amenable to experimentation.

A Great Discovery

Immediately and without help, Pasteur prepared and crystallized nineteen different salts of tartrates and paratartrates, and examined the crystals with great care under the microscope. With much satisfaction he found that they all exhibited small facets similar to those seen in quartz crystals—a fact which had escaped the attention of other observers. Then he detected that these facets did not all have the same orientation in the different crystals. More precisely, the facets in each of the tartrate salts exhibited the same orientation, whereas in each of the paratartrates, some were oriented in one direction, and some in the opposite direction. But at this point it seems best to let Pasteur describe in his own words how he made the discovery that launched him on a scientific career.

> The fortunate idea came to me to orient my crystals with reference to a plane perpendicular to the observer, and then I noticed that the confused mass of crystals of paratartrate could be divided into two groups according to the orientation of their facets of asymmetry. In one group, the facet of asymmetry nearer my body was inclined to my right with reference to the plane of orientation which I just mentioned, whereas the facet of asymmetry was inclined to my left in the other. The paratartrate appeared as a mixture of two kinds of crystals, some asymmetric to the right, some asymmetric to the left.
>
> A new and obvious idea soon occurred to me. These crystals asymmetric to the right, which I could separate manually from the others, exhibited an absolute identity of shape with those of the classical right tartrate. Pursuing my preconceived idea, in the logic of its deductions, I separated these right crystals from the crystallized paratartrate; I made the lead salt and isolated

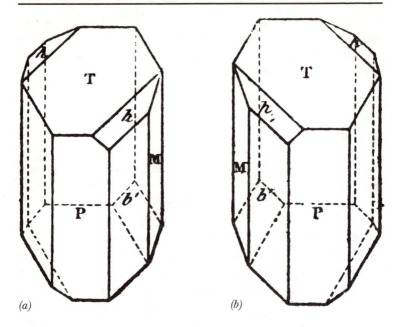

(a)   *(b)*

Pasteur's drawings of tartaric acid crystals, used to illustrate his famous paper on optical activity. (a) Left-handed crystal. (b) Right-handed crystal. Note that the two crystals are mirror images.

the acid; this acid appeared absolutely identical with the tartaric acid of grape, identical also in its action on polarized light. My happiness was even greater the day when, separating now from the paratartrate the crystals with asymmetry at their left, and making their acid, I obtained a tartaric absolutely similar to the tartaric acid of grape, but with an opposite asymmetry, and also with an opposite action on light. Its shape was identical to that of the mirror image of the right tartaric acid and, other things being equal, it rotated light to the left as much in absolute amount as the other acid did it to the right.

Finally, when I mixed solutions containing equal weights of these two acids, the mixture gave rise to a crystalline mass of paratartaric acid identical with the known paratartaric acid.

It is easy to recapture the dramatic quality of the situation and the intense excitement it must have caused in the young investigator. Pasteur was so overcome with emotion that he rushed from the laboratory, and, meeting one of the chemistry assistants in the hall, embraced him, exclaiming, "I have just made a great discovery . . . I am so happy that I am shaking all over and am unable to set my eyes again to the polarimeter!" To appreciate the magnitude of the achievement, it must be remembered that Pasteur was then barely twenty-five years old and had been working in a laboratory for only two years. Let us keep in mind also that this laboratory was very small and very primitive according to modern standards. Not only did Pasteur have to prepare all the chemicals that he used, he even had to build with his own hands the polarimeter as well as the device for measuring angles which he used in his measurements. He had no assistance, only the encouragement of his teachers and school friends, and faith in the value of his studies.

The Confirmation: A New Field of Science

The news of Pasteur's discovery soon spread through the Paris scientific circles and eventually reached Jean Baptiste Biot—the very man who three years before had presented to the Academy of Sciences the Mitscherlich paper which had perplexed Pasteur and had served as a springboard for his studies. Biot was so much interested in the new discovery that he was willing to present Pasteur's work to the scientific public, but before he did, he wanted to subject the findings to a stringent verification. Here again, let us read Pasteur's own account of his dealings with Biot.

> He [M. Biot] sent for me to repeat before his eyes the several experiments and gave me a sample of racemic acid which he had himself previously examined and found to be quite inactive toward polarized light. I prepared from it, in his presence, the sodium ammonium double salt, for which he also desired himself to provide the soda and ammonia. The solution was set aside for slow evaporation in one of the rooms of his own laboratory, and when thirty to forty grams of crystals had separated, he again

summoned me to the College de France [where Biot had his office] so that I might collect the dextro and levorotatory crystals [i.e., the crystals deviating the plane of polarized light to the right or to the left] before his eyes, and separate them according to their crystallographic character—asking me to repeat the statement that the crystals which I should place on his right hand would cause deviation to the right, and the others to the left. This done, he said that he himself would do the rest. He prepared the carefully weighed solutions, and at the moment when he was about to examine them in the polarimeter, he again called me into his laboratory. He first put into the apparatus the more interesting solution, the one which was to cause rotation to the left. At the first sight of the color tints presented by the two halves of the field in the "Soleil" polarimeter, and without having to make a reading, Biot recognized that there was a strong left-handed rotation. Then the illustrious old man, who was visibly moved, seized me by the hand, and said, "My dear son, I have loved science so deeply that this stirs my heart."

Thus, at one stroke Pasteur had established himself as a masterful experimenter and created a new field of science—namely the relation of optical activity to molecular and crystalline structure. For three years he continued in this field and made concrete and lasting contributions to the chemical aspects of crystallography.

3

Pasteur's First Steps Toward Biology

On the completion of his postgraduate work, Pasteur left the École Normale, and in 1848 he was appointed professor of chemistry at the University of Strasbourg. There he was introduced into the family of one of the university officials, and within a few weeks after having met the young daughter of the family, Marie Laurent, he asked her hand in marriage. Thus, he took this most important step of his personal life with the same impetuosity that manifested itself so often in his scientific career. His work was apparently somewhat disturbed during the few months of his courtship, at least if we believe the letters that he wrote to his fiancée.

> I have not cried so much since the death of my dear mother. I woke up suddenly with the thought that you did not love me and immediately started to cry. . . . My work no longer means anything to me. I, who so much loved my crystals, I who always used to wish in the evening that the night be shorter to come back the sooner to my studies.

(a)

(a) Louis Pasteur in 1852, when he was professor at the University of Strasbourg. (b) Pasteur's wife, Marie Laurent, a few years after their marriage.

(b)

Madame Pasteur: Companion and Collaborator

But the disturbance was only of short duration, and it is not apparent that it ever interfered seriously with Pasteur's scientific work. Soon after his marriage, in May 1849, the stream of discoveries began to flow again, as swiftly as before. I shall not speak again of Madame Pasteur, and yet her participation in Pasteur's achievements was much greater than these few lines would suggest. It is the unanimous opinion of all who knew her that she was not only a devoted wife, but also provided an ideal atmosphere for Pasteur's studious life. Jolly yet modest, she helped him through the many tragedies and struggles of his life, especially after the paralysis which struck him in 1868. She accepted in good spirit his odd mannerisms and the material limitations of their existence. She consecrated herself to his dreams, molding her behavior to fit the goal that he formulated. In other words, she identified her life completely with his work. She could write to her children in 1884: "Your father is absorbed in his thoughts, talks little, sleeps little, rises at dawn, and in one word continues the life I began with him this day thirty-five years ago."

Her intelligent devotion is perhaps best evoked by the words pronounced at the time of her death by Émile Roux, who had been Pasteur's associate for twenty years and had known the couple intimately:

> From the first days of their common life, Madame Pasteur understood what kind of man she had married; she did everything to protect him from the difficulties of life, taking onto herself the worries of the home, that he might retain the full freedom of his mind for his investigations. Madame Pasteur loved her husband to the extent of understanding his studies. During the evenings, she wrote under his dictation, calling for explanations, for she took a genuine interest in crystalline structure or in attenuated viruses. She had become aware that ideas become the clearer for being explained to others, and that nothing is more conducive to devising new experiments than describing the ones which have just been completed. Madame Pasteur was more than

an incomparable companion for her husband, she was his best collaborator.

Separating Crystals with Fungi

Pasteur's marriage was not the only romantic aspect of his life in Strasbourg. Another very different one reveals the complexity of his scientific personality—the constant interplay in his mind between rigorous, logical thinking and highly imaginative dreams about the mysteries of life. Throughout his scientific career, he engaged in thoughts of cosmic grandeur that went far beyond practical realities. But these romantic imaginings were always derived from factual observations, and often they led him to entirely new lines of investigation. It is to this aspect of his genius that we shall now turn.

As will be recalled, Pasteur's first fractionation of racemic acid of tartaric acid into its two isomeric components was the painstaking process of separating the crystals under the microscope according to the orientation of their facets. In subsequent years much less laborious methods of separation were worked out in his laboratory, but only one will be mentioned here, a very original method of chemical fractionation based on a biological phenomenon. This method was discovered in 1857, the result of one of those accidents or "chance" occurrences that are meaningless to ordinary persons and are seized upon only by trained observers whose minds are receptive to the clues offered by nature. "In experimental science," Pasteur was wont to say, "chance favors only the prepared mind."

The fact that certain fungi grow readily in solutions of calcium paratartrate during warm weather had been frequently observed, and it occurred in Pasteur's laboratory as it did in other places. The common reaction was, of course, to throw the solution down the sink because it was moldy. In contrast, Pasteur asked himself whether the two isomeric components of the solution, the half which rotated light to the left and the half which rotated it to the right, would be differently affected by the mold.

To answer this question, he investigated the optical activity of a solution of paratartrate in which a fungus had grown, and found, to his great excitement, that the solution became more active optically with time. He proved that only one of the components (the right rotating) was consumed, whereas the other component was spared. As a result, the latter component persisted alone in the solution and thus caused it to become optically active. This observation led to an entirely novel and convenient method for the separation of the two isomeric forms by means of the mold, but more importantly it led Pasteur's mind into new channels that were to take him, and science, into completely uncharted territory.

The Asymmetry of the Universe

It was already known that many organic substances, that is, substances produced by living things, are optically active. They have the ability to rotate the plane of polarized light in one direction or the other. In contrast, Pasteur was aware of the fact that if the same substances were synthesized in the laboratory, they were optically inactive. Now it appeared from the experience with paratartaric acid that at least one living thing, a fungus, exhibited a striking selectivity with regard to its action on one of the two isomeric components. Putting all these facts together and extrapolating from them, Pasteur soon formed the view that only living agents could produce optically active asymmetric compounds and that an intensive study of molecular asymmetry would eventually throw light on the origin of life. In his words, "This important criterion [molecular asymmetry] constitutes perhaps the only sharply defined difference which can be drawn at the present time between the chemistry of dead and of living matter." And to his friend Chappuis he confided in 1851, "I am on the verge of mysteries, and the veil which covers them is getting thinner and thinner. The night seems to me too long." These "mysteries" had to do with nothing less than the creation of life! He postulated that the peculiar selectivity of living processes for one or the other of isomeric forms of the same molecule might be the manifestation of asymmetric forces of the environment acting upon the living organism during the synthesis of protoplasmic constituents. In his words:

> Life, as manifested to us, is a function of the asymmetry of the universe and of the consequences of this fact. The universe is asymmetrical; for, if the whole of the bodies which compose the solar system moving with their individual movements were placed before a glass, the image in the glass could not be superposed upon the reality. Even the movement of solar light is asymmetrical. . . . Terrestrial magnetism, the opposition which exists between the north and south poles in a magnet and between positive and negative electricity, are but resultants of asymmetrical actions and movements. . . .
>
> Life is dominated by asymmetrical actions. I can even imagine that all living species are primordially, in their structure, in their external forms, functions of cosmic asymmetry.

Pasteur was bold enough to attempt some experimentation in this highly speculative domain, hoping to duplicate in the laboratory the asymmetrical effects which he assumed to preside over the synthesis of organic materials in nature. He used powerful magnets in order to introduce asymmetrical influences during the formation of crystals. He also devised a clockwork arrangement with which he intended to reverse the natural movement of the solar rays striking a plant, from its birth to its death. He was thus trying to find out whether in such an artificial world—where the sun rose, so to speak, in the west and set in the east—the optically active substances would not appear in forms opposite to those occurring in the normal order of nature! He eventually abandoned these fantastic experiments without having obtained any results, but never gave up completely his alchemist's dream of unraveling the chemical riddle of life.

Asymmetry and the Development of Biochemistry

I shall not deal further with these experiments, but I cannot refrain from mentioning that even today the fact that asymmetric molecules are always the products of living processes remains as much of a mystery as ever. Ever since Pasteur, it has been universally accepted that many organic molecules exist in two forms, the structure of one being related to that of the other as the right hand is related to the left, so that each is identical with the mirror image of other other. Both forms may occur in living organisms, but as a rule each species uses or synthesizes only one. Such asymmetric syntheses are hard to manage in the laboratory. Pasteur's preoccupation with this problem has acquired some new significance, since the chemical reactions involved in the origin of life have been widely studied over the past few decades (partly because of interest in space exploration). It has often been said that no other chemical characteristic is as distinctive of living organisms as is optical activity. It might be mentioned also that the discovery in physics of the nonconservation of parity in certain interactions of "fundamental particles" has led to a general acceptance of the notion that the structure of the universe is asymmetrical. This is what Pasteur had prophesied in 1874 before the French Academy of Sciences:

> The universe is an asymmetric system. I am convinced that life as we know it has arisen out of asymmetrical processes in the universe. *The universe is asymmetric.*

While Pasteur's studies on the biological significance of optical activity did not explain the origin of life, they have yielded a number of facts which have had far-reaching influence on the development of biochemistry. Pasteur himself recognized that the differences in structural configuration between the isomeric forms of tartaric acids, as well as of other organic compounds, are reflected in the differential behavior of these isomeric substances toward living agents, for example, in their effect on taste buds and in their susceptibility to attack by microorganisms. These observations have served as a springboard for a whole range of investigations on the chemical basis of biological specificity, a problem which is such a characteristic feature of modern biochemistry.

Although we cannot develop here the implications of the fact that biological activity is dependent on molecular structure, we must deal further with the very direct and profound influence that this phenomenon had on Pasteur's scientific life. It was from his conviction that asymmetric molecules are always the product of life that he was led to the study of fermentation, to the recognition that microorganisms play an essential role in the economy of nature, and eventually to his epoch-making discoveries in the field of infectious diseases.

4

From Crystals to Fermentation

In Strasbourg recognition for his studies in crystallography had come to Pasteur in the form of honors and prizes. Although he used the money thus earned to buy laboratory equipment—at the sacrifice of many urgent needs at home—his working facilities were still extremely limited. For this reason, he accepted the offer that was made to him in 1854 at the age of 32 to take the chair of chemistry and to become dean of sciences in the newly organized University of Lille, in the north of France (see map). It was understood that he should focus his teaching and other activities on the industrial interests of the Lille region. The surviving notes for his lectures in chemistry show that he took this recommendation to heart. The requirement that he teach the industrial applications of chemistry led him to develop a philosophy of science that guided him for the rest of his life.

Heretofore Pasteur had been a purely theoretical scientist, unconcerned with practical matters, but now he had to take an active interest in local industries. This appeared to create a conflict of interest between his former life and his new position, for then, as now, there were many who believed that the state of mind required for the successful prosecution of pure science was almost incompatible with the attitude imposed by applied science. But this was not Pasteur's opinion. Immediately he formulated the view, and taught it with passion to his students, that in fact there was no incompatibility. In his words, "There are not two different kinds of science; there is science and there are the applications of science." The two types constantly interplay, and one type cannot progress far without contact with the other. Nor were these idle words, for within one year after his arrival in Lille he had begun to concern himself with the practical problems of alcoholic *fermentation,* which was one of the chief industries of the region. From his investigations he derived clues for his theoretical problems, and soon was able to apply his new knowledge to the improvement of factory practices. As we shall see later, he retained the same philosophy throughout his life, whether he dealt with the manufacture of beer, the preservation of wine, the diseases of silkworms, or the problems of vaccination.

Living "Ferments"

Shortly after his arrival in Lille, Pasteur was approached by an industrialist named Bigo, who was engaged in the production of alcohol (ethyl alcohol, also called *ethanol*) by the fermentation of beet juice. Monsieur Bigo complained that in many cases, and for unknown reasons, the alcohol became contaminated with undesirable substances in the course of fermentation. Pasteur was totally unfamiliar with the problem of alcoholic fermentation, but nevertheless agreed to look into it. He visited the factory at frequent intervals, observed everything he could, and took samples of the fermenting juice back to his laboratory. Among other tests he put the fermenting juice under the microscope and made careful descriptions and drawings of all that he could see. He noticed in particular, as others had before him, the presence of small globules of yeast in the fermenting juice, but he saw in addition other smaller structures that did not look like yeast. He also examined the juice in his polarimeter and found that it was optically active, capable of rotating the plane of polarized light. One of the optically active components that he could isolate from the fermented beet juice was *amyl alcohol*. This immediately brought back to his mind one of his earlier interests, his belief that only living things could produce optically active organic compounds. And it was this thought that became the link between his past scientific life in chemistry and his subsequent work in biology. Shortly after finding optically active amyl alcohol in the fermenting juice, he became convinced that, contrary to general belief, the processes involved in fermentation were not merely chemical in character, but came from the activity of living things: of living "ferments" as he called them, of microbes or microorganisms as we now say.

The Nature of Fermentation

At this point, we must stop for a moment to consider what was then regarded as the scientific theory of fermentation, the point of view taught in all standard textbooks of the day. It was known that yeast always accompanied alcoholic fermentation, and several naturalists had recognized under the microscope that yeast had a definite globular shape. But according to the accepted view, yeast was nothing but a complex chemical substance, acting as catalyst in the conversion of sugar into alcohol. With less precision, but much in the same spirit, it was also known that other chemical changes in organic matter—for example, the conversion of sugar into *lactic acid*, or of alcohol into *acetic acid* (vinegar)—were likewise accompanied by the presence of complex materials, which also were assumed to act as catalysts, purely by chemical contact. This point of view was taught in all textbooks, under the sanction of the most eminent chemists of the day, particularly of the Swedish chemist Jöns Jakob Berzelius and the German chemist Justus von Liebig.

The new and very revolutionary suggestion that Pasteur made was that the yeast found during alcoholic fermentation, and the organic material associated with the production of lactic acid and acetic acid, were not lifeless catalysts but in reality were living things. He contended that the organic materials served as food for these living things and that the products accumulating in their presence were the results of their metabolic pro-

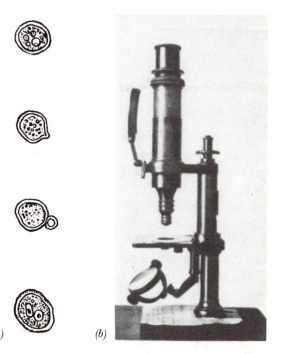

(a)   (b)

Pasteur's microscopic study of yeast convinced him that the alcoholic fermentation was a biological process. (a) Pasteur's drawings of yeast cells, illustrating the budding process. Observations of budding convinced Pasteur that yeast was alive. (b) The simple kind of microscope used by Pasteur during his studies on the alcoholic fermentation.

cesses. Thus, many phenomena that heretofore had been considered purely chemical were in his view biological in origin. Let me emphasize that Pasteur's views were at first little more than hunches of the kind that are formulated with much emphasis in heated discussions. If Pasteur had done nothing more than formulate ideas, suggested to him by the fact that optically active substances denote the presence of a living agent, his name would now be forgotten as are the names of so many other young persons who have had bright ideas but have done nothing to convert them into realities. Fortunately, Pasteur was disciplined enough to use his hunch as a working hypothesis, as a basis on which to build a solidly documented experimental structure.

Sour Milk: The Beginning of Scientific Microbiology

Here I shall not try to describe or even list the large numbers of experiments that Pasteur devised and carried out, to prove that in his words "fermentation is a phenomenon correlative of life." Rather I shall select one instance because in his view—and rightfully, I believe—it dealt with a situation crucial to the whole argument. This particular case is that of the conversion of sugar into lactic acid. This conversion occurs frequently in nature, for example, in the souring of milk, which most commonly results from the transformation of milk sugar into lactic acid. From the biochemical point of view, nothing could be simpler than this change, since it corresponds to the breakdown of one molecule of glucose into two molecules of lactic acid.

Because of its apparently simple chemical character, Pasteur selected this reaction as a test to demonstrate the role of living things in chemical changes. This move illustrates, I believe, the extraordinary sense of scientific showmanship that he displayed so often in life. What Pasteur showed in this first study—as he did even more convincingly with other more complex fermentations—was that the lactic-acid ferment consists of an immense number of microscopic organized bodies, which all resemble one another. Moreover, he demonstrated that these formed bodies could be made to increase in number if he supplied them with the proper kind of food. Once grown in the pure state and in sufficient amount, the lactic ferment could be transferred to a new sugar solution, and then it accomplished with extraordinary speed the transformation of the sugar into lactic acid.

By applying the same experimental approach to other types of fermentation, Pasteur showed furthermore that the acidity, neutrality, or alkalinity of the fermenting solutions had very profound effects on the activity of the various kinds of ferments. Thus, yeast produces alcohol most rapidly in an acid solution, whereas the lactic-acid ferment is most active at neutrality. He even recognized—for the first time—the activity of certain antiseptics. Onion juice, he found, inhibited the action of yeast, but not of the lactic-acid ferment. The ideas of a specific ferment associated with each fermentation, of disproportion between the weight of the ferment produced and the weight of matter transformed, of vital competition between two organisms simultaneously invading the same medium, resulting in the dominance of the one better adapted to the culture conditions—all these ideas, which the future was to prove valid and develop into a body of science and technology, are forcefully set forth in a short paper that he published in 1857 under the title, *Mémoire sur la fermentation appelee lactique* (Report on the lactic acid fermentation). This paper can truly be regarded as the beginning of scientific microbiology, indeed as one of the most important landmarks of biochemical and biological sciences. Its fundamental spirit can be summarized in Pasteur's own words: "The purity of a ferment, its homogeneity, its free unrestrained development from foodstuffs well adapted to its individual nature, these are some of the conditions which are essential for good fermentation."

Over One Hundred Years Later

In the light of these concepts, which appear so obvious now, but were so revolutionary over 100 years ago, it became possible to explain the defects in the industrial production of alcohol which had first brought Pasteur in direct contact with the problems of fermentation. The small globules of yeast, always associated with alcoholic fermentation, were not just bits of inanimate material catalyzing the conversion of sugar into alcohol. Yeast was a microscopic plant, with a life of its own, and alcohol was the product of its living processes. The other smaller bodies that Pasteur had detected in the defective fermentations were also living organisms. They differed from yeast not only in size and shape, but also in chemical activity, and therefore in the nature of their products. They were the cause of the defects in alcoholic fermentation, and the solution to Monsieur Bigo's difficulties was therefore to eliminate these other microscopic living agents, or to prevent them from gaining a foothold in the fermenting fluid. There were many practical details to be solved before these theoretical considerations could be made the basis of industrial processes. But at least the problem had been clearly stated, and we shall see in the following chapter how practical applications rapidly followed from these beautifully simple concepts.

As already mentioned, the ideas that Pasteur derived from the study of lactic and alcoholic fermentation constitute the fundamental basis of microbiological sciences, and it is truly remarkable that the *Report on the lactic-acid fermentation*, in which these ideas first appeared, was published hardly more than two years after he had begun to work on the problems of fermentation! In this preliminary paper he even suggested, though without evidence, that the same principles might contribute to the understanding of infectious diseases! In view of the historical importance of this short paper, it is not unusual that the hundredth anniversary of its publication should have been celebrated, in 1957, as marking the beginning of a new era for science and technology. During the celebration many speakers from all over the world emphasized that much of our present knowledge of biochemistry has evolved from the point of view first enunciated by Pasteur with regard to lactic acid and alcoholic fermentation; others showed how this knowledge constitutes the basis of many important biological industries—in particular those concerned with the production of organic substances by microorganisms; still others focused attention upon the medical consequences of the event, the germ theory of disease, and the production of drugs (antibiotics) to combat infection. We shall have occasion to come back to some of these modern developments.

5

A Crowded Life

In 1857 Pasteur was appointed assistant director in charge of scientific studies and of general administration at the school from which he graduated, the École Normale Supérieure in Paris. In addition to organization of the curriculum, his administrative duties included the supervision of housing, board, medical care, and general discipline of the students, as well as the relations between the school and parents and other educational establishments. As shown by his reports, he did not take these new responsibilities lightly. He administered the problems of household management with as much thoroughness and vigor as he devoted to the reorganization of advanced studies. Moreover, Pasteur, who was now widely known in academic circles, soon became involved in larger problems of national interest. His prestige, and his combative nature, progressively led him into controversies which often went beyond scientific subjects. Yet despite all these intereferences, his laboratory work in Paris became even more intense and more productive than it had been in Strasbourg and in Lille.

Working Conditions in Paris

Before proceeding to a description of his discoveries during that period, a few words must be said concerning the conditions under which he worked in Paris. His title of director of scientific studies at the École Normale might give the impression that he had at his disposal large and well-equipped laboratories, with many assistants and generous budgets, but in fact he had limited facilities. During the early years after his return to Paris he worked alone and had to make many of his instruments.

He found in the attic of the school two very small unused rooms, and he converted them into a laboratory which he equipped with funds from the family budget. The studies on alcoholic fermentation begun in Lille were completed in these miserable quarters. Eventually he obtained from the authorities an assistant whose time was to be given entirely to investigative work—an arrangement hitherto unheard of in France. He was, furthermore, allowed to move his laboratory into a primitive "pavilion," consisting of five small rooms on two floors, which had been built for the school architect and his clerks. Crowded for space, and pinched for funds, he improvised under the stairway an incubator for temperature control of his cultures. The only way he could enter it was by crawling on hands and knees, yet it was in this cramped room that Pasteur spent long hours daily observing the countless flasks which he used in his studies on "spontaneous generation" (see Chapter 6). After a few years, the small laboratory was enlarged by additional construction, and from these few rooms—so modest by modern standards—came the studies which made Pasteur's name famous in many fields of learning. He could carry out his research work only because he was willing to put into practice Benjamin Franklin's admonition that a good workman should know how to saw with a file and to file with a saw. For those who believe that science can prosper only through the lavish working facilities provided in the modern research institutions, there is a lesson in the fact that the earliest of the great research institutes, the

Pasteur Institute in Paris, did not open its doors until 1888, when Pasteur's own working days were almost over!

A Single Gigantic Problem

Pasteur's return to Paris marked the beginning of an era of incredible activity. From 1857 until 1888 his notebooks and publications reveal a multitude of projects—including theoretical studies, practical applications, and passionate debates—all carried out more or less simultaneously. All his activities were so intermingled that it would be impossible to continue their account along chronological lines. For the sake of convenience, we shall therefore postpone until the end of this book most of the facts concerning Pasteur's activities as a philosopher of science, a citizen, and a controversionalist. His investigative work can conveniently be divided into two periods separated by the year 1877. From that year on, he devoted most of his energy to the study of animal and human diseases. The scientific activities of the period 1857–77 can be considered under several separate scientific headings, but it must be emphasized again that these headings are arbitrary and justified only by reasons of convenience in presentation. In reality, the subjects that will be discussed in the following pages do not constitute unrelated topics, but rather the multiple facets of a single gigantic problem that Pasteur studied with passion and almost without interruption for a period of twenty years. This study dealt with the problem of spontaneous generation.

6

Spontaneous Generation

Let us start with a problem that was not the first Pasteur undertook after his return to Paris, but certainly was in his mind
from the beginning of his studies with microorganisms. If, as
he believed, the souring of milk, the alcoholic fermentation of
sugar beet juice, the conversion of grape juice into wine, the
conversion of wine into vinegar, the putrefaction of meat, and
so many other dramatic changes in organic matter, were really
caused by microbial action, where did the microorganisms responsible for these changes originate? Were they generated anew
in milk, sugar beet juice, grape juice, wine, meat, etc., or did
they already exist somewhere ready to start their activities as
soon as conditions proved favorable for them? This question
was not original with Pasteur; it had been debated by philosophers and experimenters for more than twenty centuries. But
it was a very exciting question, raising as it did the problem of
the origin of life. Those who believed that microorganisms could
arise without parents, in fermenting or putrefying materials,
did in fact accept that life was continually being created anew

from inanimate matter. This belief came to be known as the doctrine of *spontaneous generation*. In contrast, many scientists and philosophers denied this possibility and asserted that every living thing arises from living things with similar characteristics. The faith of those who denied that spontaneous generation ever occurred was summarized in Rudolf Virchow's Latin dictum: "*Omnis cellula e cellula*" (only from cells arise cells).

We shall not review here all the facts and reasons, or rather pseudo facts and pseudo reasons, which had accumulated on both sides of the spontaneous generation debate over the preceding centuries. Let it merely be mentioned that before Pasteur entered the arena, the attitude of reasonable, unprejudiced persons was uncertain, or evenly divided between the two parties. After Pasteur had done his work, there was no longer any reason to believe that spontaneous generation ever occurs—under ordinary conditions at least. This clarification of the age-old controversy is the best possible evidence not only of Pasteur's skill as an experimenter and as a theoretical scientist, but also of the uniqueness of his contributions to this field.

There is no way at the present time of judging whether Pasteur undertook this problem with any prejudiced view. Time and time again, he asserted that he was ready to believe in spontaneous generation if it could be shown to occur, and indeed he did try many different ways to provide conditions under which it had a chance to occur. But all was in vain. Never did any growth of any sort develop when all precautions had been taken to keep out the microorganisms that he assumed to be in the surrounding air or on nearby objects. But the precautions that had to be taken were infinite, and earlier investigators who thought they had observed spontaneous generation had not been aware of these difficulties. This was where Pasteur revealed in the most spectacular manner his resourcefulness as an experimenter.

Grapes With and Without Yeasts

It would take a long volume to describe the many different kinds of experiments that he performed while dealing with the problem of spontaneous generation. A spectacular one was to remove with a fine needle the juice from grapes with undamaged skin, and to show that if this was done with all precautions necessary to avoid contact with air or objects, the juice did not ferment until yeast had been added to it. This experiment he repeated late in 1878 in a modified and much extended form to counteract new claims by the famous French scientist Claude Bernard, who suggested that the spontaneous generation of yeast was possible after all. In addition to its scientific interest, this episode has the merit of illustrating Pasteur's working methods, his ardor in returning to already conquered positions when they were threatened, and the suddenness with which he took decisions when he judged that an important issue was at stake. "Without too much care for expense," he wrote, "I ordered in all haste several greenhouses with the intention of transporting them to the Jura Mountains, where I possess a vineyard some dozens of square meters in size. There was not a moment to lose. And this is why."

> I have shown . . . that the germs of yeast are not yet present on the grape . . . at the end of July. . . . By taking this moment to cover some vine with greenhouses almost hermetically closed, I could have, in October at grape harvest time, vines bearing ripe grapes without any yeasts on the surface. These grapes, being crushed with the precautions necessary to exclude yeast from the air, should not be able to ferment or to make wine.
>
> The fourth of August, 1987, my greenhouses were finished and ready to be installed. . . . During and after their installation, I searched with care to see if yeasts were really absent from the clusters. . . . The result was what I expected . . . the vines covered by the greenhouses bore no trace of yeast. . . .
>
> Toward the tenth of October, the grapes in the greenhouses were ripe; one could clearly distinguish the seeds through their

skin and they were as sweet in taste as the majority of the grapes grown outside. . . .

On the tenth of October, I made my first experiment on the grapes of the uncovered clusters. . . . The result, I may say, surpassed my expectation. . . . Today, after a multitude of trials, I am just where I started, that is to say, it has been impossible for me to obtain one *single time* the alcoholic yeast fermentation from clusters protected with cotton.

A comparative experiment naturally suggested itself. . . . It was to be expected that if I exposed greenhouse clusters in the open . . . they would now ferment under the influence of the yeasts which they could not fail to receive in their new location. This was precisely the result that I obtained.

The Swan-neck Flask

Among the many other types of experiments that Pasteur designed to rule out spontaneous generation, one is worth some emphasis by virtue of its very simplicity and decisiveness and because it finally silenced his opponents and settled the issue—at least for the time being. A fermentable fluid was put into a flask, the long neck of which was then heated and drawn into the form of an S tube (hence the name "swan-neck flask"). When the liquid was boiled, the vapor forced the air out through the orifice of the neck. As the fluid became cool again, the air slowly returned to the flask, but was washed in the moisture that condensed in the curves of the neck after heating was interrupted. Under these conditions, any dust or particle carried by the air was trapped in the neck, and the fluid in the flask remained clear, sterile. However, when the neck of the flask was broken, and the unwashed air allowed to come into contact with the fluid, then microscopic life immediately began to develop.

Despite the spectacular success of these experiments, there were still unforeseen difficulties to overcome. They arose from the fact, then unknown but now well understood, that certain species of bacteria form *heat-resistant spores*. In some of the early experiments these spores persisted in the fluid that was pre-

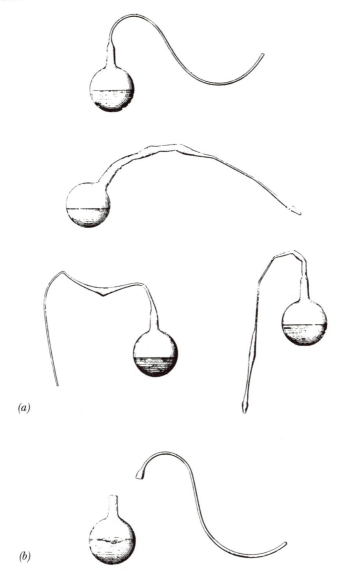

(a)

(b)

Pasteur's own drawings of the swan-necked flasks he used in his experiments on spontaneous generation. (a) Various shapes of flasks. (b) Flask with neck removed, exposing the liquid to contamination from the air.

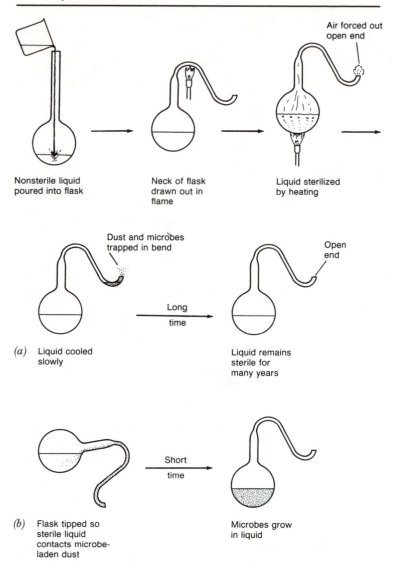

Air forced out
open end

Nonsterile liquid
poured into flask

Neck of flask
drawn out in
flame

Liquid sterilized
by heating

Dust and microbes
trapped in bend

Open
end

Long
time

(a) Liquid cooled
slowly

Liquid remains
sterile for
many years

Short
time

(b) Flask tipped so
sterile liquid
contacts microbe-
laden dust

Microbes grow
in liquid

Pasteur's experiment with the swan-necked flask. (a) If the flask remains upright, no microbial growth occurs. (b) If microorganisms trapped in the neck reach the sterile liquid, they grow rapidly. These experiments show that microbial growth occurs only if preexisting organisms reach the liquid.

sumed to have been sterilized by heating, and when they germinated, they gave rise to bacterial growth even though access to outside air had been prevented. These difficulties arising from the presence of heat-resistant spores were eventually overcome, and Pasteur was able to prepare his swan-neck flasks in such a manner that the broth remained sterile in them all. Some of these flasks prepared over 100 years ago can still be seen today at the Pasteur Institute in Paris, the fluid as limpid as the day it was sterilized.

Pasteur was careful to emphasize over and over again that his experiments did not deal with the problem of the origin of life, but merely with the fact that microorganisms do not generate from nonliving materials in sterile broth or in other organic materials. Nevertheless, for years studies of spontaneous generation were carried out in an atmosphere of intense excitement and of passionate controversy because it was erroneously thought by some of the participants that the problem involved religious issues—a view which Pasteur denied strenuously. One of the high points of this debate was a lecture that Pasteur delivered in 1864 at one of the "scientific evenings" of the Sorbonne University in Paris. Before a brilliant public, which included celebrities in addition to professors and students, Pasteur outlined the historical background of the controversy, the technical aspects of his experiments, their significance, and their limitations. Presenting to his audience the swan-neck flasks in which heated infusions had remained sterile in contact with natural air, he formulated his conclusion in these words of singular beauty:

> And, therefore, gentlemen, I could point to that liquid and say to you, I have taken my drop of water from the immensity of creation, and I have taken it full of the elements appropriated to the development of microscopic organisms. And I wait, I watch, I question it!—begging it to recommence for me the beautiful spectacle of the first creation. But it is dumb, dumb since these experiments were begun several years ago; it is dumb because I have kept it from the only thing the human mind does

not know how to produce: from the germs which float in the air, from Life, for Life is a germ and a germ is Life. Never will the doctrine of spontaneous generation recover from the mortal blow of this simple experiment.

The Germ Theory

The doctrine of spontaneous generation has not recovered yet; it may never. Today, after more than a century, the fluids in these very same flasks stand unaltered, witness to the fact that organic matter can be protected from the destructive action of living forces, but that the secret of organizing matter into Life has not yet been learned.

However, it must be emphasized that what had been settled by Pasteur was not a theory of the origin of life. Nothing had been learned of the conditions under which Life had first appeared, and no one knows even today whether it is still emerging anew from inanimate matter. The fact that had been established was that microbial life would not appear in an organic medium that had been adequately sterilized, and subsequently protected from outside contamination. *The germ theory is not a philosophical theory of life, but merely a body of factual observations from a series of practical operations. It teaches that fermentation, decomposition, putrefaction are caused by living microorganisms, ubiquitous in nature; that these microorganisms are not begotten by the decomposing or fermenting fluid, but come into it from the outside; that sterile liquid exposed to sterile air will remain sterile forever.*

It was this concept that Pasteur expounded in his Sorbonne lecture before an amphitheater overflowing with a fashionable audience that had come expecting to hear a statement concerning the origin, nature, and meaning of life. But wisely he refrained from philosophizing. He did not deny that spontaneous generation was a possibility; he merely affirmed that it had never been shown to occur. The words he pronounced on that occasion constitute the permanent rock on which were built whole sections of biological sciences:

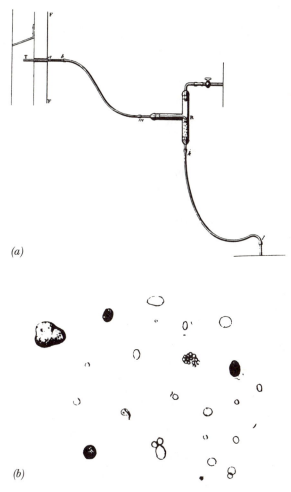

(a)

(b)

One of the crucial studies that Pasteur made showed that microorganisms were present in ordinary air. (a) Pasteur's method for studying the microbial content of air. The tube T, in the outside air, passes through a hole in the window of the laboratory (F-F) to a filter (A-B) containing guncotton. The apparatus R is connected to a vacuum source. A known volume of air is pulled through the filter. After the gun cotton is dissolved in alcohol, the entrapped particles are examined under the microscope. (b) One of Pasteur's drawings of the structures he observed. The structures were stained with iodine so that they were more visible in the microscope.

There is no known circumstance in which it has been shown that microscopic beings come into the world without germs, without parents similar to themselves. Those who affirm it have been duped by illusions, by ill-conducted experiments, by errors that they either did not perceive, or did not know how to avoid.

Interestingly enough, there is at the present time a renewal of interest in the origin of life, being stimulated by the activities in the exploration of outer space. On the one hand, many efforts are being made to imagine types of chemical reactions that would be self-reproducing and thus exhibit one of the most distinctive properties of life. On the other hand, the discovery that genes and viruses are amenable to chemical analysis has led us close to a detailed understanding of the chemical structures characteristic of living processes. Only time will tell to what extent these efforts really bear on the perennial problem of the origin of life, a problem which constitutes one of the common grounds of science and philosophy. But what is certain is that none of the present developments conflicts in any way with the conclusions of Pasteur's work on spontaneous generation. It can be said, in fact, that no constructive thinking on the problem of the origin of life was possible until the ghost of spontaneous generation had been slain. Science may eventually show that there is something fundamentally true in the ancient notion that life may have arisen from a kind of primeval ooze. But it is certain that microbes do not arise casually from nonliving materials such as fermenting fluids and putrefying meat, and in this limited sense Pasteur was absolutely right. Never will the doctrine of spontaneous generation recover from the mortal blow of his beautiful experiments!

The New Science of Bacteriology

In addition to settling the controversy on spontaneous generation, Pasteur's efforts served to establish the new science of bacteriology on a solid technical basis. Exacting procedures had

Equipment used in Pasteur's laboratory for aseptic manipulation of microorganisms. Left, autoclave with pressure gauge, for heating materials to temperatures above the boiling point; center, incubator, for culturing at temperatures above room temperature; right, steamer. Note also the culture flasks in the incubator and in the foreground.

to be devised to prevent the introduction of germs from the outside into the system under study, and also to destroy germs already present in it. Because of this necessity, the fundamental techniques of *aseptic manipulation* and of *sterilization* were worked out between 1860 and 1880. Incidental to the controversy also, there were discovered many facts concerning the distribution of microorganisms in our surroundings, in air and in water. It was also found that the blood and urine of normal animals and of humans are free of microbes and can be preserved without exhibiting putrefying changes if collected with suitable aseptic precautions. All these observations constitute the concrete basis on which was eventually erected our understanding of the natural history of microbial life. Moreover, as we shall see, Pasteur derived from his studies of spontaneous generation the germ theory of disease and many of the laws of how diseases spread. The controversy on spontaneous generation was the exacting school at which bacteriology became aware of its problems and learned its methodology.

51

7

Pasteurization

The demonstration that microbes do not generate spontaneously encouraged the development of techniques to destroy them and to prevent or minimize subsequent contamination. Immediately these advances brought about profound technological changes in the preparation and preservation of food products and subsequently in other industrial processes as well.

Pasteur's awareness of the fact that microorganisms can interfere with biological processes arose from his early experiences with alcoholic fermentation in Lille. He had then noticed that typical yeast globules were the only structures seen under the microscope when the fermentation was healthy, whereas smaller microscopic forms became prevalent when fermentation was defective. While on vacation in his country home at Arbois, in September 1858, he had occasion to submit some spoiled wines to microscopic examination and saw in them microorganisms similar in shape to the lactic-acid bacteria which he had just discovered. This observation, and his experience in the Lille distillery, probably led him to conclude that the "dis-

(a)

(b)

(a) In this house in Arbois Pasteur set up a temporary laboratory for studies on diseases of wine. (b) Laboratory in Arbois where Pasteur worked in the summers.

eases" of fermentations were caused by microorganisms which competed with yeast in the fermenting fluid. His studies of vinegar production provided further evidence for this view.

Wine, Vinegar, and Beer

Souring is one of the most common types of deterioration affecting wine; and Pasteur soon discovered that this change resulted from the oxidation of alcohol to acetic acid by a process similar to or identical with that carried out by the bacteria that carry out the transformation of wine into vinegar. In addition to souring, there are many other types of alterations that unfavorably affect the quality of wines; the Bordeaux wines "turn," the Burgundy wines become "bitter," the Champagnes become "ropy." Fortunately, Pasteur was well placed to test by experimentation his general thesis that these "diseases" also came from contamination by foreign organisms, for some of his childhood friends owned well-stocked wine cellars at Arbois. There, in an improvised laboratory, he examined systematically under the microscope all the healthy and diseased wines that were submitted to him. From the very beginning success rewarded his efforts, for whenever a sample had been found defective in some respect, he discovered, mingled with the yeast cells, other distinct microscopic forms. So skillful did he become in the detection of these various germs that he soon was able to predict the particular flavor of a wine from an examination of the sediment. In "healthy" wines the foreign bodies were absent and yeast cells alone were to be seen. More or less simultaneously, he made similar observations with regard to vinegar manufacture, finding that here again defects in the quality of the product could be related to the presence of microorganisms other than the organism called *Mycoderma aceti* that was the active vinegar microbe.

Like wine and vinegar, beer was often found to undergo

spontaneous alterations, to become acid, and even putrid, especially in the summer. Pasteur demonstrated that these alterations were always caused by microscopic organisms, and he described his findings in a book published in 1877 under the title *Studies on beer, its diseases, and their causes.* He had taken up the study of brewing techniques after the Franco-Prussian War of 1870–71, in a pathetic attempt to enhance French prestige by improving the quality of French beer and thus surpassing Germany in one of her most famous products. These studies, carried out in Pasteur's own laboratory converted for a while into a pilot brewery, and also at the Whitbread brewery in London, led to the conclusion that, as in wine, the defects that occur "in the wort, and in the beer itself, are due to the presence of microscopic organisms of a nature totally different from those belonging to the yeast proper."

> As all the disease germs of wort and beer are destroyed in the copper vessels in which the wort is heated, and as the introduction of pure yeast from a pure beer cannot introduce in the latter any ferment of a detrimental nature, it follows that it ought to be possible to prepare beers incapable of developing any mischievous foreign ferments whatever. This can be done provided that the wort coming from the copper vessels is protected from ordinary air . . . and fermented with pure yeast, and that the beer is placed in vessels carefully freed from ferments at the end of fermentation.

It was soon discovered that the introduction of microorganisms in biological products can be minimized by an intelligent and rigorous control of the technological operations, but cannot be prevented entirely. The problem therefore was to inhibit the further development of these organisms after they had been introduced into the product. To this end, Pasteur first tried to add a variety of *antiseptics*, but the results were mediocre and, after much hesitation, he considered the possibility of using heat as a sterilizing agent.

Partial Sterilization or "Pasteurization"

His first studies of heat as a preserving agent were carried out with wine. As will be recalled, he had grown up in one of the best wine districts in France, and, as a connoisseur of the beverage, he was much disturbed at the thought that heating might alter its flavor and bouquet. He therefore proceeded with very great caution and eventually convinced himself that heating at 55°C would not alter appreciably the bouquet of wine if the

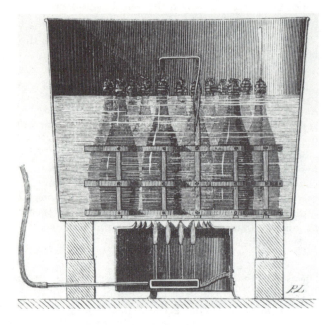

Pasteur's procedure for heating small numbers of bottles of wine. The bottles, held in a rack, were submerged in water in a metal container so that just the tops of the bottles were out of water. A gas fire was used to heat the water bath. During heating, the wine in the bottles expanded and tended to push out the stopper, but the stoppers were held with string or wire. A small amount of wine oozed out harmlessly from around the stopper. After cooling, the volume decreased in the bottle, creating a slight vacuum. The stopper was then hammered down firmly and the bottle placed in the wine cellar for storage.

treatment was applied only after the oxygen originally present in the bottle had become exhausted. These considerations led to the process of *partial sterilization*, which soon became known the world over under the name of *"pasteurization,"* and which was found applicable to wine, beer, cider, vinegar, milk, and countless other perishable beverages, foods, and organic products.

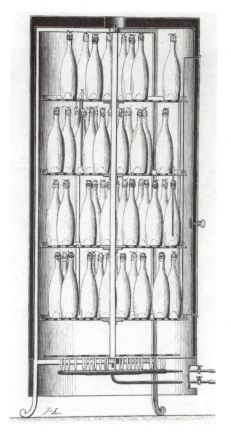

One of Pasteur's designs for a larger chamber that could be used to heat up to 200 bottles of wine. Hot air rather than hot water is used. The gas burner at the bottom heats a metal plate. Pasteur recognized that in this apparatus it was difficult to get every bottle to the same temperature.

It was characteristic of Pasteur that he did not remain satisfied with formulating the theoretical basis of heat sterilization, but took an active interest in designing industrial equipment adapted to the heating of fluids in large volumes and at low cost. His treatises on vinegar, wine, and beer are illustrated with drawings and photographs of this type of equipment, and describe in detail the operations involved in the process. The

Procedure for heating small barrels of wine, of 30 liter volume. A metal container served as a water bath, with sufficient water added so that the wine barrel was covered just up to the bung (which was inserted loosely). The water was heated with gas up to a temperature of 70 to 80°C. It took 5–6 hours of heating for the wine in the barrel to reach a temperature of 60°C. As the wine expanded during heating a small amount seeped out through the bung; but only a small amount of wine was lost. After the barrel cooled, the bung was pounded down tightly and the barrel taken to the wine cellar for storage. Pasteur tested this method by leaving barrels of wine that had been heated outside on a terrace for many months. The wine retained its flavor and odor and remained perfectly clear.

word "pasteurization" is, indeed, a symbol of his scientific life; it recalls the part he played in establishing the theoretical basis of the germ theory, and the phenomenal effort that he devoted to making it useful to his fellow humans. It reminds us also of his well-known statement: "There are no such things as pure and applied science—there are only science, and the applications of science."

Pasteur's suggestion for a device that could be used to heat wine in barrels in a large-scale installation. Pictured is a metal coil which could be inserted directly into the wine barrel through the bung. The apparatus was sealed loosely in the barrel by the cork stopper (*a b*). Steam passing through the coil heated the wine to the desired temperature. After the heating was complete, the coil was removed and a bung added. Pasteur suggested that such coils should be made of silver-plated copper. In a large installation, the steam could be passed from one coil to another in series.

While it is of no scientific interest, it might be worth mentioning an incident that bears on a point of ethics of increasing relevance to the behavior of university scientists in modern industrial societies. Pasteur was not a wealthy man, and there is no doubt that his family responsibilities often weighed on his mind. After he had developed techniques for the preservation of vinegar, wine, and beer with the use of heat, he took patents to protect the rights to his discovery. That there were discussions within his family concerning the possible financial exploitation of these patents is revealed in one of his letters: "My wife . . . who worries concerning the future of our children, gives me good reasons for overcoming my scruples." Nevertheless, he decided to release his patents to the public, and he did not derive financial profit even from the development or sale of large-scale industrial equipment devised for pasteurization.

For American readers, it will be of interest to learn that pasteurization of wine was immediately adopted in the United States, even in far-away and as yet undeveloped California. Pasteur took great pride in this recognition of his work so far away from France, and he stated in one of his articles: "It is inspiring to hear from the citizen of a country where the grapevine did not exist twenty years ago, that, to credit a French discovery, he has experimented at one stroke on 100,000 liters of wine. These men go forward with giant steps, while we timidly place one foot in front of the other."

New Understanding of Ancient Practices

Pasteurization was not, of course, the first practical technique devised for the preservation of foodstuffs. In fact, many other techniques had been developed empirically in the past throughout the world, and are still being used today. Thus, sun-drying, or *desiccation*, has been a practice from time immemorial for the preservation of strips of meat and of some fruit in subtropical countries. The smoke used in curing meat possesses antiseptic properties which prevent or at least retard putrefaction, and to a certain extent this is probably true of some of the spices commonly added to foodstuffs. The high concentration of salt in brine also acts as *inhibitor* of bacterial growth as does the acetic acid of vinegar in pickled products and the lactic acid in sauerkraut. Until Pasteur's time, the most effective method of food preservation had been the controlled heating introduced by Nicholas Appert around 1810, a forerunner of the practices used at the present time in the canning industry.

Nicholas Appert (1752–1841), the father of canning. In 1810, Appert first published a book describing his method for preserving foods by heating. Appert's method involved heating at a high temperature so that the food was sterilized. Pasteur later developed the method of heating at a lower temperature (partial sterilization) that came to be known as *pasteurization*. As Pasteur wrote: "When I published the results of my first experiments on the preservation of wine by heat, I was merely presenting a new application of Appert's method, but I was completely ignorant of the fact that Appert had thought of this same procedure long before me."

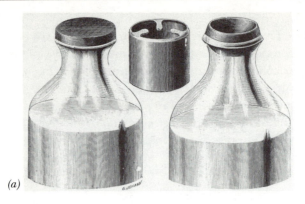

(a)

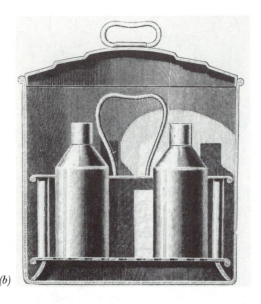

(b)

Pasteurization of milk. Pasteur's method of partial sterilization by heat was gradually applied to milk. Initially there was strong resistance to pasteurization of milk because the flavor and color of this liquid is altered easily by heat. Eventually, appropriate methods were developed, and experience showed the public health significance, especially for infants and young children. The first person to pasteurize milk was the German chemist F. Soxhlet, who published his work in 1886. (a) Soxhlet's special bottle for milk pasteurization. (b) Soxhlet's home milk pasteurization apparatus.

It is of interest to note in passing that, at the time of the controversies on spontaneous generation, soups, meats, vegetables, and fruit had been canned on an extensive scale for fifty years by Appert's method, so that it may seem that Pasteur was demonstrating the obvious. But there is always a lag in many scientists' apprehension of the implications of the practical man's work. One could say facetiously that Pasteur had to demonstrate to scientists what the homemaker already knew.

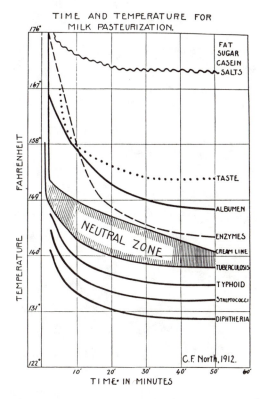

TIME AND TEMPERATURE FOR MILK PASTEURIZATION.

Early scientific studies on the pasteurization process established the proper time and temperature that provides the best microbial control with the least disturbance of the milk. The neutral zone shows the time and temperature at which milk may be pasteurized with the least disturbance.

(a)

(b)

(a) The American philanthropist Nathan Straus was a strong promoter of milk pasteurization. Here is a photograph of the pasteurizing oven used in his New York dairy. (b) Van used by the Nathan Straus dairy to distribute pasteurized milk quickly throughout New York City. (c) Nathan Straus' first public milk station, on the pier at East Third Street, in lower New York City, 1893.

(c)

All the examples mentioned show how much had been discovered by trial and error long before the days of experimental science. What Pasteur brought to the problem was the concept that most food spoilage is caused by microorganisms of various kinds, and he thus provided a new understanding that gave increased significance to the ancient empirical techniques. Scientific knowledge permitted rapid improvements with entirely new techniques.

Although not much more than one century has elapsed since Pasteur introduced the scientific approach to the preservation of foodstuffs, more progress has been made in that relatively short time than had been accomplished through millennia of trial and error! Such is the superiority of experimental science over empiricism! There is no doubt, moreover, that further progress is in the offing. Heating (pasteurization) is only one of the techniques that can destroy or inhibit microorganisms. It is quite satisfactory for the preservation of milk, beverages, and for the canning of certain other foodstuffs, but it has limitations with regard to more delicate products. Foodstuffs can also be preserved by radiation, and even though its use in foodstuffs has not yet been generally sanctioned, it is possible that radiation eventually will find a place in food sterilization and other technological procedures. Progress is now rapid, because it is no longer empirical. Ever since Pasteur, the problems of food spoilage have been well defined. Much is known about the microorganisms that have to be dealt with in each particular situation, and it is therefore possible to plan technological procedures in such a way that they achieve the desired end with the least amount of alteration in the food product.

8

Utilizing Microbes

Pasteurization with its subsequent developments was only one of the many technological applications that followed from Pasteur's discoveries. Other and even more important practical consequences grew out of his demonstration that microorganisms of all sorts play a dominant role in the changes that organic matter endlessly undergoes in nature. In 1867, in a letter written to an important French public official, he outlined his views regarding the power of microbial life:

> We know that the substances extracted from plants ferment when they are abandoned to themselves, and disappear little by little in contact with the air. We know that the cadavers of animals undergo putrefaction and that soon only their skeletons remain. This destruction of dead organic matter is one of the necessities of the perpetuation of life.
>
> If the remnants of dead plants and animals were not destroyed, the surface of the earth would soon be encumbered with organic matter, and life would become impossible because the cycle of transformation . . . could no longer be closed.

It is necessary that the fibrin of our muscles, the albumin of our blood, the gelatin of our bones, the urea of our urine, the ligneous matter of plants, and sugar of their fruits, the starch of their seeds ... be progressively converted into water, ammonia and carbon dioxide so that the elementary principles of these complex organic substances be taken up again by plants, elaborated anew, to serve as food for new living beings similar to those that gave birth to them, and so on *ad infinitum* to the end of the centuries.

The Indispensable Links

Without denying that ordinary chemical forces can slowly attack organic matter, Pasteur thus affirmed his belief that *decomposition is chiefly caused by microorganisms*. And indeed, it is now realized that substances of animal or plant origin undergo sooner or later a chain of chemical alterations which break them down, step by step, into simpler and simpler compounds, and that in this fashion the chemical elements are returned to nature after death for the support of new life. "All are of the dust, and all turn to dust again." It was one of Pasteur's greatest achievements to show that all the structures and products of plants, animals, and other forms of life eventually become food for countless types of microorganisms, which in an orderly progressive manner make use of them for building their own bodies and which in their turn die to make these materials available for other forms of life. *Microorganisms constitute, therefore, indispensable links in the eternal chain that binds life to inanimate matter.*

Pasteur foresaw, and it is now known as a fact, that soil harbors huge numbers of microorganisms of all sorts which endlessly transform organic matter, while others play a similar role with regard to the nitrogen of the air and the minerals of the rocks. The immense amounts of refuse that find their way into sewage are broken down by microorganisms and thus can be more readily utilized, or disposed of. There is no end to the list that could be made of the activities of microorganisms in the economy of nature—whether they be the rusting of iron pipes, the genesis of petroleum, or the decomposition of leaves on the forest floor. Truly as Pasteur was wont to say,

> The role of the infinitely small in nature is infinitely great.

The Benefits of Precise Knowledge

Since for almost every type of substance there exists in nature some microorganisms peculiarly adapted to its destruction or modification, it follows that humans should be able to take advantage of this diversity and versatility of the microbial world for useful purposes. In fact, from time immemorial and all over the world, microorganisms have been used empirically in many varied technological processes. We have mentioned several times in preceding pages the production of wine, of beer, of vinegar, and of sour milk, but these fermentations constitute only a few examples among the ancient processes in which microbes take a part—all the way from cheese making to the retting of flax, from the preparation of cocoa beans to the ripening of clay. Here again, Pasteur's contribution was to show how procedures devised in the past by trial and error could be improved through precise knowledge of the microbes and of their chemical activities. Although he applied this understanding chiefly to the production of wine, vinegar, and beer, he saw much further than these limited applications would indicate. Realizing that microorganisms can be adapted to the performance of almost any kind of biochemical reaction, he was bold enough to state: "A day will come, I am convinced, when microorganisms will be utilized in certain industrial operations on account of their ability to transform organic matter." This prophecy has been fulfilled, and today we are in the era of *biotechnology* when organic acids, various solvents, vitamins, drugs, and enzymes are produced on an enormous scale by microbial processes—all this a logical development of Pasteur's work.

For example, the commercial production with microorganisms of *lactic acid* and of *citric acid* began around the turn of the century. *Butanol and acetone*, as well as *glycerol*, were produced on a large scale by fermentation during the First World War. The first commercial production of *gluconic acid* and of *riboflavin* dates from 1938, and by now other vitamins are also produced totally or partially by microbial fermentation. One of the most dramatic is the industrial production of antibacterial drugs by microorganisms—*penicillin* being the first and most famous of the *antibiotics*. But these are not the only drugs of microbial origin; *ergot*, for example, is a product of the fungus *Claviceps purpurea*, which has great importance in medical practice. Among other chemicals of industrial importance produced by various types of microorganisms, one should also mention many types of *enzymes*—diastases, proteases, pectases—which are used widely in food products and in a great variety of industrial processes.

Amino acids constitute an important group of microbial products related to nutrition, which looms very large in importance. Plant proteins from seeds and tubers are often deficient in the amino acids methionine, lysine, tryptophan, threonine, and proline, and for this reason have a low nutritional value. A cheap source of amino acids would therefore be of enormous importance for supplementing animal feeds, and also for improving human nutrition, especially in the underprivileged parts of the world. Several essential amino acids are now produced commercially by fermentation. In theory, it should be possible, by the judicious selection of microbial strains, to produce almost any amino acid with the help of microorganisms. In practice, of course, many difficulties arise. Nevertheless, processes for microbial production of *glutamic acid* (used as a flavor enhancer), *lysine*, *tryptophan*, and *phenylalanine* (used in the production of the artificial sweetener *aspartame*) are in place.

As a last example of biotechnology, I shall mention the large-scale production of yeast cells, a subject very closely related to

Pasteur's legacy: Major corporations with microbiological and biotechnological interests.

Company	Sales, billions $$	Areas of major interest
Exxon	88	Oil, chemicals
Mobil	55	Oil
duPont	35	Chemicals
Std. Oil Indiana	28	Oil, chemicals
Shell	19.7	Oil, chemicals
Phillips Petroleum	15.2	Oil, chemicals
Proctor and Gamble	12.4	Consumer products, food
Dow Chemical	11	Chemicals, agriculture
Allied Corp.	10.3	Conglomerate
Beatrice Foods	9.0	Foods, consumer products
General Foods	8.0	Foods
PepsiCo	7.8	Beverages
3-M	7.0	Chemicals, minerals
Coca-Cola	6.9	Beverages
Consolidated Foods	6.5	Foods
Monsanto	6.3	Chemicals, agriculture
W.R. Grace	6.2	Fertilizers, chemicals, agriculture
Anheuser-Busch	6.0	Brewing
Nabisco Brands	5.9	Foods
Johnson and Johnson	5.9	Health care
General Mills	5.5	Foods
Ralston Purina	4.9	Foods
Colgate-Palmolive	4.9	Consumer products
Archer-Daniels-Midland	4.3	Chemicals, high-fructose syrup
Borden	4.3	Foods
CPC International	4.0	Chemicals, food
Bristol-Myers	3.9	Pharmaceuticals
Pfizer	3.7	Pharmaceuticals, chemicals
H.J. Heinz	3.7	Foods
Pillsbury	3.7	Foods
American Cyanamid	3.5	Pharmaceuticals, chemicals
United Brands	3.5	Foods
Owens-Illinois	3.4	Chemicals
Carnation	3.3	Foods
Campbell Soup	3.3	Foods
Merck	3.2	Pharmaceuticals
SmithKline Beckman	3.1	Pharmaceuticals
Warner-Lambert	3.1	Pharmaceuticals
Eli Lilly	3.0	Pharmaceuticals
Abbott Laboratories	2.9	Pharmaceuticals
National Distillers	2.3	Alcoholic beverages
Upjohn	1.9	Pharmaceuticals
Rohm and Haas	1.9	Chemicals, agriculture
Baxter Travenol	1.8	Pharmaceuticals
Schering-Pough	1.8	Pharmaceuticals
Squibb	1.8	Pharmaceuticals

Pasteur's early scientific interests. In addition to its practical importance, this industry provides a wonderful illustration of the influence that theoretical studies exert on technological processes. Pasteur had shown that when yeast is grown in the absence of oxygen, there results a wasteful utilization of sugar with accumulation of alcohol. This is, of course, a desirable result in the production of wine, beer, and in other fermentations in which alcohol is the desired product. But the yield of yeast cells is very small during alcoholic fermentation in the absence of oxygen. In contrast, hardly any alcohol is produced from sugar when oxygen is readily available, and the yield of yeast cells is then very large. For this reason, the yeast grower always provides intense aeration of the culture medium whenever the aim is to produce yeast cells to be used in the baking industry, in the home, or as a source of food.

Thus, Pasteur demonstrated that with the proper knowledge one could control the biochemical activities of microorganisms, and make them produce almost any type of chemical compound, the most complicated as well as the simplest. Thousands of years ago, we learned to domesticate certain plants and animals, and have continued to use these on farms or in homes in much the same way as did our ancestors. It can be said that the domestication of microbial life entered the scientific era with Pasteur, and that, thanks to him, microbial industries reached within two generations a very high level of diversification and of efficiency.

9

Biochemistry and Life

We must now go back to the year 1857 and watch in more detail Pasteur's early struggles with the problems of alcoholic and lactic-acid fermentation. The first task he assumed after returning to the École Normale was to prove beyond doubt that yeast and the lactic-acid ferment were really living things. It is not easy for us to realize the skepticism, indeed the hostility, which prevailed at that time in the scientific world against the view that microscopic living creatures could perform important chemical reactions. The extent of the scorn that scientists professed for this view appears in a skit published by Friedrich Wöhler (1800–1882)—the famous chemist who had synthesized the first organic chemical, urea. In this sarcastic document Wöhler described yeast with a considerable degree of anatomical realism, as consisting of eggs which developed into minute animals shaped like distilling apparatus. These creatures took in sugar as food and digested it into carbonic acid (CO_2) and alcohol, which were separately excreted. The famous chemist and biologist, Justus von Liebig, dismissed the germ theory of fermentation with a shrug of the shoulders, regarding Pasteur's view that microbes could cause fermentation as ridiculous and naíve, as the opinion of a child "who would explain the rapidity of the Rhine current by attributing it to the violent movement of the many millwheels at Mainz."

Pasteur Persists

Fortunately, Pasteur was not intimidated by the haughty scorn of his scientific elders, and he countered their heavy witticism with an experiment of incredible simplicity and elegance. It turned out to have an enormous influence on the subsequent history of biochemical sciences. Very boldly he undertook to grow yeast in a simple medium devoid of complex organic nitrogenous compounds—a liquid containing only sugar, ammonia, and some mineral salts to supply the yeast globules with their structural elements. He had the ingenious idea of adding to his nutrient medium the ashes of incinerated yeast in addition to the salts of phosphoric acid, potassium, magnesium, and iron, hoping to supply thereby the unknown mineral elements required by the small plant. He acknowledged that, under these conditions, yeast grew less readily than it did in the juice of the grape or in beer brew, probably because it had to synthesize all its tissue constituents instead of finding many of the metabolic factors ready-made in the natural organic fluids. Nevertheless, he could report in 1860 that he had obtained fermentation in his synthetic medium inoculated with minute amounts of yeast, and that the amount of alcohol produced ran parallel with the multiplication of the yeast. With less refinement, but a like method, he applied similar techniques to lactic-acid fermentation and then to other reactions that he proved were the results of microbial activities. Of all these studies we shall mention only two that illustrate the breadth of his understanding of biochemical phenomena.

It had long been known that the production of vinegar from wine, as in the French Orleans process, or from dilute alcohol as practiced in Germany, was essentially the result of an oxidation converting the alcohol into acetic acid. In the French process oxidation was favored by exposing the wine to the air in very shallow layers; in the German process by making the dilute alcohol trickle down over wood shavings so as to secure intense aeration. It was also known that this oxidation was "catalyzed" by the presence of a slimy organic material called "mother of vinegar." Here again, as with yeast, Pasteur estab-

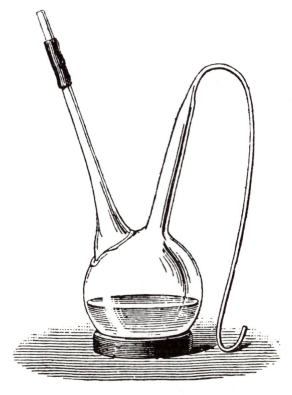

Pasteur's drawing of the kind of flask he used for studying yeast fermentations. This is a simple modification of the flask he used in his studies on spontaneous generation, but permitted periodic sampling so that the progress of the fermentation could be monitored.

lished that when minute amounts of the mother of vinegar were transferred to a synthetic solution containing dilute alcohol, ammonia, and mineral salts, the slimy material increased in abundance, and simultaneously produced acetic acid. He saw under the microscope that the whole process was accompanied by the multiplication of minute bacteria which adhered together to form the mother of vinegar, and he even recognized the presence of the bacteria on the surface of acidifying wine or on the wood shavings used in the German process. This understanding led to rapid improvements in the processes of vinegar production, and moreover, it greatly enlarged understanding of the chemical potentialities of microorganisms.

The Discovery of "Anaerobic" Life

Even more thought-provoking was the unexpected discovery that certain types of bacteria could live without air. According to Pasteur's account, he had once placed under the microscope a drop of sugar solution that was in the process of changing into butyric acid. The drop contained bacteria, which were at first rapidly motile. Then he observed the odd fact that whereas the bacteria in the center of the drop continued to move, those at the periphery soon came to a standstill. From this simple observation he guessed that air was toxic for these bacteria and that they probably lived without oxygen. Accurate as it is, this account gives only a very incomplete picture of what had happened in Pasteur's mind as he was looking at the drop of fluid under the microscope. He had repeatedly observed that butyric acid was more likely to appear in sugar solutions that were either kept free of air altogether, or at least poorly aerated. Subconsciously in other words, his mind had stored facts that were compatible with the view that butyric fermentation did take place in the absence of oxygen, and what he saw under the microscope immediately acquired meaning in the light of these subconscious thoughts. Once again, chance had favored him, but only because many days of observation and thought had prepared him and made him receptive to the new findings. There was no precedent for the view that life could occur in the absence of oxygen; in fact, this view went against all accepted notions. Yet, not only did Pasteur recognize this possibility, but he immediately incorporated it in his thinking and without further ado soon coined the adjective "anaerobic" to refer to life without oxygen, in contrast to "aerobic" for life

Pasteur's device for studying microorganisms under the microscope in the complete absence of air. A, flask filled to the top; B, overflow into a jar of mercury, preventing the entrance of oxygen from the air; V, reservoir of excess culture medium.

as usually known in the presence of air.

As pointed out before, it is unfortunate that all these discoveries of Pasteur must be stated individually, for they did not occur as separate events, as well-defined experiments planned today, carried out tomorrow, and written up immediately. In reality all the aspects of this work on fermentations were continuously reacting one with the other, influencing each other, giving new significance to old observations and leading to new hypotheses. In an attempt to coordinate the multiple factors of this extraordinary intellectual feat and so give it some sort of unity, we shall state briefly here some of the general conclusions Pasteur had reached when he came to the end of this phase of his activities. The most complete statement of his views in this field is found on his book on beer, published in 1876. The circumstances were sufficiently odd to warrant a few words at this point.

It will be recalled that Pasteur came from one of the parts of France famous for good wine and that he worked on the improvement of beer manufacture after the Franco-Prussian War of 1870–71, merely as a way of advancing French competition with Germany in the economic and gustatory field! On reading his book, one gets the impression that he found relief from working on a subject that he disliked—beer—by thinking about a problem in which he was deeply interested—the nature of fermentation. Thus did it come about that the book on beer gave him the opportunity to summarize much of the biochemical wisdom and understanding he had derived from his earlier studies on fermentation.

Let us go back to the various types of microbial activity that Pasteur had studied in greatest detail. One, the production of acetic acid, involved the use of large amounts of oxygen for the oxidation of alcohol. In contrast, the conversion of sugar into butyric acid corresponded to a chemical reduction in which oxygen did not intervene and did in fact inhibit the activity of the butyric-acid ferment. The lactic-acid fermentation corresponded to still another type of reaction which occurred more or less independently of oxygen through an apparently simple splitting of one glucose molecule into two molecules of lactic acid. At first sight, it seemed that each and every one of these microbial activities constituted a phenomenon completely apart from the other, not having anything in common. However, Pasteur came to an entirely different conclusion, in large part, it would seem, on the basis of his profound and original studies of the life of yeast.

Point of Synthesis: The Utilization of Oxygen

The great advantage of yeast for these studies was that it can grow both in the absence and in the presence of air. Moreover, and this turned out to be the key to the whole problem, the mode of growth of yeast is very different depending upon the intensity of aeration during its contact with sugar. Yeast grows slowly and fermentation takes a long time in the complete absence of air, but the amount of sugar transformed into carbon dioxide and alcohol per unit of yeast is then extremely high. For example, 0.5–0.7 g (grams) of yeast was sufficient in Pasteur's experiments to transform 100 g of sugar into alcohol in the absence of air, a ratio of 1 to 150 or 1 to 200. On the other hand, as the amount of air admitted during fermentation is increased, the development of yeast becomes more rapid and more abundant, and the ratio of weight of sugar fermented to weight of yeast becomes smaller. When an excess of oxygen is provided throughout the process, hardly any alcohol is formed, although the development of yeast is very abundant and the ratio of sugar consumed to yeast produced falls to approximately 5. Some alteration of the size and shape of the yeast cells also occurs simultaneously with these dramatic changes in physiological behavior.

These extraordinary differences in the chemical behavior of yeast depending upon the availability of oxygen led Pasteur to postulate that living cells can obtain energy from foodstuffs through two very different types of mechanisms. One involves utilization of oxygen and is very effective because the complete oxidation of foodstuffs with little waste product releases a great deal of energy, most of which becomes available to the cell. Another mechanism occurs without oxygen, but is very wasteful. For example, the conversion of sugar into lactic acid, alcohol, or butyric acid provides the cell with chemical energy but only in very small amounts. The process is wasteful because lactic acid, butyric acid, or alcohol can be regarded as waste products that the particular bacterium or yeast cannot utilize because it cannot oxidize it. The fact that these waste products happen to be useful is, of course, another story. Yeast proved to be the best organism for the analysis of this problem: it can live aerobically with an effective utilization of sugar for energy production through almost complete oxidation by means of oxygen, or it can live anaerobically with a wasteful utilization of sugar, leaving alcohol as an unoxidized byproduct. In brief, fermentation was the method used by yeast to derive energy from sugar under anaerobic conditions. In 1872 Pasteur restated these views in more precise terms: "Under ordinary conditions, the heat (energy) necessary for development comes from the oxidation of foodstuffs (except in the case of utilization of solar light). In fermentation, it comes from the decomposition of the fermentable matter. The ratio of the weight of fermentable matter decomposed to the weight of yeast produced will be higher or lower depending upon the extent of action of free oxygen. The maximum will correspond to life with participation of free oxygen."

A Definition of Fermentation

Eventually, Pasteur summarized his understanding of these complex phenomena in a few arresting formulae, the gist of which is that "fermentation is respiration in the absence of air." Moreover, he recognized that what he had observed was not peculiar to yeast and bacteria, but was instead a phenomenon of great generality. For example, he noticed that, while plums kept in an open container took up oxygen and became soft and sweet, they remained firm, lost sugar, and produced alcohol if placed in an atmosphere of carbon dioxide. Time and time again he restated his belief that: "Fermentation should be possible in all types of cells. . . . Fermentation by yeast is only a particular case of a very general phenomenon. All living beings are ferments under certain conditions of their life."

Specifically he suggested that the same principles apply also to animal tissues, for example, to muscle. And in fact it is now well established that muscle cells, and probably all animal tissue cells, can derive some energy from the conversion of sugar into lactic acid, just as bacteria do. But this is a very wasteful process, and, moreover, its outcome is the accumulation of lactic acid which soon proves to have toxic effects. In normal life, therefore, the production of energy is rendered much more economical and efficient, and the accumulation of toxic products prevented, by the respiratory mechanisms which bring oxygen into the reaction to complete oxidative processes. Thus did Pasteur elevate some specialized observations on microbial activities to the level of one of the most fundamental biochemical laws of life.

The Chemical Mystery of Life

The detailed study of yeast led Pasteur to still another broad biological generalization. He had shown that yeast could be grown in a simple broth containing sugar and mineral salts as its main constituents. Likewise, he succeeded in cultivating in well-defined culture media many other types of bacteria. His first graduate student at the École Normale, Jules Raulin, greatly advanced the knowledge of microbial nutrition by working out the requirements of a mold, *Aspergillus niger*, and showing in particular that certain metals and other rare mineral elements are required for its normal growth. As early as 1860 Pasteur himself pointed out that these findings made in his laboratory would permit physiology to attack the fundamental chemical problems of life. The bodies of plants and animals consist of an immense number of cells, but in microorganisms the living agent is reduced to the single-cell level. By studying microbial physiology, therefore, it is possible to analyze the chemical phenomena which determine the function of the individual cell—the fundamental unit of life—be it that of a plant, a microorganism, an animal, or even a human. In practice it is today possible to grow *in vitro* (in test tubes) almost every kind of living cell and thus to define its particular requirements. And this general technique has revealed the fascinating fact that living cells possess many characteristics in common. For example, it is now known that most vitamins intervene in the metabolism of all cells. The fact that some cells require and others do not require a particular vitamin for growth is of little importance in this respect, because those that do not require the vitamin manufacture it themselves and use it just as the others do in the course of their biochemical living processes.

Thus, it can be said that Pasteur's work led inescapably to the doctrine of the biochemical unity of life, truly one of the most important philosophical concepts of modern science.

While Pasteur's studies of the biological significance of stereoisomerism did not throw any light on the genesis of life, they have yielded a number of facts that have had far-reaching influence on the development of biochemistry. Pasteur himself recognized that the differences in structural configuration between the isomeric forms of tartaric acids, as well as of other organic compounds, are reflected in the differential behavior of these isomeric substances toward living agents, for example, in their effect on taste buds and in their susceptibility to attack by microorganisms. These observations have served as a starting point for a whole range of investigations of the chemical basis of biological specificity, a problem so characteristic of modern biochemistry.

But while he recognized that the fundamental metabolic and nutritional processes are common to all known forms of life,

Pasteur pondered endlessly over the mechanisms whereby each living organism transmits to its progeny its unique hereditary characteristics. Once he had convinced himself—and the world—that spontaneous generation does not occur in ordinary circumstances, he came to regard the transmissibility of hereditary traits as the unique characteristic of life. As he wrote, "The mystery of life does not reside in its manifestations in adult beings, but rather and solely in the existence of the germ and of its becoming. . . . Once the germ exists, it needs only inanimate substances and proper conditions of temperature to obey the laws of its development. . . . It will then grow and manifest all the phenomena that we call 'vital,' but vital phenomena are only physical and chemical phenomena; it is the law of their succession which constitutes the unknown of life." Modern molecular genetics has now attacked successfully this fascinating problem of such passionate interest to Pasteur.

10

Victory Over Disease

The year 1877 constitutes a landmark in the life of Pasteur and in the history of medicine. That April he published the first of his studies on *anthrax*—a disease of farm animals and humans—and this paper bears to the *germ theory of disease* the same relation that his 1857 paper on lactic acid bears to the germ theory of fermentation. Before discussion in detail the facts revealed by Pasteur's studies of infection, however, we must stop to consider how it happened that he was led to devote the rest of his life to biological and medical problems, even though he was trained as a chemist and had never studied biology, let alone medicine.

First, let us make clear that while it is true that the germ theory of disease was accepted in medical circles only after 1877, the ground for acceptance had been prepared by many centuries of solid observations and shrewd thinking. Like most other scientific theories, the belief that microbes can cause disease had emerged as an abstract concept—a hunch—long before it was possible to state the facts clearly or to test them by experiment. Over many years, the theory evolved progressively from a vague awareness to the level of precise understanding.

Contagion and the Potato Blight

From time immemorial it has been known that certain diseases are catching—like colds or tuberculosis—and that others are specially prevalent in certain places—malaria in swampy regions, for example. Awareness of these facts led very early to the concept that certain diseases can be transmitted from one person to the next by contact, or can be caused by something present in the air. The history of the expression "contagious" disease symbolizes this ancient knowledge. The word contagion comes from the Latin *contagio* which means contact. Contagion, in other words, implies the transmission of disease by direct or indirect contact. There have been many hypotheses concerning transmission of disease by contact. Some physicians believed the agent to be something volatile. Thus, the Italian word malaria means "bad air"—something noxious arising from marshes and other wet places. For other physicians the transmissible causes of disease were invisible particles in suspension in the air. Minute invisible animalcules had been implicated very early, but there was no way of proving their existence. Lack of precise knowledge concerning the nature of the transmissible agents responsible for disease did not, however, prevent practical men from establishing sanitary policies to minimize contagion. During epidemics of plague, for instance, the inhabitants of the stricken cities or districts were forbidden to move into unaffected areas for fear they would spread the disease. The policy of quarantine derives its name from the fact that in Venice ships arriving from foreign lands were held in the harbor for forty days (*quarante* in Italian) before the crew or passengers could land. Pasteur knew these facts, and it is certain that he saw in them evidence for his view that microbes were responsible for contagion.

The first direct evidence that microbes could play a part in disease was obtained around 1850. The occasion was the potato blight, a terrible scourge which devastated the potato fields all over Ireland for several years in succession. The potato blight is of enormous importance in political and economic history because more than one million people died of the famine in Ireland; the country was ruined, all sorts of diseases became rampant among farm and city people; many of those who survived were so impoverished that they had to emigrate, especially to America, and as a result of the disaster the Irish population fell from eight million to under four million. The potato blight is also important in the history of science because it contributed much to the understanding of disease causation.

Everyone knew that the spring had been cold in Ireland the year of the blight, with much rain and fog, and the conclusion was natural that the bad weather had been responsible for the disease. A few botanists pointed out, however, that the blighted potato plants had been invaded by a microscopic fungus, *Phytophthora infestans*, and they contended that this fungus was the real cause of the disaster. As we shall see later, the discussions that followed and that have continued to our day have thrown much light on the real meaning of the expression "cause of a disease." But there is no evidence that the facts discovered around 1850 by the botanists concerning the potato blight had any influence on the thinking of physicians with regard to the nature of contagious diseases of man. At that time, it was apparently difficult to recognize that there was a close analogy between the spoiling of potatoes and the diseases of humans.

Pasteur had never heard of the invasion of the Irish potato fields by the fungus *Phytophthora infestans*, and this is unfortunate because he would have grasped the broad significance of the phenomenon for human and veterinary medicine. Nevertheless, early in his work on fermentation he had become convinced by intuition that microbes could cause disease. He stated this conviction very explicitly as early as 1857 in his preliminary paper on lactic-acid fermentation—and he continued from then on to reiterate his hypothesis in letters, articles, and lectures. For example, in the course of his studies on spontaneous generation, he wrote in 1861: "It would be interesting to carry out frequent microscopic analysis of the dust floating in the air at the different seasons, and in different localities. The understanding of the phenomena of contagion, especially during the periods of epidemic diseases, would have much to gain from such studies." And somewhat later, he came back to the same suggestion in words that were really prophetic:

> In Paris, during the month of July when the fruit trade is active, there must be large numbers of yeasts floating in the air of the streets. *If fermentations were diseases, one could speak of epidemics of fermentation.*

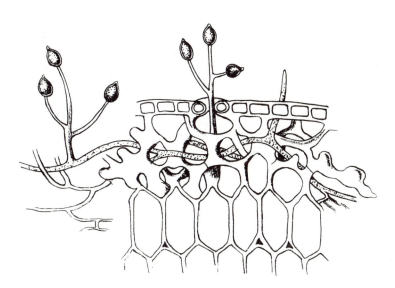

The Irish potato blight was one of the first diseases to be shown to be caused by a microorganism. Drawing by M. J. Berkeley, made in 1846. Irish potato blight was responsible for the great famine in Ireland. Berkeley's drawing shows the manner by which the fungus grows around and through the cells of the potato leaf.

Can we fail to observe that the further we penetrate into the
experimental study of germs, the more we perceive unexpected
lights and ideas leading to the knowledge of the causes of contagious diseases! Is it not worth noting that in this vineyard . . .
every particle of soil was capable of inducing alcoholic fermentation, whereas the soil of the greenhouses was inactive in this
respect. And why? Because I had taken the precaution of covering this soil with glass at the proper time. The death, if I may
use this expression, of a grape falling on the ground of any
vineyard, is always accompanied by the multiplication of the grape
of the yeast cells; in contrast, this kind of death is impossible in
the corner of soil protected by my greenhouses. . . . As the yeast
cells reach the grapes only at a certain time of the year, it is
possible to protect them by means of a shelter placed at the
proper time, just as Europe can be protected from cholera and
plague by adequate quarantine measures.

Lister Acknowledges a Debt

Pasteur had been so emphatic in suggesting that contagious
diseases might be related to fermentation and putrefaction that
in 1864 his writings reached the Scottish surgeon Joseph Lister
(1827–1912). Lister had studied in detail the development of
noxious pus in wounds, a process called *suppuration*. Under
Pasteur's influence Lister postulated that microorganisms can
cause wound suppuration, just as they cause fermentation and
putrefaction. For this reason, Lister suggested that microorganisms should be prevented at all costs from reaching the
hands of the surgeon, his instruments, and the very air surrounding the operating field. To achieve this, Lister used a spray
of phenol throughout the operations he performed, taking his
lead from the fact that this substance was then employed for
the treatment of sewage and excreta. Lister's approach was
highly successful in reducing tissue damage and death of the
patient. Thus began the era of modern surgery. In a most generous manner Lister often acknowledged publicly his intellectual debt to Pasteur, for example in the following letter that
he wrote to him from Edinburgh in February 1874:

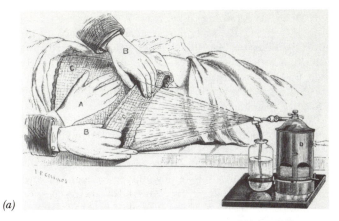

(a)

(b)

The technique of antiseptic surgery, as developed by Joseph Lister after reading Pasteur's work on fermentation. (a) Lister's antiseptic spray apparatus in use in changing a surgical dressing. The metal container labeled *D* was a small kerosene-fired steam generator, and steam pressure caused the antiseptic in the glass reservoir to vaporize. The reservoir was filled with carbolic acid (phenol). (b) An operation in progress. A fine mist of antiseptic spray covers the region where the surgical incision is made. Note that the surgeon and assistants are dressed in ordinary street clothes and are working with their bare hands. Both (a) and (b) were drawings to illustrate an 1882 English book on Lister's antiseptic principles.

My Dear Sir: Allow me to beg your acceptance of a pamphlet, which I sent by the same post, containing an account of some investigations into the subject which you have done so much to elucidate, the germ theory of fermentative changes. I flatter myself that you may read with some interest what I have written on the organisms which you were the first to describe in your *Study on the lactic fermentation.*

I do not know whether the records of British Surgery ever meet your eye. If so, you will have seen from time to time notices of the antiseptic system of treatment, which I have been labouring for the last nine years to bring to perfection.

Allow me to take this opportunity to tender you my most cordial thanks for having, by your brilliant researches, demonstrated to me the truth of the germ theory of putrefaction, and thus furnished me with the principle upon which alone the antiseptic system can be carried out. Should you at any time visit Edinburgh it would, I believe, give you sincere gratification to see at our hospital how largely mankind is being benefited by your labours.

I need hardly add that it would afford me the highest gratification to show you how greatly surgery is indebted to you.

Forgive the freedom with which a common love of science inspires me, and

Believe me, with profound respect,

Yours very sincerely,

Joseph Lister.

Lister again gave generous recognition to Pasteur in the introduction to his classical paper, *On the Antiseptic Principle in the Practice of Surgery.* In his words:

When it had been shown by the researches of Pasteur that the septic property of the atmosphere depended, not on the oxygen or a gaseous constituent, but on minute organisms suspended in it, which owed their energy to their vitality, it occurred to me that decomposition in the injured part might be avoided without excluding the air, by applying as a dressing some material capable of destroying the life of the floating particles.

Diseased Silkworms: Another Triumph

While it was a purely intellectual process that had led Pasteur to the conviction that microbes can cause disease in human beings, it was through accidental circumstances that he came to work on an actual disease. But his first patients were not human beings, they were *silkworms*! The production of silk from silkworms was then an important agricultural industry in certain regions of the center and south of France. However, toward the middle of the nineteenth century a mysterious disease began to attack the French silkworm nurseries. By 1865 the disease had spread to most silkworm-producing areas, and the industry was near ruin in France, and also, to a lesser degree, in the rest of Western Europe.

One of Pasteur's former professors of chemistry, Jean Baptiste Dumas, came from the afflicted region, and asked him as a favor to head a commission organized by the Ministry of Agriculture to investigate the problem. Needless to say, Pasteur knew nothing of silkworms or of their diseases, but he accepted the challenge. In part, his acceptance came from a desire to meet the wishes of his respected master, and to justify the faith that he had put in him. To Pasteur's remark that he was totally unfamiliar with the subject, Dumas had replied one day: "So much the better! For ideas, you will have only those which shall come to you as a result of your own observations!"

It is probable also that Pasteur welcomed the opportunity to approach the field of experimental pathology, as is suggested by a sentence in his letter of acceptance: "The subject . . . may even come within the range of my present studies." He had long foreseen that his work on fermentation would be of significance in the study of the physiological and pathological processes of humans and animals. But he was aware of his unfamiliarity with biological problems, and Dumas' insistence helped

(a)

Pasteur worked on silkworm diseases at Alès in the south of France. (a) House where Pasteur set up his laboratory. (b) Examining silkworm eggs for evidence of infection. Emile Duclaux at the microscope. (c) Pasteur's drawing of the silkworm larva for his book on silkworm diseases.

(b)

(c)

him to face an experience that he both desired and dreaded.

Pasteur's studies of silkworm diseases lasted from 1865 to 1870. They constituted one of the most dramatic and spectacular feats of his scientific life. Most of the work on silkworms was carried out in a rather primitive house converted into a makeshift laboratory in Alès, right in the heart of the silkworm district, in the remote and mountainous Cévennes region. There Pasteur had to familiarize himself with the anatomy and physiology of the worms, and with the techniques of silk production. After three years of heartbreaking work, he established that there were at least two entirely different diseases, one the *pébrine* caused by a parasite protozoan, another the *flacherie*, primarily nutritional in origin. He worked out very effective and simple techniques for breeding worms not contaminated by the protozoan of *pébrine*, and for improving hygienic conditions in the silkworm nurseries. He organized a vigorous educational campaign to teach the silkworm producers how to apply his procedures under practical conditions, and simultaneously he engaged in passionate controversies with those who denied the value of his work. Because of the urgency of the practical problems, he was under the public eye all the time, compelled to divulge the laboratory discoveries as soon as they were made to express opinions as to how they were applicable to industrial and agricultural practices.

Personal Tragedy: The Indomitable Will

During the same period multiple tragedies came to afflict his personal life. In 1865 he had lost his father and one of his daughters, Camille, then two years old. Another daughter, Cecile, died of typhoid fever at the age of twelve in May 1866. As the weight of these sorrows and the burden of the immense responsibilities which he had undertaken were leaving a mark on his health, Madame Pasteur, accompanied by their last surviving daughter, Marie-Louise, came to join the hard-working group around her husband. Then in 1868 Pasteur was stricken by a cerebral hemorrhage, which endangered his life and caused a permanent paralysis of the left arm and leg. As soon as he began to regain his faculties, a week after the attack of paralysis, he wrote a scientific communication, dictating it to his student Désiré Gernez, who was watching over him during the night. Within a few weeks, he started again for the Cévennes mountains to resume his studies of silkworm diseases, despite the difficulties of the trip, the lack of comfort in his provincial quarters, and contrary to the advice of his physicians. This performance revealed once more that Pasteur was a man of indomitable will. It was not only his opponents that he wanted

Pasteur in 1868.

Paris, 5 September 1867

Sir,

My studies on fermentation and on the role of microscopic organisms have opened vast new visions in the field of physiological chemistry, which are now beginning to find practical use in agriculture and medicine. But the fields remaining to be investigated are immense. My greatest desire would be to continue my studies much more vigorously, and without being limited by lack of facilities and supplies.

I wish to have a much larger laboratory, to which would be attached a wing where experiments on putrid and infectious diseases could be carried out without endangering the public health. How could research be carried out on gangrene, or viruses, and how could animal inoculations be done, without a building suitable for housing live and dead animals?... The so-called splenic fever costs the district of Beauce about 4 million francs annually. It would be essential to go to this district and spend some weeks during several summers making careful observations.

These studies, and a thousand others that could be mentioned, deal, according to my mind, with the major processes occurring during the transformation of organic matter after death, returning the organic elements to the soil and to the atmosphere. Such studies can only be done if a large and well-funded laboratory is available.

The time has come to liberate experimental science from the poverty in which it works. Everything brings us to this. We are in the midst of your great reign and there is an urgent necessity to maintain the scientific superiority of France over our rivals.

Following the general design outlined above, I am proposing to His Excellence the Minister of Public Instruction that a laboratory be established, under my direction, that would be largely dedicated to work in physiological chemistry....

May I dare to hope, Your Majesty, that you will approve my project...?

L. Pasteur
Member, Academy of Science

Pasteur's letter to the Emperor Napoleon III, dated September 5, 1867, requesting financial support for a new laboratory to study infectious diseases. This letter was written at the time Pasteur was studying silkworm diseases. The Emperor immediately agreed to Pasteur's request and work on the new laboratory began, but Pasteur's stroke and the Franco-Prussian War greatly delayed its completion.

to overpower; it was also nature—it was himself.

There is no doubt that Pasteur's studies of silkworm diseases had great practical results and thus constitute the first practical triumph of laboratory science in the control of infectious disease. But as in the case of the potato blight, these studies did not affect medical thinking. For most physicians there was no relation between the ills of humans and the death of silkworms, but this was not Pasteur's opinion. He was aware that the work on silkworm diseases had been his apprenticeship in the study of pathological problems, and he was wont to tell those who later came to work in his laboratory: "Read the studies on silkworm diseases; it will be, I believe, a good preparation for the investigations that we are about to undertake."

11

The Germ Theory Is Established

We are now in a better situation to evaluate the events of 1877 when Pasteur began his work on anthrax. Contrary to general belief, the year does not deserve a place in history for the first demonstration that microbes can cause disease. This had been shown for the potato blight in 1850 and for the *pébrine* of silkworms in 1868. What does make the years 1876–77 a landmark in the history of medicine is the fact that for the first time a microbe was shown to be capable of causing an important disease affecting higher animals and humans. The disease was anthrax, then very common on farms all over Europe. Strangely enough, it turned out that just as Pasteur was beginning to work on anthrax, its microbial origin was also being studied by a young German physician who was soon to become immensely famous, Robert Koch. Let us salute in passing this great German scientist who shares with Pasteur the honor of having founded medical microbiology. To symbolize the magnitude of Koch's discoveries, we need only mention that shortly after the completion of his studies on anthrax he electrified the world by discovering the microbes responsible for *cholera* and for *tuberculosis*—two of the most destructive enemies of humankind.

Anthrax: A Final Proof

In reality, several veterinarians and physicians had suspected long before Pasteur and Koch that bacteria were responsible for anthrax. They had seen bacteria in the blood and organs of sick animals, and, furthermore, they had transferred the disease by injecting into healthy animals a few drops of infected blood. But, for a number of technical reasons beyond the scope of this book, these observations were far from convincing, and it took the experimental genius of Koch and Pasteur to demonstrate once and for all what the observation of their predecessors had merely suggested.

Koch's great experiment was to sow fragments of tissues from sick animals into a drop of blood serum of normal rabbits. He saw that bacteria similar to those originally present in the organs multiplied extensively in the serum and with the culture thus obtained he inoculated another drop of serum. After repeating the process eight times he found to his great satisfaction that the last culture injected into a healthy mouse was as capable of producing anthrax as was blood taken directly from an animal just dead of the disease. Koch also made the important discovery that the bacterium associated with anthrax produced heat-resistant spores and that these spores were part of the life cycle of the organism. These experiments appeared convincing, but despite their thoroughness and elegance, they still left a loophole for those who believed that there was in the blood something other than the bacteria capable of inducing anthrax. Although Koch had transferred his cultures eight times in succession, this was not sufficient to rule out the possibility that some hypothetical component of the blood had been carried over from the original drop and was responsible, instead of the bacteria, for transmitting the infection to the inoculated animal.

Robert Koch, the great German bacteriologist and co-founder, with Pasteur, of the field of medical microbiology. Koch discovered the life cycle of the anthrax bacillus and developed pure culture methods that enabled him to isolate and characterize the causal agents of two dread scourges of humankind, tuberculosis and cholera. "Koch's Postulates," listed below, became the cornerstone of research on pathogenic microorganisms.

1. The organism must always be present in an individual suffering from the disease;
2. The organism must be cultivated in pure culture away from the infected individual;
3. Such a pure culture, when inoculated into a susceptible host (experimental animal), must initiate an infection with the characteristic disease symptoms.

It was this debatable point that Pasteur's experiments were designed to settle.

Pasteur knew from his earlier studies on spontaneous generation that the blood of a healthy animal, taken aseptically during life and added to any kind of nutrient fluid, would not putrefy or give rise to any living microorganism. He expected, therefore, that the blood of an anthrax animal handled with aseptic precautions should give cultures containing only the anthrax bacillus. Experiment soon showed this to be so, and showed also that rapid and abundant growth of the bacillus could be obtained by cultivating it in neutral urine; these cultures could be readily maintained through many generations by transfers in the same medium. Pasteur added one drop of blood to fifty cubic centimeters (nearly two ounces) of sterile urine and then, after incubation and multiplication of the bacilli, transferred one drop of this culture into a new flask containing fifty cubic centimeters of urine. After repeating this process one hundred times in succession, he arrived at a culture in which the dilution of the original blood was so great—of the order of 1 part in 100^{100}—that not even one molecule of it was left in the final material. Only the bacteria could escape the dilution, because they continued to multiply with each transfer. And yet, a drop of the hundredth culture killed a guinea pig or a rabbit as rapidly as a drop of the original infected blood, thus demonstrating that the "virulence principle" rested in the bacterium, or was produced by it.

Pasteur devised many other ingenious experiments to secure additional evidence that the anthrax bacillus was the cause of disease. He filtered cultures through membranes fine enough to hold back the bacteria and showed that the clear filtrate injected into a rabbit did not make it sick. He allowed flasks of culture to rest undisturbed in places at low and constant temperature, until the bacteria had settled to the bottom; again the clear supernatant fluid was found incapable of establishing the disease in experimental animals, but a drop of the deposit, containing the bacterial bodies, killed them with anthrax. These results constituted the strongest possible evidence that the anthrax bacillus itself was responsible for the infection. The germ theory of disease was now firmly established.

Rabies: The Discovery of Filterable Viruses

The three decades that followed the original studies on anthrax saw the discovery of many other bacterial agents of disease by Pasteur, Koch, their associates, and their followers. The spectacular achievements of this period, which has been called the "golden age of microbiology," had great import for the welfare of the human race. Startling as they were, these discoveries constitute merely the technical exploitation of the fundamental methods established by Koch and Pasteur, methods which rapidly became standard practice in the bacteriological laboratories of the world. It is of extraordinary interest, however, that the next great theoretical advance in the germ theory of disease was to be made by Pasteur himself when he discovered that disease can be caused by agents so small as to be invisible under the microscope and able to pass through filters, and so peculiar as to fail to grow in the ordinary culture media of the bacteriologists. These agents of disease are now known as *filterable viruses* or simply, *viruses*.

The new discovery came from the study of *rabies*. Rabies was then known as a disease contracted by humans or a few species of animals from the bite of rabid dogs or wolves. Bacteriological studies—and this must have been very disheartening—failed to reveal to Pasteur a bacterial cause for rabies. Attempts were made to cultivate a microorganism in spinal fluid, and even in fresh nerve substance obtained from normal animals, but all in vain. His failure is not to be wondered at, for it is now known that rabies is caused by a filterable virus, which cannot be seen by ordinary microscopy, and which cannot be cultivated in lifeless bacteriological media. With an uncommon and truly admirable intellectual agility, Pasteur then gave up the *in vitro*

The Golden Age of Microbiology

Year	Disease	Organism	Discoverer
1877	Anthrax	*Bacillus anthracis*	Koch, R.
1878	Suppuration	*Staphylococcus*	Koch, R.
1879	Gonorrhea	*Neisseria gonorrhoeae*	Neisser, A.L.S.
1880	Typhoid fever	*Salmonella typhi*	Eberth, C.J.
1881	Suppuration	*Streptococcus*	Ogston, A.
1882	Tuberculosis	*Mycobacterium tuberculosis*	Koch, R.
1883	Cholera	*Vibrio cholerae*	Koch, R.
1883	Diphtheria	*Corynebacterium diphtheriae*	Klebs, T.A.E.
1884	Tetanus	*Clostridium tetani*	Nicholaier, A.
1885	Diarrhea	*Escherichia coli*	Escherich, T.
1886	Pneumonia	*Streptococcus pneumoniae*	Fraenkel, A.
1887	Meningitis	*Neisseria meningitidis*	Weischselbaum, A.
1888	Food poisoning	*Salmonella enteritidis*	Gaertner, A.A.H.
1892	Gas gangrene	*Clostridium perfringens*	Welch, W.H.
1894	Plague	*Yersinia pestis*	Kitasato, S., Yersin, A.J.E. (independently)
1896	Botulism	*Clostridium botulinum*	van Ermengem, E.M.P.
1898	Dysentery	*Shigella dysenteriae*	Shiga, K.
1900	Paratyphoid	*Salmonella paratyphi*	Schottmüller, H.
1903	Syphilis	*Treponema pallidum*	Schaudinn, F.R., and Hoffmann, E.
1906	Whooping cough	*Bordtella pertussis*	Bordet, J., and Gengou, O.

cultural techniques, to the development of which he had contributed so much. Heretofore, he had emphasized the necessity of discovering for each type of microorganism the nutrient medium most selectively adapted to its cultivation. He now conceived the idea of using the susceptible tissues of experimental animals, instead of sterile nutrient solutions, to cultivate the virus of the disease; the concept of selectivity of cultural conditions was thus simply carried over from lifeless media to receptive living cells.

Rabies had been a widespread disease since dogs were first domesticated. This is a 17th century drawing from a book which warned of the dangers of mad dogs. Infection with rabies virus frequently induces a marked change in the behavior of the dog. The animal becomes extremely aggressive (*rabid*), very restless, and begins to run wild, viciously biting other dogs or humans. In most cases, infection with the rabies virus is fatal.

Extension of the Experimental Method

The general symptoms of rabies suggested that the nervous system was attacked during the disease. Nerve tissue seemed to be an ideal medium for the virus of rabies, and to fulfill the condition of selectivity, which was the foundation of the cultural method. As the main problem was to gain access to this tissue under aseptic conditions, the surest way was to attempt to inoculate dogs under the dura mater (the fibrous membrane surrounding the brain), by boring a hole through the skull (a technique called *trephining*). "The thought that the skull of a dog was to be perforated was disagreeable to him," wrote his assistant, Emile Roux. "He desired intensely that the experiment be made, but he dreaded to see it undertaken. I performed it one day in his absence; the next day, when I told him that the intracranial inoculation presented no difficulty, he was moved with pity for the dog: 'Poor beast. Its brain is certainly badly wounded. It must be paralyzed.' Without replying, I went below to look for the animal and had him brought into the laboratory. Pasteur did not love dogs; but when he saw this one full of life, curiously ferreting about everywhere he showed the greatest satisfaction and straightaway lavished upon him the kindest words."

The dog inoculated by trephination developed rabies fourteen days later, and all the dogs treated in the same fashion behaved in a similar manner. Now that the cultivation of the virus in the animal body was possible the work could progress at a rapid pace, as in the case of anthrax, and other bacterial diseases.

Thus was discovered a technique for the cultivation of an unknown infectious agent in the receptive tissues of a susceptible animal. This technique has permitted the study of those agents of disease that are not cultivable in lifeless media, and has brought them within the fold of the germ theory of disease. The demonstration that invisible viruses could be handled almost as readily as cultivable bacteria was a great technical feat,

(a)

(b)

Trephination, Pasteur's technique for inoculating rabies virus directly into the brain of an experimental animal. (a) Trephination of a rabbit in Pasteur's laboratory, from a 19th century illustration. Pasteur, on the left, never did this operation himself. (b) A trephine is a small circular saw with a center pin. As the handle is rotated, a circular disk is cut out of the skull, exposing the underlying brain tissue.

Pasteur's legacy: Some major discoveries in virus research

Date	Person	Discovery
1798	Edward Jenner	Smallpox vaccine
1881	Louis Pasteur	First paper on rabies
1892	D.I. Ivanovski	First description of the filterability of a virus (tobacco mosaic)
1898	F. Loeffler, and P. Frosch	First description of the filterability of an animal virus (foot-and-mouth disease)
1898	M.W. Beijerinck	Proof that viruses only multiply within living cells
1901	Walter Reed	Discovery of yellow fever virus
1903	A. Negri	Description of cellular bodies formed after rabies infection (Negri bodies)
1903	P. Remlinger, and Riffat-Bey	Discovery of the rabies virus
1909	S. Flexner, and P.A. Lewis	Discovery of polio virus
1911	J. Goldberger, and J.F. Anderson	Discovery of measles virus
1911	P. Rous	Discovery of tumor virus (Rous sarcoma of chickens)
1915–1917	F.W. Twort, and F.d'Herelle	Discovery of bacterial viruses (bacteriophage)
1934	C.D. Johnson, and E.W. Goodpasture	Discovery of mumps virus
1935	W.M. Stanley	First crystallization of a virus (tobacco mosaic virus)
1939	G.A. Kausche, E. Pfankuch, and H. Ruska	First visualization of a virus under the electron microscope
1949	J.H. Enders, T.H. Weller, and F.C. Robbins	First cultivation of polio virus in tissue culture (opening way for rational vaccine development)
1955	F.L. Schaffer, and C.E. Schwerdt	First crystallization of an animal virus (polio virus)
1955	J. Salk	First successful polio vaccine
1962	A. Sabin	Live virus vaccine for polio

Based on Hughes, S.S. 1977. *The Virus. A History of the Concept*. Heinemann, London.

and its theoretical and practical consequences have been immense. Even more impressive, perhaps, is the spectacle of Pasteur, then almost sixty years of age and semiparalyzed, attacking with undiminished vigor and energy a technical problem for which his previous experience had not prepared him. Throughout his life the concept of selectivity of chemical and biological reactions had served him as the master key to open the doors through which were revealed many of nature's secrets. From the separation of left- and right-handed crystals of tartaric acid by selective procedures or agents, through the cultivation of yeast and of various bacteria in chemically defined media, to the differentiation of the anthrax bacillus from other microorganisms by infection of experimental animals, he had in the course of twenty-five years applied the concept of selectivity to many different situations. The propagation of the rabies virus in receptive nervous tissue demonstrated that the same concept, if used with imagination, was applicable to still other biological problems. In his hands, the experimental method was not a set of recipes, but a living philosophy adaptable to the ever-changing circumstances of natural phenomena.

12

The Birth of Immunology

One of the first bacterial diseases that Pasteur undertook to study after anthrax was *fowl cholera*. He had no difficulty isolating its causative agent, and there would be no reason to single out this disease for particular discussion, if it were not for the fact that its study led to the discovery of vaccination—an achievement as remarkable in its practical consequences as in its theoretical implications.

Pasteur had begun experiments on chickens infected with fowl cholera in the spring of 1879, but an unexpected difficulty interrupted the work after the summer vacation. The cultures of the chicken cholera bacillus that had been kept in the laboratory during the summer failed to produce disease when inoculated into chickens in the early fall. A new, virulent culture was obtained from a natural outbreak, and it was inoculated into new animals, as well as into the chickens which had resisted the old cultures. The new animals, just brought from the market, succumbed to the infection in the customary length of time, thus showing that the fresh culture was very active. But to every-

(a)

(b)

(a) Edward Jenner, the English physician who discovered vaccination.
(b) One of Jenner's drawings showing the development of characteristic
pustules on the arm of a person inoculated with cowpox vaccine.

one's astonishment, and the astonishment of Pasteur himself, almost all the chickens that had previously been infected with the nonvirulent culture survived the infection. According to the accounts left by one of his collaborators, Pasteur remained silent for a minute, then exclaimed as if he had seen a vision, "Don't you see that these animals have been *vaccinated!*"

The Origins of Vaccination

To the modern reader, there is nothing remarkable in the use of the word "vaccination," which has become part of everyday language. But this was over a century ago. Then the word *vaccination* was used only to refer to the special case of injection of *cowpox* material for inducing protection against *smallpox*. We must stop for a minute, therefore, to retrace the steps that led Pasteur to see a relation between the protective effect of cowpox against smallpox, and the survival of the chickens in his accidental experiment.

In eighteenth-century England some people believed that anyone who had had cowpox, a skin infection contracted by contact with an infected cow and somewhat similar to smallpox, was thereby rendered incapable of contracting the latter disease. It is reported that Edward Jenner (1749–1823) was led to study the matter by the statement of a Gloucestershire dairy-maid who had come to him as a patient. When he suggested that she was suffering from smallpox, she immediately replied: "I cannot take the smallpox because I have had the cowpox." Jenner attempted to give scientific foundation to the popular belief by studying systematically the protective effect of cowpox injection in human beings, and he soon convinced himself, and the world, that this treatment did in fact give protection against exposure to virulent smallpox.

Thus was introduced into the Western world the practice of immunization against smallpox by the injection of material originating from skin lesions in the cow; the word "vaccination," under which the method came to be known, is derived from the Latin word *vacca*, a cow.

Jenner soon had many followers in England, but it was perhaps in America that the method received the most vigorous support. Benjamin Waterhouse in Boston took up the cudgels for vaccination, and, having received vaccine virus from England, he vaccinated his own family in July 1800 and dared expose his children to infection in the smallpox hospital in order to demonstrate that they were immune. In 1801 he sent some of Jenner's vaccine to President Thomas Jefferson, who had his own family vaccinated, as well as some of their neighbors and a few Indians.

Pasteur was familiar with Jenner's work, of course, and with the practice of vaccination against smallpox. And soon after the beginning of his work on infectious diseases he became convinced that something similar to vaccination was the best approach to their control. It was this conviction that made him perceive immediately the meaning of the accidental experiment with chickens. By transferring to humans pox material from the cow, Jenner had so modified the human constitution as to render it no longer receptive to smallpox. Pasteur recognized that this effect was the manifestation of a general law, and that his odd cultures of fowl cholera bacteria, which had become "attenuated" during the summer, had brought about some transformation in the body of the inoculated chickens making them less receptive to the virulent form of the microorganism. Jenner's discovery was only a special case for developing attenuated cultures that could be used in immunization procedures. More generally, vaccination could be regarded as a technique for specifically increasing the resistance of the body to an inimical agent. To make more emphatic the analogy between his and Jenner's discoveries, Pasteur chose to describe the phenomenon that he had observed in chickens under the name "vaccination." Thus, as has happened to many words, the meaning of "vaccination" progressively evolved from the description of a concrete procedure (Jenner's procedure for smallpox) into the expression of an abstract scientific concept.

From Vision to Practice

The discoveries of Jenner and Pasteur have implications which transcend immunological science. They reveal in what subtle manner and how profoundly the behavior of living things can be affected by influences that reach them from the external world. Humans or fowl, once having received a minute amount of material from cowpox or from the culture of a bacterium, are indelibly marked by this apparently trivial experience; they thereby become somewhat different living beings. Pasteur realized immediately that his observations of fowl cholera brought the phenomenon of immunity within the range of study by microbiological techniques. As he could cultivate the causative bacillus of fowl cholera *in vitro*, and as attenuation of the bacillus had occurred spontaneously in some of his cultures, Pasteur became convinced that it should be possible to produce vaccines at will in the laboratory. Instead of depending upon the chance finding of naturally occurring immunizing agents, as cowpox was for smallpox, vaccination could then become a general technique, applicable to all infectious diseases. Within the incredibly short period of four years, Pasteur succeeded in demonstrating the practical possibilities of this visionary concept for fowl cholera, anthrax, swine erysipelas, and rabies. I shall select a few of the aspects of the work on vaccination against anthrax and rabies to illustrate not the specialized techniques employed, but rather the amazing intellectual courage that Pasteur displayed in the prosecution of his work.

As soon as he had obtained an attenuated culture of the anthrax bacillus and worked out the technique of vaccination against the disease in his Paris laboratory, Pasteur expressed the desire to put the technique to the test in farm animals under field conditions. Anthrax was then a disease of great economic importance, and the possibility of finding a protection against it constituted a lively subject of discussion in veterinary circles. The germ theory of disease was still in its infancy, and few were the physicians and veterinarians who had any concept of the scientific meaning of immunization.

In the spring of 1881 a veterinarian named Rossignol succeeded in enlisting the support of many farmers of the Brie district, near Paris, to finance a large-scale test of anthrax immunization. Pasteur was well aware of the fact that many veterinarians and physicians were highly skeptical of his claims, and he recognized that many saw in the proposed test an occasion to cover the germ theory with ridicule. Nothing, therefore, could set in bolder relief his confidence and gameness of spirit than his acceptance of the incredibly drastic terms of the protocol submitted to him. Rossignol publicized the test widely, and the experiment thus became an event of international importance. It took place in the presence of a great assembly of people of all kinds, including the Paris correspondent of the *Times* of London, Mr. De Blowitz, who for a few days focused the eyes of his readers throughout the world on the farm at Pouilly le Fort, where the test was being conducted.

In the experiment twenty-four sheep, one goat, and six cows were inoculated on May 5 with five drops of a living attenuated culture of anthrax bacillus. On May 17 all these animals were revaccinated with a second dose of a less-attenuated culture. On May 31 all the immunized animals were then infected with a highly virulent anthrax culture, and the same culture was injected as well into twenty-nine normal animals: twenty-four sheep, one goat, and four cows. When Pasteur arrived on the field on the second day of June with his assistants Chamberland, Roux, and Thuillier, he was greeted with loud acclamation. All the vaccinated sheep were well. Twenty-one of the control sheep and the single goat were dead of anthrax, two other control sheep died in front of the spectators, and the last unprotected sheep died at the end of the day. The six vaccinated cows were well and showed no symptoms, whereas the four control cows had extensive swellings at the site of inoculation and febrile reactions. The triumph was complete.

As soon as he became convinced of the value of anthrax vaccination, Pasteur undertook to make himself the promoter of the new method. In order to convince those who wished to touch and to see before believing, he arranged for vaccination experiments to be repeated in different places in France and abroad. To the secluded life in the laboratory where the studies of rabies had already begun, he now added a public life not less active, involving detailed analysis of the results of field experiments, replies to the demands for information, answers to the complaints, and defense in the face of criticism and sly attacks, as well as of open warfare.

Thanks to prodigious efforts, anthrax vaccination soon became an established practice. By 1894 3,400,000 sheep and 438,000 cattle had been vaccinated with respective mortalities

The farm at Pouilly le Fort where Pasteur's famous public trial of his anthrax vaccine took place in May 1881.

(a)

of 1 and 0.3 percent under natural conditions of field exposure. Just as the demonstration of the pathogenic role of the anthrax bacillus had been the touchstone of the germ theory of disease, it was the vaccination against anthrax that revealed to the medical and lay mind the practical possibilities of the new science of immunity.

The Dramatic Prophylaxis of Rabies

It is, however, the antirabies treatment which is usually cited as Pasteur's greatest triumph and claim to immortality, and which established microbiological sciences in the popular mind and in the practice of medicine. Rabies had long had a firm

(b)

The rabies vaccine. (a) Pasteur in his laboratory examining one of his spinal cord preparations. From a 19th century painting. (b) An original preparation of Pasteur's, still preserved in the Pasteur Institute, showing the manner in which he dried the spinal cords of rabbits to alternate the virulence of the rabies virus.

hold on public imagination and was the epitome of terror and mystery. It was therefore well suited to satisfy Pasteur's longing for romantic problems. It combined a supreme challenge to the experimenter and his method, and the chance to capture the interest of the medical and lay public by a spectacular achievement. In fact, Pasteur was right in the selection of this seemingly hopeless problem. The Pouilly le Fort experiment on anthrax had rendered the public conversant with the doctrine of immunization, but it was the prophylaxis of rabies that made of microbiological science an established religion and surrounded its creator with the halo of sainthood.

In the first phase of the rabies work, Pasteur showed that the spinal cords of rabbits dead of the disease could be rendered almost nonvirulent by keeping them for two weeks in sterile dried air. Specifically, the technique consisted in keeping the spinal cord in a container with caustic potash to prevent putrefaction, and allowing penetration of oxygen to attenuate the virus. The famous portrait painted by Edelfeldt shows Pasteur absorbed in the contemplation of one of these flasks. By inoculating dogs with emulsions of progressively less attenuated cord, it was possible to protect the animal against inoculation with the most virulent form of virus. Under normal conditions of exposure rabies develops slowly in humans as well as in animals. For example, a person bitten by a mad dog ordinarily does not display symptoms of the disease until a month or more after the bite. This period of incubation therefore appeared long enough to suggest the possibility of establishing resistance by vaccinating even after the bite had been inflicted. Experiments made on dogs bitten by rabid animals, and then treated with the vaccine, gave promising results. Would the same method be applicable to human beings bitten by rabid animals and still in the incubation period of the disease?

The story of the mental anguish Pasteur experienced before daring to proceed from animal experiments to the treatment of human disease has often been told. The decision to apply rabies vaccination to the human was forced upon him when a young boy, Joseph Meister, was brought from Alsace for treatment on July 6, 1885, suffering from rabid dog bites on the hands, legs, and thighs. After consulting with physicians who assured him that the boy was doomed, Pasteur reluctantly decided to administer the vaccine. On July 7, sixty hours after the accident, Joseph Meister was injected with rabbit spinal cord attenuated by fourteen days' drying. In twelve successive inoculations he received stronger and stronger virus until, on July 16, he received an inoculation of still fully virulent spinal cord which had been removed the day before from the body of a rabbit that had died following inoculation with the virus. Joseph Meister exhibited no symptom and returned to Alsace in good health. He later became gatekeeper of the Pasteur Institute. In 1940, fifty-five years after the accident that gave him a lasting place in medical history, he committed suicide rather than open Pasteur's burial crypt for the German invaders.

The second case treated by Pasteur was that of a shepherd, Jean Baptiste Jupille, aged fifteen. Seeing a dog about to attack some children, Jupille had seized his whip in an attempt to drive it away, but was severely bitten; he finally managed to wind his whip around the muzzle of the animal and to crush its skull with his wooden shoe. The dog was subsequently declared rabid, and Jupille was brought to Paris for treatment six days after being bitten. He survived, and his deed was commemorated in a statue which stands today in front of the Pasteur Institute in Paris.

These two dramatic successes encouraged numerous patients to go to Pasteur for treatment after being bitten by animals known or presumed to be rabid. By October 1886, fifteen months after Joseph Meister had first been treated, no fewer than 2,490 persons had received the vaccine. Thus, like Jenner, Pasteur saw his method become an established practice within a short time of its inception, but as had happened to smallpox vaccination, the rabies treatment was immediately attacked as valueless, and capable of causing the very disease it was designed to control.

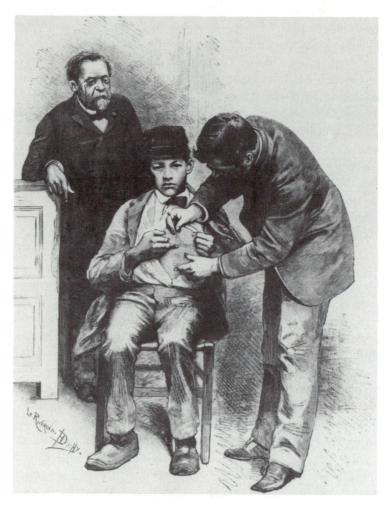

A drawing from a 19th century illustrated French magazine, showing Pasteur supervising the rabies vaccination of Jean Baptiste Jupille.

(a)

(b)

Pasteur's initial successes attracted large numbers of people seeking the vaccine. (a) Pasteur photographed amidst a group of children who had received rabies vaccine after having been bitten by rabid dogs. (b) A group of Russians bitten by a rabid wolf who came to Paris to receive the Pasteur treatment.

I cannot discuss here the very complex technical problems posed by the antirabies treatment in humans. Granted the real difficulties associated with Pasteur's vaccination techniques, it is on much broader issues that his achievements must be judged. Pasteur had demonstrated the possibility of investigating by rigorous techniques the infectious diseases caused by invisible, noncultivable viruses; he had shown that their pathogenic potentialities could be modified by various laboratory artifices; he

Pasteur depicted as the savior of children threatened by rabid dogs. Cartoon from a 19th century illustrated magazine.

had established beyond doubt that a solid immunity could be brought about without endangering the life or health of the vaccinated animals. Thanks to the rabies epic, a new science developed which eventually led to the development of vaccination techniques against yellow fever and several other virus diseases. Even more important, immunization became recognized as a general law of nature. All these achievements were the fruit of Pasteur's boldness as an experimenter, and of his mental courage in the face of natural odds and of human opposition.

The Dream of "Chemical Vaccines"

After so many struggles, intellectual effort, and dramatic successes, almost any other human being would have judged that the time had come to stop, or at least to settle down to a well-established and comfortable routine. But this was not Pasteur's bent. Although tired and sick, and sixty-five, he began to think about new avenues of approach to the problem of immunity. His vaccines against fowl cholera, anthrax, swine erysipelas, and rabies consisted of living microbes, attenuated in virulence true enough, but still capable of multiplying in the body. In fact, Pasteur believed, and he was right, that the immunity elicited by these vaccines depended precisely upon the fact that they did multiply to a limited extent in the vaccinated individual. However, some accidental findings made in the course of this work led him to think that it might be possible to cause immunity by injecting not the living microbes themselves, but instead lifeless material made up of some of their constituents or products. For example, the bacteria of fowl cholera released in the culture medium a soluble substance toxic for animals. Would it not be possible to immunize the fowl by injecting this toxic material into them? With anthrax and rabies also some experiments seemed to suggest that immunity could be produced without multiplication of the living attenuated microbes.

Because of ill health Pasteur had to abandon experimental work before he could put these original ideas to the test. But his statements that the future of immunity might reside in what he called "chemical vaccines," in contrast to the living vaccines with which he had worked so far, clearly indicated the direction he would have followed if he had been able to work for another decade. Nor were these the thoughts of a senile, irresponsible man. Even in his lifetime others showed that immunity against *diphtheria* and against *tetanus* could be produced by injecting not the diphtheria or tetanus bacilli themselves, but instead

Pasteur's legacy: Available vaccines today for infectious diseases in humans

Disease	Type of vaccine used
Bacterial diseases	
Diphtheria	Toxoid
Tetanus	Toxoid
Pertussis	Killed bacteria
Typhoid fever	Killed bacteria
Paratyphoid fever	Killed bacteria
Cholera	Killed cells or cell extract
Plague	Killed cells or cell extract
Tuberculosis	Attenuated strain (BCG)
Meningitis	Purified bacterial polysaccharide
Bacterial pneumonia	Purified bacterial polysaccharide
Typhus fever	Killed bacteria
Viral diseases	
Smallpox	Attenuated virus
Yellow fever	Attenuated virus
Measles	Attenuated virus
Mumps	Attenuated virus
Rubella	Attenuated virus
Polio	Attenuated virus
Influenza	Inactivated virus
Rabies	Inactivated virus (human) or attenuated virus (dogs and other animals)

their lifeless, soluble toxic products. Then it was found sometime later that immunity against certain bacteria and viruses could be produced by injecting these bacteria and viruses previously killed by heat or by certain antiseptics. One of the *polio vaccines* (the Salk vaccine) belongs to this class, consisting as it does of a suspension of polio viruses killed by treatment with formalin. The other polio vaccine, the Sabine vaccine, consists of attenuated virus. Then finally, it has been demonstrated that immunity against some of the microbes that cause pneumonia can be produced by injecting a synthetic chemical substance similar in composition to the gum which forms a protective envelope around these microbes. Truly, the "chemical vaccines" dreamed of by Pasteur have now come into being.

From Folklore to Knowledge

Let us emphasize once more that all Pasteur's work on vaccination was carried out within a very few years, at the end of his scientific life, and against immense odds. Let us conclude this chapter, as Pasteur would have liked, by pointing out that the story of vaccination provides one of the most spectacular examples of the power of experimental science, and of the manner in which folklore evolves into rational knowledge.

For thousands of years it had been known that persons recovered from a given disease were more likely to be more resistant than their fellow humans to the same disease. Either by accident or by trial and error, certain simple techniques of immunization had been developed to bring about this state of increased resistance. One of these techniques had grown from the knowledge among dairymaids in England that they did not develop smallpox if they had had an attack of cowpox—a folklore experience that Jenner had converted into a practical technique of vaccination. One century after Jenner, Pasteur guessed that vaccination against smallpox with cowpox was in reality the specialized application of a general law of nature—namely, that one can vaccinate against many types of microbial diseases by using related microorganisms of attenuated virulence. This generalization led to the development of general techniques for the production of vaccines. It gave birth to the science of immunology and encouraged chemists to study the nature of the substances in microorganisms that are capable of inducing resistance to infection. Thus, the biological science of immunology progressively evolved into its chemical counterpart, immunochemistry. In other words, close to 200 years of systematic experimental science have transformed the empirical knowledge of the dairymaid into the refined understanding of the professional immunochemist.

This example makes clear that, while knowledge often begins with observations and operations within the reach of most perceptive and intelligent persons, it can grow rapidly, and in depth, only when pursued systematically by the techniques of experimental science.

13

Further Applications of the Germ Theory of Disease

As we have seen, Pasteur showed very early in his scientific life an uncanny skill in converting the results of theoretical studies into practical applications. Just as the experiments on fermentation led him to develop practical procedures for preserving foodstuffs with controlled heating, so did the experiments on the germ theory of disease lead him to become involved in practical problems of medicine and surgery. The studies of vaccination which have just been recounted constitute the most spectacular phase of his achievements in this field, and also the most productive in practical results. But he devoted himself to many other types of practical applications, some of which have come to fruit only in recent years.

Biological Control and Warfare with Microbes

One of Pasteur's most original ideas was to use microorganisms for the control of animal and plant parasites. The first suggestion of his interest in this field appears as a casual laboratory note of 1882. It concerns phylloxera, a plant louse that was then destroying the vineyards of France and of the rest of Europe. "The insect . . . must have some contagious disease of its own," Pasteur wrote, "and it should not be impossible to isolate the causative microorganism of this disease. One would next . . . produce artificial foci of infection in countries affected by the phylloxera." Pasteur never followed this idea, but he came back to it five years later, with regard to the control of the rabbits which had become a plague threatening the economy of Australia and New Zealand. In a letter to an English journal, he suggested that the most promising approach to the eradication of rabbits was to introduce into Australia a microbial species that would start a fatal infection among them. "So far, one had employed chemical poisons to control this plague. . . . Is it not preferable to use, in order to destroy living beings, a poison endowed with life and capable of multiplying at a great speed?. . . . I should like to see the agent of death carried into the burrows by communicating to rabbits a disease that might become epidemic."

He carried out a field test of his idea on an estate in France, having cultures of the bacillus *Pasteurella multocida*, which is virulent for rabbits, spread on alfalfa around burrows. Although many rabbits died after eating the contaminated alfalfa, practical reasons prevented him from going further with this technique. In fact, it is most unlikely that infection with *Pasteurella multocida* would have proved effective as a method of rabbit control on a large scale, because it is now known that this organism could not have established a widespread rabbit epidemic with a progressive course. Nevertheless, many attempts have since been made to control animal and plant plagues with other microbial parasites, and a few of these attempts have produced spectacular results—for a while at least. For example, the introduction into Australia of the virus which causes the fatal disease known as *myxomatosis* has brought about a destructive epidemic among the rabbits in these countries. Although the ultimate outcome of the epidemic cannot yet be predicted (the Australian rabbits have become rapidly resistant to the virus), there is no doubt that Pasteur clearly visualized the practical potentialities of biological control of plant and animal pests through the activities of microorganisms. It is a sad commentary on the role of the scientists in the modern world that huge research programs during and shortly after World War II were devoted to the search for ways to utilize these potentialities in military conflicts. What Pasteur had suggested as a possible method of biological control of pests became chiefly a possible technique of biological warfare.

Antibiotics and Aseptic Surgery

Pasteur's name has often been mentioned with reference to the discovery of *antimicrobial drugs* produced by microorganisms— the so-called *antibiotics*. All historians of the subject point to his original observation that cultures of the anthrax bacillus with which he was working lost their virulence when they became contaminated with soil microorganisms. Amazingly enough, it is never mentioned that his first realization that certain living things produce substances capable of exerting selective antimicrobial effects antedates his anthrax work by twenty years. In his very first paper on lactic-acid fermentation, published as we have seen in 1857, he reported that onion juice added to a sugar solution prevented the development of yeast. There is no doubt that he had clearly seen the practical potentialities of these observations, as shown by his statement in 1878 that "these facts perhaps justify the highest hopes for therapeutics." This prophecy was completely fulfilled half a century later with the discovery of penicillin, and today it is still inspiring countless workers all over the world in their attempts to obtain new anti-infectious drugs from microorganisms.

In view of the success of this prophetic vision, it seems at first sight odd that Pasteur never actually concerned himself with the development and use of drugs for the treatment of infectious diseases. The reason is to be found in his belief that prevention is better than cure. "When meditating over a disease," he wrote, "I never think of finding a remedy for it but, instead, search for means to prevent it." This was the medical philosophy that prompted him to devote so much effort to the problems of vaccination and of sanitation.

As he began to frequent hospital wards, Pasteur became more and more convinced that the very objects surrounding the patients were the source of dangerous microorganisms and that even the doctors and nurses often acted as carriers of infection. He—who did not have a medical degree—was bold enough to scold physicians on this score. In a famous lecture delivered before the Academy of Medicine in Paris he issued warnings which created a great sensation: "This water, this sponge, this lint with which you wash or cover a wound, may deposit germs which have the power of multiplying rapidly within the tissues. . . . If I had the honor of being a surgeon, impressed as I am with the dangers to which the patient is exposed from the microbes present over the surface of all objects, particularly in hospitals, not only would I use none but perfectly clean instruments, but I would clean my hands with the greatest care, and subject them to a rapid flaming. . . . I would use only lint, bandages, and sponges previously exposed to a temperature of 130° to 150°C." This memorable statement has become the basis of *aseptic surgery*, which aims at preventing access of microorganisms to the operative field rather than trying to kill them with antiseptics applied to the tissues.

It is not necessary to emphasize further the contributions made by the germ theory of disease to the development of sanitary measures. As everyone knows, awareness of the dangers of infection is now universal in our communities, and specialized control laboratories watch over the water we drink, the food we eat, the objects we touch, and the air we breathe, in an attempt to eliminate from our environment any microorganism potentially capable of causing disease. Sanitation has now become almost synonymous with Western civilization and there is no doubt that it has greatly contributed to the decrease in the prevalence of microbial disease during recent decades.

A Neglected Lesson

So great, indeed, have been the practical achievements that have grown out of bacteriological knowledge that there has been a tendency to regard the control of disease as absolutely dependent on the use of techniques directed against the microorganisms. In reality, however, there are many other factors to be considered in the study of microbial diseases. For example, the hereditary constitution of the patient, nutritional state, emotional equilibrium, the season of the year, and the climate are among the factors that can affect the course of infection. Today, many physicians and medical scientists lament the fact that, under the influence of the germ theory of disease, all these factors tend to be neglected and even ignored. I believe that if Pasteur were living today, he, too, would feel very much disturbed that his followers have emphasized only one aspect of his teaching, and have lost view of his broader philosophy of disease causation.

14

Pasteur's Dilemma—The Road Not Taken*

Pasteur had been trained not in biology or pathology but in physics and organic chemistry. He first achieved international fame at the age of 27 by his crystallographical studies and his discovery of isomerism. It was through measurements of optical rotation of organic acids that he was led, by many indirect steps, to recognize that the conversion of sugar into alcohol or lactic acid is caused by microbes. In his first biological paper, published in 1857 at age 35, he boldly formulated what he called the germ theory of fermentation—namely that each particular type of fermentation is caused by a specific kind of microbe. In the same preliminary paper he suggested, without any evidence, that this theory could be generalized, and he boldly announced a specific microbial etiology of disease. Eventually the doctrine of specific etiology led him to the practice of specific vaccinations.

---

*Adapted from ASM News 40:703–709 (1974).

Throughout his life, Pasteur stated that he had been led by an inescapable logic from crystals and optical rotation to fermentations and their control, and eventually to microbial diseases and specific vaccinations. One can recognize indeed a majestic "ordonnance" in Pasteur's scientific achievements. Yet I shall try to show that the trend of his logic was not as inescapable as he thought. He could have followed other trends which would have led him just as logically into other lines of work and to other worthwhile achievements. He had been prevented by other tasks from continuing his early work on isomerism, but he had followed developments in the field. Indeed, he never lost his early conviction that studies in crystalline assymetry would contribute to an understanding of life and of its origins.

What of his work on disease? Pasteur had entered the field of pathology through his work on the diseases of silkworms, almost by accident at the request of his former teacher Jean Baptiste Dumas. After several false starts based on his belief that these diseases were nutritional and physiological in nature, he had shown that they were in reality caused by microbes and could be controlled by measures designed to protect the worms from contamination. But despite the outstanding success of his purely antimicrobial control methods, he gained the impression that the physiological well-being of the silk worms greatly influenced their resistance to infection. In his book on silkworm diseases he made the following statement which reveals an aspect of his thoughts which he did not have the time to develop scientifically. "If I were to undertake new studies on the silkworm diseases, I would direct my efforts to the environmental conditions that increase their vigor and resistance. . . . I am convinced that it would be possible to discover techniques for improving the physiological state of the worms and thereby increase their resistance to disease."

His enduring conviction that health is an expression of the physiological status is reflected also in the lectures he delivered at the École des Beaux Arts in Paris from 1863 to 1867. While teaching the applications of physics and chemistry to architecture, he discussed at length and illustrated with experiments how health and physiological well-being are influenced by the composition of the air in living quarters.

I shall now briefly mention a few of Pasteur's laboratory observations that led him very early to believe that environmental control might be as essential as control of the specific microorganisms for a good management of fermentations and of microbial diseases.

The central dogma of the germ theory is that each particular type of fermentation or of disease is caused by a specific kind of microbe. But this does not mean that fermentations and diseases can only be controlled by acting on their direct causes, for example, by pasteurization or vaccination or with antiseptics and other antimicrobial drugs. There is evidence indeed that Pasteur was at first interested in the potentialities of control by manipulation of the physicochemical environment—what he called the "terrain." In his very first preliminary paper on fermentation—the 1857 "Mémoire sur la fermentation lactique"—he emphasized that, when glucose solutions are left opened in contact with the air, the sugar is converted into lactic acid by bacteria if the solution is acidic and into alcohol by yeast if the solution is alkaline. He guessed that bacteria and yeast are ubiquitous in the air and therefore find their way naturally into the solution under usual circumstances, but that acidity or alkalinity decides which type of microorganism will gain the upper hand.

To the end of his life, Pasteur reiterated his belief—almost as an obsession—that the structure and activities of microorganisms are always conditioned by the nature of their environment. For example, he described how the very shape and size of yeasts and molds are determined by cultural conditions and especially by oxygen tension. Some of his most remarkable metabolic studies are concerned with the influence of oxygen on the amount of alcohol, organic acids, carbon dioxide, and cellular protoplasm produced by a particular microbial species from a given type and amount of substrate. Since Pasteur's primary training was in chemistry, there is no doubt that the logic of his work could have led him much further than he went in the direction of microbial physiology—had not his energy been monopolized by the problems of infectious pathology and vaccination.

Whereas Pasteur's studies on the relation between environmental factors and metabolic activities are well known because they led him to spectacular discoveries, his awareness of the importance of the terrain in infection is hardly ever mentioned, because he did not convert it into experimental work. Yet, his scientific philosophy in this regard was sophisticated, taking into account genetic and evolutionary concepts of adaptation. I shall try to present his views in the form of a few statements, each documented by direct quotations extracted from his own writings.

Early in his work on disease, he recognized that it was a biological necessity for living things to be endowed with natural resistance to the agents of destruction ubiquitous in their environment. As he saw it, populations—be they of microbes or humans—usually achieve some sort of evolutionary adaptation to their environment which renders them better able to resist the causes of disease with which they frequently come into contact. Furthermore, he took it for granted that the body in a state of normal physiological health exhibits a striking resistance to many types of microbial agents.

As he pointed out, the various body surfaces and the intestinal tract are full of microorganisms which can cause damage only when the body is weakened. Likewise, infection often fails to take hold even when antiseptic measures are neglected in the course of surgery. Indeed, human nature possesses a remarkable ability to overcome foci of infection.

As already mentioned, Pasteur's attitude regarding the importance of physiological well-being in resistance to infection had developed during his studies with silkworms. He had then become aware of profound differences in the pathogenesis of the two diseases that he had encountered in these insects. In the case of the disease pebrine, the presence of the specific protozoan was a sufficient cause of the disease, provided the infective dose was large enough. But in the case of the other disease, flacherie, the resistance of the worms to infection was profoundly influenced by environmental factors. Among these, Pasteur considered that excessive heat and humidity, inadequate aeration, stormy weather, and poor food were inimical to the general physiological health of the insects. As he put it, the proliferation of microorganisms in the intestinal tract of worms suffering from flacherie was more an effect than a cause of the disease.

Pasteur did not hesitate to extend these views to the most important human diseases. He accepted that resistance to tuberculosis was an expression of native hereditary endowment on the one hand, and that it was influenced on the other hand by the state of nutrition and by certain factors of the environment, including the climate. Even more boldly, he suggested that the mental state affected resistance to infection.

This point of view naturally led Pasteur to conclude that resistance to infection could probably be increased by improving the physiological state of the infected individual. He urged his collaborator, Duclaux, to look for procedures that would increase the general resistance of silkworms. And he expressed the opinion that in humans also successful therapy often depended upon the ability of the physician to restore physiological conditions favorable to natural resistance.

Although circumstances did not allow Pasteur to deal effectively with the physiological determinants of infectious diseases, he carried out at least one spectacular experiment concerning the effect of temperature on susceptibility to infection. Puzzled by the fact that hens are refractory to anthrax, he had wondered whether this might not be explained by their body temperature, which is higher than that of animals susceptible to the disease. To test this hypothesis, he inoculated hens and placed them in a cold bath to lower their body temperature. Animals so treated died the next day, showing numerous bacilli in their blood, spleen, lungs, and liver. Another hen, similarly infected and maintained in the cold bath until the disease was in full progress, was then taken out of the water, dried, and placed under conditions that allowed rapid increase in body temperature. Amazingly, it made a complete recovery. Thus, the mere fall of temperature from 42°C (the normal temperature of hens) to 38°C was sufficient to render birds almost as receptive to anthrax as are rabbits or guinea pigs. The interpretation of this change in susceptibility is probably more complex than was assumed by Pasteur, but, whatever the exact mechanism involved, his experiment illustrates how the environment profoundly affects the response of the body to infectious agents.

Pasteur once formulated another hypothesis which, long regarded as naïve, is acquiring new significance from recent studies on the effect of nutrition on infection. He had postulated that the immunity following recovery from infection might be due to the fact that the body becomes depleted in some nutritional factor essential to the parasite. "One could imagine that cesium or rubidium are elements necessary for the life of the microbe under consideration, that there exists only a small amount of these elements in its tissues and that this amount has been exhausted by a first growth of the microbes; this animal, then, will remain refractory until its tissues have recuperated these elements." The "exhaustion theory" was soon abandoned by Pasteur himself. Yet, research now suggests that there was a grain of truth in it.

Given the state of scientific knowledge in the mid-nineteenth century, Pasteur certainly took the right path in the kind of logic he followed—from specific causes of fermentation to specific causes of infectious diseases and then to specific vaccination. Biological sciences could not have gone far without the precise knowledge and the intellectual discipline provided by the concept of specificity. But microbiologists are now profitably thinking along other lines of logic, for example, by orienting their thoughts toward ecology—with regard not only to pathological processes but also to the creative interplay of microorganisms with all sorts of natural systems, even on a global scale.

As already mentioned, Pasteur himself had recognized the implications of the ecological point of view in his early work on fermentation and had kept it in mind during all his subsequent studies. Early in his scientific life, he expressed it with a passionate eloquence in long letters (1862–1867) to important French officials of the time, including Emperor Napoleon III. In these letters, he advocated support for the microbiological sciences on the ground that they would provide an explanation for the cycles of chemical elements in nature—from complex organic matter to simpler chemical substances and back into life processes.

Under his influence, the ecological view of microbiological activities soon became one of the dominant aspects of soil science. Ecological concepts were used early also in problems as different as sewage purification and cheese making. It is now possible to analyze and synthesize the many roles that microbial life plays in the economy of nature. But instead of considering microbial activities from this cosmic point of view, I shall discuss only one ecological problem, selected to illustrate the creative effects of biological associations involving various microorganisms.

My one example concerns germfree life. Pasteur had been inclined to believe that animals could not possibly survive without harboring microbes in their bodies. However, he had encouraged his associates, particularly Duclaux, to put the question to experimental test. Precise techniques have now been worked out to raise many species of animals under germfree conditions. Since animals obtained and maintained under germfree conditions can develop, achieve normal life spans, and reproduce for several generations, it would seem at first sight that Pasteur had been mistaken in his assumption. And yet he was partially right, because germfree animals exhibit biological abnormalities which would make them unable to compete with normal animals in the open world.

The subtitle of the present chapter "The Road Not Taken" is from the poem in which Robert Frost suggests that by selecting one particular road we lose the opportunity to experience what another road would have offered. Pasteur's writings make clear that he was conscious of the scientific opportunities he had neglected by taking, so to speak, the "pure culture" road in his microbiological studies, at the expense of the physiological and ecological points of view. But I am convinced that he was right in orienting his work toward the specificity aspect of biological processes, because this was an indispensable phase in the study of natural systems. The time has come, however, when it will be extremely profitable to take the road—in Robert Frost's words "less travelled by"—namely, the road that will lead to physiological and ecological studies. The limited experience available has already proven that the most creative processes emerge from the integration of complex systems, rather than from the analytic breakdown of their component parts.

For almost a century, microbiological sciences have provided models, materials, and techniques that have greatly facilitated the understanding of the mechanisms responsible for the operation of isolated biological processes. In my opinion our science can now once more provide models, materials, and techniques for a new step in the study of life. Just as microbiologists have been pioneers in modern developments of metabolism and genetics, so they can now participate in the effort to understand the integration of individual biological units into more complex social structures—including human societies.

15

A Dedicated Life

Pasteur possessed several personality traits rarely found together in one individual. His devotion to scientific research was complete, and, despite the stroke that partly paralyzed him at the age of forty-six, he worked with incredible intensity until his health completely failed. He was a masterful technician but also highly intuitive. He derived problems from industrial or medical questions, and never shied away from practical problems, but he also pursued the large theoretical concepts involved in his studies and thus reached fundamental scientific generalizations. He worked almost in isolation, with very few collaborators, but had an immense gift for public debate. In many famous controversies he overcame his opponents by the spoken and written word, and also by elegant and dramatic demonstrations. While worshiping experimental science, he also maintained that their exist spiritual values that transcend scientific approach—a thesis which he defended in a celebrated debate with the philosopher Ernest Renan at the time of his reception into the French Academy of Letters.

Pasteur and Family

We cannot deal here with the more personal aspects of his life, even though this would make an inspiring story. Let us merely mention that the responsiveness of his temperament and the warmth of his feelings were manifested in a most engaging manner in the wonderful relations that he had with his father, mother, sisters, as well as with his wife and children, his school friends, and his teachers. The following quotations from the letter that he wrote his wife on the night of his father's death may help to convey the warmth of his temperament.

> I have been thinking all day of the marks of affection I have had from my father. For thirty years I have been his constant care, I owe everything to him. When I was young he kept me from bad company and instilled into me the habit of working and the example of the most loyal and best-filled life. He was far above his position both in mind and in character. . . . You did not know him, dearest Marie, at the time when he and my mother were working so hard for the children they loved, for me especially, whose books and schooling cost so much. . . . And the touching part of his affection for me is that it never was mixed with ambition. You remember that he would have been pleased to see me the headmaster of Arbois College? He foresaw that advancement would mean hard work, perhaps detrimental to my health. And yet I am sure that some of the success in my scientific career must have filled him with joy and pride; his son! his name! the child he had guided and cherished!

Some twenty years later, the dedication of a memorial plaque placed on the house where he was born in Dôle gave Pasteur once more the occasion to express in public his feelings toward his parents. Answering the speeches of congratulation addressed to him, he replied in the following words:

> Your sympathy has joined on that memorial plate the two great things which have been the passion and the delight of my life: *the love of Science and the cult of the home.*
> Oh! my father, my mother, dear departed ones, who lived so humbly in this little house, it is to you that I owe everything.

(a)

(b)

(c)

(d)

Pasteur and his family. (a) Pasteur at his villa at Pont-Gisquet dictating a paper to Madame Pasteur. (b) Madame Pasteur and the daughter Marie-Louise Pasteur. The photo was taken in the garden of the École Normale around 1877. (c) Pasteur surrounded by his family in the garden of his summer place at Arbois, in 1892. From left to right; front row: Madame Pasteur, grandson Louis Pasteur Vallery-Radot, Pasteur, granddaughter Camile Vallery-Radot; back row: nephew Laurent, son-in-law René Vallery-Radot, daughter Marie-Louise (married to René Vallery-Radot). (d) Pasteur in 1891 on the beach at Saint-Aubin, with his grandchildren.

Your enthusiasm, my brave-hearted mother, you have instilled it into me. If I have always associated the greatness of science with the greatness of France, it is because I was impregnated with the feelings that you had inspired. And you, dearest father, whose father was as hard as your hard trade, you have shown to me what patience and protracted effort can accomplish. It is to you that I owe perseverance in daily work. Not only did you have the qualities which go to make a useful life, but also admiration for great men and great things. To look upwards, learn to the utmost, to seek to rise ever higher, such was your teaching. I can see you now, after a hard day's work, reading in the evening some story of the battles in the glorious epoch of which you were a witness. Whilst teaching me to read, your care was that I should learn the greatness of France.

Pasteur and Country

Pasteur's devotion was not limited to his family. He expressed repeatedly his indebtedness to some of his teachers; he remained attached to his native province, and above all he had a passionate love for France. "The thought of France supported my courage during the difficult hours which are an inevitable part of prolonged efforts. I associated her greatness with the greatness of science." Following the French disasters in the Franco-Prussian War of 1870–71, the Italian Government offered him a chair of chemistry at the University of Pisa, with a high salary and very great personal advantages, but after much hesitation he refused, "I should feel like a deserter if I sought, away from my country in distress, a material situation better than that which it can offer me."

His national pride was deeply wounded when France was defeated by Prussia in 1871, and he seized upon the occasion to point out to his countrymen that the disaster came in part from their neglect of science. Appealing to public opinion as well as to governmental bodies, he pleaded for more vigorous support of scientific research and of other intellectual pursuits. In 1871 he issued a pamphlet in which he lamented the material circumstances that prevented young French scholars from devoting their energies to academic research; he contrasted the miserable state of laboratories in France with the magnificent support they were receiving abroad and particularly in Germany; he recalled the prominent part played by French science in helping the country to overcome the onslaught of Europe during the Revolution and the Napoleonic Wars.

Some of the public statements that he made at that time are meaningful for us today, when national survival depends so much on the proper attitude toward science and general culture. Time and time again, he spoke of the "close correlation that exists between theoretical science and the life of nations." He pointed out that the material prosperity that France enjoyed in the late nineteenth century had its origin in the discoveries of the preceding generations, and that to neglect theoretical science was "to allow the sources of wealth to go dry." Furthermore, while he emphasized science's essential role in the maintenance of national wealth and power, he never lost sight of its larger values. "In the present state of modern civilization," he wrote, *the cultivation of the highest forms of science is perhaps even more necessary to the moral state of a nation than to its material prosperity.*"

He described with enthusiasm how, by virtue of her leadership in scientific research during the fifty years before the Revolution, the France of 1792 had multiplied her forces through the genius of invention and had found, wherever needed, men capable of organizing victory. And in words of overwhelming conviction he exclaimed, "Oh my country! You who so long held the scepter of thought, why did you neglect your noblest creations? They are the divine torch which illuminates the world, the live source of the highest sentiments, which keep us from sacrificing everything to material satisfactions."

A Higher Dedication

However, his devotion to the French cause did not blind him to the larger truth that science transcends natural borders and interest. He knew well that science is of equal relevance to all people, and is one of the few human activities of universal value.

> I am imbued with two deep impressions; the first, that science knows no country; the second, which seems to contradict the first, although it is in reality a direct consequence of it, that science is the highest personification of the nation. Science knows no country, because knowledge belongs to humanity, and is the torch which illuminates the world. Science is the highest personification of the nation because that nation will remain the first which carries the furthest the works of thought and intelligence.

It was not in an abstract manner that he worshiped science. He said himself that it had been "the dominating passion" of his life, and that he had "lived only for it." On many occasions he found words filled with emotion to express the happiness that he had derived from his studious hours. At every phase of his life, he approached his work with such a sense of dedication that he could truly speak of "enthusiasm" as the internal god that had constantly sustained him. Across almost a century, his voice brings a message which can help many of us today in the achievement of great tasks. "The Greeks have given us one of the most beautiful words of our language, the word 'enthusiasm'—a God within. The grandeur of the acts of men is measured by the inspiration from which they spring. *Happy is he who bears a God within.*"

It was this enthusiasm, this belief in the greatness of the cause for which he was working, that made him speak with such love of the institutions of learning, the laboratories, and the libraries in which most of his waking hours had been spent. He was trying to convey this love to laymen when he wrote in an oft-quoted sentence, "*Take interest, I beseech you, in those sacred institutions which we designate under the expressive name of labora-*

tories. Demand that they be multiplied and adorned; they are the temples of wealth and of the future. There it is that humanity grows, becomes stronger and better. There it learns to read in the works of nature, symbols of progress and of universal harmony, whereas the works of mankind are too often those of fanaticism and destruction."

In his romantic student days Pasteur had thought that he would be devoting his scientific life to the solution of abstract problems pertaining to the nature of life. But circumstances had engaged him in other more concrete pursuits, such as industrial fermentations and the control of infectious diseases. In 1888, as he opened the new research institute to be named for him, the Pasteur Institute, he dedicated it with the following words: "Two contrary laws seem to be wrestling with each other nowadays: the one, a law of blood and of death, ever imagining new means of destruction and forcing nations to be constantly ready for the battlefield—the other, a law of peace, work and health, ever evolving new means for delivering man from the scourges which beset him."

Four years later, his seventieth birthday was the occasion of a solemn jubilee in the great amphitheater of the Sorbonne, attended by the President of the French Republic and by delegations of French and foreign institutions of learning. As emphasized by one of the official orators, it was not merely a great scientist who was the hero of the day, but a man who had devoted all his strength, his heart, and his genius to the service of mankind.

Unable to speak for emotion, and compelled to extend his thanks through the voice of his son, Pasteur then expressed for a last time in public his conviction that science would some day bring happiness to man.

> Delegates from foreign nations, who have come from so far to give France a proof of sympathy: you bring me the deepest joy that can be felt by a man whose invincible belief is that Science and Peace will triumph over Ignorance and War, that nations will unite, not to destroy, but to build, and that the future will belong to those who will have done most for suffering humanity.

The Pasteur Institute, as illustrated in a 19th century engraving. Inaugurated November 14, 1888, the Pasteur Institute was initially primarily a center for treatment of rabies and other contagious diseases, but has developed into a major center for microbiological research. Emile Roux, Pasteur's successor, defined the Pasteur Institute as: "a cooperative scientific venture where each scientist strives toward a common end, while at the same time retaining independence of ideas and approaches."

The modern Pasteur Institute employs more than 2000 people and has numerous buildings both in Paris and elsewhere. It produces serums and vaccines for medical and veterinary use as well as laboratory products for research. Among the vaccines and serums that it produces are antitoxins for diphtheria, tetanus, botulism, and staphylococcal infection, BCG vaccine for tuberculosis, and vaccines for polio, typhoid fever, paratyphoid fever, whooping cough, cholera, and influenza. The Pasteur Institute is also a leader in research on acquired immunodeficiency syndrome (AIDS), and is the codiscoverer of the blood test for AIDS infection.

The following Nobel Prize Winners were at the Pasteur Institute: 1907: Charles Laveran. Discovery of the protozoan which causes malaria; 1908: Elie Metchnikoff. Discovery of the process of phagocytosis; 1919: Jules Bordet. Discovery of complement and other discoveries in immunology; 1928: Charles Nicolle. Discovery that typhus fever is transmitted by the body louse; 1957: Daniel Bovet. Production of artificial curare (South American poison) for use as a muscle relaxant; 1965: Andre Lwoff, Jacques Monod, and François Jacob. Fundamental discoveries in molecular genetics and cellular biochemistry.

Addressing the students, he recalled the rich satisfactions he had derived from his years of toil and expressed his undying confidence in the power of the experimental method to improve the lot of man on earth.

> Young men, have faith in those powerful and safe methods, of which we do not yet know all the secrets. And, whatever your career may be, do not let yourselves be discouraged by the sadness of certain hours which pass over nations. *Live in the serene peace of laboratories and libraries.*

Of His Time and Timeless

The account of Pasteur's deeds and words leaves the impression that his was truly an enchanted life—with prodigious achievements, both theoretical and practical, spectacular triumphs over his opponents, and a worldwide fame that made him a legendary character during his lifetime. We have seen, however, that all this had been gained at the cost of arduous and constant labor, against all kinds of odds and much opposition. Certainly also, Pasteur suffered in his later life from having been compelled by practical necessities to abandon some of the theoretical problems dearest to his heart. Time and time again, he stated that he had been "enchained" by an inescapable forward-moving logic that had led him from the study of crystals to the study of fermentation and spontaneous generation, and then of contagious diseases. Yet the desire of his early days to work on the nature of life had remained one of his haunting dreams. He came to believe that it was only through accidental circumstances that he was involved in practical problems—important of course, but not as deep in their significance as those he had visualized early in life. Pasteur's grandson, Professor Louis Pasteur Vallery-Radot, has told a moving story which reveals the pathetic intensity of this inner conflict during Pasteur's later years.

I see again that face, that appeared to be carved from a block of granite—that high and large forehead, those grayish-green eyes, with such a deep and kind look. He was partly paralyzed on his left side, and it was with this terrible incapacity that he carried on his research on infectious diseases.

He seemed to me serious and sad. He was probably sad because of all the things he had dreamed of but not realized.

I remember one evening, at the Pasteur Institute. He was writing quietly at his desk, his head bent on his right hand, in a familiar pose. I was at the corner of the table, not moving or speaking. I had been taught to respect his silences. He stood up and, feeling the need to express his thoughts to the nearest person, even a child, he told me: "*Ah! my boy, I wish I had a new life before me! With how much joy I should like to undertake again my studies on crystals!*" To have given up his research on crystals was the eternal sorrow of his life.

In reality, however, Pasteur could not have escaped entirely the appeal of practical problems. He worked during the second part of the nineteenth century, a period when, for the first time, the findings of experimental science were being converted into practical applications on a large scale. As a man of the nineteenth century, he was bound to focus his efforts on those aspects of his science likely to yield concrete results. What is remarkable is that the urge to work on concrete problems did not prevent him from seeing beyond the immediate needs of his time, and from dealing intellectually with subjects that were not yet ripe for practical application.

All scientists, like artists, naturally reflect the characteristics of the civilization and of the times in which they arise. A few of the great ones, however, have visions that appear to be without roots in their cultural past and which are therefore difficult to explain rationally in terms of obvious direct influences. Yet even these creators should not be regarded as aberrations in the natural sequence of cultural events. They constitute rather peculiar mentalities through which emerge and become manifest social undercurrents that remain hidden to less perceptive minds. Some of them succeed in converting their visions—which are really signs from the social and cultural subconscious—into messages and products meaningful and of immediate value to their fellow humans. They become then the popular scientific heroes of their own society. Others perceive the hopes and the tasks of the more distant future, but without providing precise or practical solutions. They give warnings of the problems to come, but these anticipations are usually not understood by their contemporaries and acquire meaning only much later. Pasteur belonged in all these categories. Because of his immense practical skill in converting theoretical knowledge into technological processes, he was one of the most productive men of the nineteenth century. By synthesizing almost unconsciously the known facts of biology and biochemistry into original concepts of fermentation and disease, he created a new science which immediately met urgent needs in his social environment. And by visualizing microbial life as an essential part of the ecological complex, he foresaw an aspect of science that is yet to develop.

All the discoveries that he made have stood the test of time, and some of his prophetic visions are now acquiring increased significance as we add new dimensions to the magnificent structure that he began to build. His writings carry a message that will encourage us as we try to reach beyond the conventional theories of fermentation and infection. His thought is still a living force reflected in many phases of contemporary biochemical, biological, and medical science. To him can be applied the words that he once used in writing of his great fellow countryman, the chemist Antoine Lavoisier: "His scientific creation remains eternally young. Certain details of it may have aged, as have the fashions of yesteryear, but its spirit and its method will survive. They constitute one of the great achievements of human thought."

Chronology

1822 Pasteur born 27 December at two o'clock in the morning in Dôle, France

1831 Completed primary school at Arbois

1839 Completed secondary school at Arbois

1842 Completed college at Besançon

1847 Completed doctorate degree in physics and chemistry at École Normale Supérieure in Paris

1846–1849 Assistant in chemistry, École Normale

1848 Announced his first discoveries on asymmetry of crystals

1849–1854 Professor of chemistry, Faculty of Sciences, Strasbourg

1849 Married Marie Laurent, the daughter of the Rector of the University of Strasbourg

1850 Birth of Pasteur's first child, a daughter, Jeanne (died 1859)

1851 Birth of Pasteur's son, Jean-Baptiste (named for Jean-Baptiste Biot, Pasteur's mentor)

1853 Awarded medal (Legion of Honor) for his work on crystals and awarded a prize of the Pharmacy Society of Paris

1853 Birth of Pasteur's daughter, Cécile (died, 1866)

1854–1857 Professor of chemistry and Dean of the Faculty of Sciences, Lille

1857 Awarded Rumford Medal of the Royal Society of London (for his work on crystallography)

1857 Published first paper on fermentation

1857–1867 Administrator and director of scientific studies, École Normale Supérieure, Paris

1858 Birth of Pasteur's daughter, Marie-Louise

1858 Set up his "miserable" laboratory in an attic of the École Normale, rue d'Ulm, Paris

1860 Received a prize in experimental physiology from the Académie des Sciences for his work on fermentation

1861 Published famous paper on spontaneous generation

1861 Published paper on life without air

1862 Elected member of the Académie des Sciences

1863 Birth of Pasteur's son, Camille (died, 1865)

1865 Initiated work at Alès on silkworm diseases

1866 Published book on diseases of wine and their prevention; first description of the pasteurization process

1866–1867 Awarded medals and prizes for his work on diseases of wine and the pasteurization process

1867–1874 Professor of chemistry, University of Paris (Sorbonne)

1867–1888 Director of the Laboratory of Physiological Chemistry, École Normale, Paris

1868 Honorary M.D., University of Bonn (returned during Franco-Prussian War of 1870–1871)

1868 Suffered a stroke, leaving him partially paralyzed for life on his left side

1869 Elected Fellow of the Royal Society of London

1870 Franco-Prussian War. Pasteur avoids the siege of Paris by moving to Arbois

1870 Published book on diseases of silkworms

1873 Elected member of the Académie de Médecine

1873–1882 Awarded many medals and prizes

1876 Published book on diseases of beer

1877 Published first work on anthrax

1879 Marie-Louise Pasteur (Pasteur's daughter) marries René Vallery-Radot (later Pasteur's biographer)

1880–1881 Published paper on attenuation and immunization of fowl cholera

1880 Birth of Pasteur's first grandchild, Camille Vallery-Radot

1881 Famous experiment on anthrax vaccination at Pouilly le Fort

1881 First paper on rabies

1882 Elected to the Académie Française

1885 Joseph Meister vaccinated for rabies, first treatment of a human

1886 Birth of Pasteur's grandson, Louis Pasteur Vallery-Radot

1888 Opening of the Pasteur Institute, Paris

1892 Seventy-year Jubilee celebration at the Sorbonne

1895 Pasteur died, 28 September, at Chateau Villeneure-l'Étang (near Paris)

Glossary

Acetic acid An organic acid containing three carbon atoms that is produced by acetic acid bacteria and is the principle ingredient in vinegar.

Aerobe An organism that grows in the presence of O_2; may be facultative or obligate.

Amino acid An organic acid containing nitrogen in the form of an amino group; building block of protein.

Amyl alcohol A five-carbon alcohol produced as a fermentation product by certain bacteria.

Anthrax A bacterial disease caused by *Bacillus anthracis* that affects predominantly domestic animals but may also affect humans.

Anaerobe An organism that grows in the absence of oxygen.

Antibiotic A chemical agent produced by one organism that is harmful to other organisms.

Antibody A protein present in serum or other body fluid that combines specifically with antigen.

Antigen A substance, usually macromolecular, that induces specific antibody formation.

Antimicrobial Harmful to microorganisms by either killing or inhibiting growth.

Antiseptic An agent that kills or inhibits growth, but is not harmful to human tissue.

Antiserum A serum containing antibodies.

Antitoxin An antibody active against a toxin.

Aseptic Absence of living microorganisms.

Aseptic surgery Surgery under conditions that prevent the entry of microorganisms to the site of the operation.

155

Attenuation Selection from a pathogen of nonvirulent strains still capable of immunizing.

Axenic Pure, uncontaminated; an axenic culture is a pure culture.

Bacteriology The study of bacteria. Sometimes used synonymously with microbiology.

Bacterium (plural, bacteria) The smallest and simplest type of living organism.

Bactericidal Capable of killing bacteria.

Cholera A bacterial disease caused by *Vibrio cholerae*; generally transmitted by polluted water.

Citric acid A six-carbon organic acid produced by certain bacteria and fungi.

Complement A complex of proteins in the blood serum that acts in concert with specific antibody in certain kinds of antigen-antibody reactions.

Contagious Transmissible from one person to another.

Cowpox A disease of cows related to smallpox in humans.

Crystallography Study of the structure and composition of crystals.

Culture A particular strain or kind of organism growing in a laboratory medium.

Decomposition Natural process by which organic matter is broken down; generally brought about by microorganisms.

Desiccation Drying.

Diphtheria Bacterial disease of humans caused by *Corynebacterium diphtheriae*.

Disinfectant An agent that kills microorganisms, but may be harmful to human tissue.

Endospore A bacterial spore formed within the cell and extremely resistant to heat as well as to other harmful agents.

Enzymes Proteins present in cells that speed up the rate of chemical reactions.

Fermentation Catabolic reactions producing ATP in which organic compounds serve as both primary electron donor and ultimate electron acceptor.

Fermentation (industrial) A large-scale microbial process.

Filterable Capable of passing through a filter able to hold back the smallest bacteria. Generally used in reference to viruses, as *filterable viruses*.

Flacherie A disease of silkworms.

Fowl cholera A disease of chickens and other birds that resembles cholera in humans but is caused by a different organism.

Germ theory of disease Theory that infectious diseases are caused by living organisms (generally bacteria).

Heat-resistant Not killed by treatment at high temperature. Generally refers to spores.

Host An organism capable of supporting the growth of a virus or parasite.

Immune Able to resist infectious disease.

Immunization Induction of specific immunity by injecting antigen or antibodies.

Immunological Refers to processes of antibody formation and antigen-antibody reactions, whether or not immunity to infectious disease results.

In vivo In the body, in a living organism.

In vitro In glass, in culture.

Infection Growth of an organism within the body.

Inhibitor Substance capable of preventing the growth of a living organism.

Lactic acid A three-carbon organic acid produced by many bacteria during fermentation; also produced by animal muscle.

Metabolism All biochemical reactions in a cell, both anabolic and catabolic.

Microorganism A living organism that is only visible under a microscope.

Microscope Optical device for looking at very small objects.

Microbiology The study of microorganisms.

Nutrient A substance taken by a cell from its environment and used in metabolic reactions.

Obligate A qualifying adjective referring to an environmental factor always required for growth (e.g., "obligate anaerobe").

Oxidation A process by which a compound gives up electrons, acting as an electron donor, and becomes oxidized.

Parasite An organism able to live on and cause damage to another organism.

Pasteurization A process using mild heat to reduce the microbial level in heat-sensitive materials.

Pathogen An organism able to inflict damage on a host it infects.

Penicillin An antibiotic.

Prophylactic Treatment, usually immunologic, designed to protect an individual from a future attack by a pathogen.

Pure culture An organism growing in the absence of all other organisms.

Quarantine The limitation of the freedom of movement of an individual, to prevent the spread of a disease to other members of a population.

Rabid An animal that is suffering from rabies. Symptoms include frothing at the mouth, vicious biting.

Rabies A virus disease that affects primarily the nervous system.

Septicemia Invasion of the bloodstream by microorganisms; bacteremia.

Serum Fluid portion of blood remaining after the blood cells and materials responsible for clotting are removed.

Smallpox A virus disease of humans that was at one time very prevalent and occasionally fatal. Now eradicated from the world.

Spontaneous generation The theory that life could arise spontaneously in organic materials.

Spore A general term for resistant resting structures formed by many bacteria and fungi.

Sterile Free of living organisms.

Sterilization Treatment resulting in death of all living organisms and viruses in a material.

Suppuration Growth of bacteria in body tissues leading to the accumulation of massive amounts of fluid and pus.

Tartaric acid A four-carbon organic acid produced as a fermentation product by some microorganisms. Often present in wine.

Tetanus A disease of humans due to the bacterium *Clostridium tetani*. Often highly fatal.

Toxin A microbial substance able to induce host damage.

Trephine A surgical instrument used to drill a hole through the skull.

Vaccine Material used to induce antibody formation resulting in immunity.

Viable Alive; able to reproduce.

Virulence Degree of pathogenicity of a parasite.

Virus An infectious agent small enough to pass through a filter that holds back all bacteria.

Further Reading

Cadeddu, Antonio. 1985. Pasteur et le choléra des poules: révision critiquè d'un récit historique. *History and Philosophy of the Life Sciences* 7:87–104.

Dubos, René. 1950. *Louis Pasteur: Free Lance of Science.* Little Brown, Boston.

Duclaux, Émile. 1973. *Pasteur: The History of a Mind,* with a Foreword by René Dubos. Scarecrow Reprint Corporation: Metuchen, N.J.

Farley, John, and Gerald L. Geison. 1974. Science, Politics, and Spontaneous Generation in Nineteenth-Century France: The Pasteur-Pouchet Debate. *Bulletin of the History of Medicine* 48:161–198.

Geison, Gerald L. 1974. Louis Pasteur. *Dictionary of Scientific Biography,* ed. C. C. Gillispie, 16 vols. Charles Scribner's Sons, New York, N.Y., 1970–), vol. X (1974), pp. 350–416.

Geison, Gerald L., and James A. Secord. 1988. Pasteur and the Process of Discovery: The Case of Optical Isomers. *Isis* 79:6–36.

Vallery-Radot, Pasteur. 1958. *Louis Pasteur: A Great Life in Brief,* translated by Alfred Joseph. New York.

Vallery-Radot, René. 1927. *The Life of Pasteur,* translated by Mrs. R. L. Devonshire. Doubleday, New York.

Index

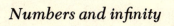

Numbers and infinity

Numbers and infinity

A historical account of mathematical concepts

ERNST SONDHEIMER

AND

ALAN ROGERSON

Westfield College, University of London

CAMBRIDGE UNIVERSITY PRESS

Cambridge

London   New York   New Rochelle

Melbourne   Sydney

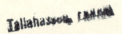
Published by the Press Syndicate of the University of Cambridge
The Pitt Building, Trumpington Street, Cambridge CB2 1RP
32 East 57th Street, New York, NY 10022, USA
296 Beaconsfield Parade, Middle Park, Melbourne 3206, Australia

© Cambridge University Press 1981

First published 1981

Printed in Great Britain at the University Press, Cambridge

Library of Congress catalogue card number: 81-7660

British Library Cataloguing in Publication Data

Sondheimer, Ernst
Numbers and infinity.
1. Mathematics – 1961-
I. Title II. Rogerson, Alan
510   QA36
ISBN 0 521 24091 3 hard covers
ISBN 0 521 28433 3 paperback

CONTENTS

PREFACE

In this book we treat mathematical ideas in a historical setting. Our principal themes are the concepts of *number* (Chapters 1–7) and *infinity* (Chapters 8–11). Within this context we have selected a number of topics for discussion with an eye to their history. Mathematical knowledge of roughly A-level standard is presupposed, and the book is addressed primarily to mathematics students in the sixth form at school and the first year at university who have an interest in historical aspects of their subject. The reader is presented with mathematical argument from time to time so that he may rise above the level of generalities and anecdotes. We hope that this will not deter any intelligent layman who wishes to find out about the development of ideas in mathematics. The more technical passages can simply be skipped or taken for granted.

The book differs both from conventional histories of mathematics and from mathematics textbooks. The history of mathematics is a vast, fascinating and difficult subject, much of it of specialised interest and of little direct concern to the mathematician of today. Many excellent accounts exist (see the bibliography for some recommended titles). We are not here primarily interested in an account of 'what happened in history', with its many blind alleys and side-issues, but we have tried to give some indication of the way men's ideas about mathematics have changed through time. In a good modern mathematics course the subject is, quite properly, developed logically on the basis of the most up-to-date views of its nature. There is usually little time to question or discuss the underlying assumptions and methods, and the complex evolution of mathematical ideas over the ages tends to be little mentioned. The student is thus presented with a beautiful and impressive logical structure.

This may give him the impression that the assumptions made, and the methods used, in handling basic concepts like number, function, continuity, should be quite obvious to him. (Only a fool would think otherwise!) In fact many of the ideas about the nature of mathematics which are taken for granted today are of very recent origin, and it may reassure the student, as he grapples with concepts that he finds difficult and that are not at all 'obvious' to him, to know that these concepts were also not obvious to people in the past, and that it took much argument, confusion and searching for the 'right' answer before the modern approach was created. Thus some knowledge of the historical background to modern mathematics should help to elucidate modern mathematics itself.

Rarely indeed were new concepts discovered all at once or immediately accepted. In the case of complex numbers (involving $\sqrt{(-1)}$) there was no particular year in which someone 'discovered' or 'invented' the idea. These numbers (which now seem so basic and clear cut) hovered on the fringe of mathematics for hundreds of years, half-understood, argued about, accepted (more or less) by some, rejected by others. Nor is the development of ideas in a discipline necessarily a smooth continuous evolutionary process. It is subject to long periods of non-development, to sudden jumps or changes in understanding and even at times to 'backward' steps. If the ideas of Popper, Kuhn and Lakatos are of interest to the reader, he will find in their works stimulating views of the progress of scientific thought, all of which see development as being essentially discontinuous. It must of course be remembered that the contemporary writer is looking back with hindsight and that his judgements are contemporary ones. He selects the results that are now considered to be significant. A historical account of mathematical ideas written in the twentieth century will inevitably reflect what twentieth-century mathematicians think is important in mathematics. But this must not lead the historical writer, when he describes the work of authors of the past, into ascribing to *them* the modern knowledge and the modern ways of thinking on which his own judgements are based. He has thus a difficult task: he must at one and the same time try to

understand the way people thought in the past and evaluate the
evidence in the light of his knowledge of the present.

Our style is deliberately informal, and we proceed by example
rather than proof. Mathematicians will not find our book
'respectable' in matters of definition; existence and uniqueness
are usually taken for granted. Thus in Chapter 7, where we talk
about hypercomplex numbers, we unashamedly treat notions
such as 'space', 'rotation', 'dimension', as intuitively given. In
modern mathematics these words receive a precise technical
definition and become more general and abstract than the
everyday notions from which they arose. This is a necessary
process from which mathematics derives its power and flexi-
bility, and the point has not been ignored in our text. But there is
often a loss of contact between the mathematician's abstract
definitions and the scientist's need to use similar concepts in
situations of practical interest; sometimes the problem is just
one of confusion of language when the specialists in different
disciplines try to communicate. We strongly believe that our
education system should aim to produce both mathematically
educated scientists and mathematicians able to apply their
knowledge. If our book does a little towards bridging existing
gaps we shall be delighted.

Having said all this we must also admit that there is much
arbitrariness in our choice of topics. The field of mathematics is
far too vast for everything of interest to be mentioned in a work
of modest compass which attempts a treatment that is not
purely superficial. For the same reason we have, usually, resisted the temptation to take the story into the twentieth century –
or sometimes even far into the nineteenth. These limitations
were also enforced by our restriction to elementary mathematics, and (not least) by our own mathematical ignorance. We
sincerely hope, however, that no reader will think that we are
only talking about old issues which are dead-and-buried today.
Many of the topics treated are still very much alive and can
furthermore be tackled much more powerfully with modern
mathematical technique. We have tried to indicate this in a few
places, but the elementary nature of our book has prevented us
from emphasising the point as much as it deserves. The

mathematically knowledgeable reader will be only too aware of all that we have omitted. (A parallel book could, and should, be written on geometry, for instance.) Finally, at our level of treatment we claim no original insights. Nor have we made direct use of primary sources, although we have tried to avoid perpetuating popular misconceptions about the history of mathematics. Our indebtedness to other authors will be obvious from a reading of the books recommended in the bibliography. We have taken what we needed from these excellent secondary sources without explicit acknowledgement on each occasion. Our thanks and apologies are tendered herewith.

The book grew out of a lecture course given (by E.S.) to first year undergraduates at Westfield College. The students were expected to participate by writing essays. This brings us to another comment on mathematics teaching. Mathematics students when they go into careers in management and administration often find that they are handicapped because their education has not trained them in the skill of English writing. A study of the history of mathematics provides an opportunity to remedy this. A list of suggested essay topics is included in the appendix, but the reader will have no difficulty in thinking of other titles.

A number of colleagues have helped with this book, either with specific suggestions or with general encouragement. In particular, our thanks go to Bryan Thwaites for encouraging us to turn the lecture notes into a book, to Patricia Bennett, Geoffrey Howson and Eira Scourfield for a critical reading of the entire manuscript and to Janet Sondheimer for help with the preface. The authors of course accept full responsibility for all errors and defects remaining in the text.

1

Representation of numbers

Let us look at the way we write numbers. Take whole numbers (positive integers) first, for example the number of days in a normal year, a number which we write as 365. This is quite a subtle way of writing such a large number. It uses a *decimal system* with *base* 10, and *place values*: thus 5 measures the 'units', 6 the 'tens' and 3 the 'hundreds', so that 365 stands for

$$3 \times 10^2 + 6 \times 10^1 + 5 \times 10^0.$$

The arrangement of the digits matters: 563 is quite a different number from 365. We need 9 digits $(1, 2, \ldots, 9)$ together with the zero (the symbol for an empty place), and these are sufficient to write any number. The zero symbol is needed, for example, to distinguish 35 from 305. This so-called 'Hindu–Arab' system of writing numbers became established in the West during the late Middle Ages, gradually displacing an earlier more primitive Roman system which can still be seen on some old clocks.

Let us consider some other ways of writing numbers. The most primitive system uses notches in a tally stick or the equivalent: knots on a string, heaps of pebbles, and so on. Here 12 appears as | | | | | | | | | | | | , or perhaps in bundles: |||| |||| || . In this system it is a laborious task to carve out the notches which represent the number of days in a year. Such methods were used by primitive tribes and may still be used nowadays by a scorekeeper in a ball game. The earliest known tally stick is the radius bone of a wolf which has 55 notches, the first 25 in groups of 5. It dates from the Old Stone Age, more than 10 000 years ago. Bundles were usually heaps of 5, 10 or 20, presumably because counting was done with the aid of the fingers on one hand, on both hands, or with fingers and toes; later special symbols were introduced to represent 5, 10, etc. Our modern ciphers 2 and 3 are believed to have originated from the primitive $=$ and $\equiv$ by connecting the horizontal lines in cursive writing.

Primitive number systems of this kind were used for thousands of years. The most familiar to us is the Roman system, an additive decimal system with special signs for the higher units, but without the notion of place values. Thus 1867 is written as MDCCCLXVII, which stands for

$$1000 + 500 + (3 \times 100) + 50 + 10 + 5 + (2 \times 1).$$

Note that V stands for half of X, D for half of ⅅ which is the old symbol for 1000. The system was very awkward for computation: try multiplying the above number by LXVII using only Roman numerals. It needed experts to do such sums.

Long before the time of the Romans, mathematics developed in the civilisations of the Ancient Orient: Egypt, Mesopotamia (Babylon), China and India. The study and elucidation of the mathematics of these ancient times is the business of archaeologists. A great deal has been discovered quite recently, although certain knowledge is hard to obtain; there is much argument about the correct interpretation of the sources (see Neugebauer 1969 for a detailed account). The Egyptian *hieroglyphic* numeration is found in carvings on tombs and monuments, and some of it is 5000 years old (as old as the pyramids). It uses a decimal system similar to the Roman, with separate symbols for powers of ten (thus 10 is ⌒, a heel bone, 100 is ⌐, a scroll, 1000 is ⚘, a lotus flower, and so on). Using this system the Egyptians found it easy to write numbers as large as a million. For Egyptian mathematics of a later period the sources are papyrus records such as the famous *Rhind papyrus* in the British Museum. This papyrus was discovered in 1858 and is known to have been written about 1650 B.C. (but it contains older material). The Rhind papyrus is not written in hieroglyphics but in a running script called *hieratic* (or 'sacred', to distinguish it from a still later *demotic* or 'popular' script). The hieratic numerals make an important advance in that they introduce the use of special signs to represent the digits from 1

to 9: thus 8 is no longer represented by repetition of the unit:
||||
||||, but by the single symbol $=$.

From Babylonia we have well-preserved clay tablets with mathematical texts. These have revealed a level of calculating skill much higher than the Egyptian. As early as 2000 B.C. the Babylonians used a number system based on the number 60 (a 'sexagesimal' system) which, remarkably enough, incorporated the place value idea: thus 4,2,7 would stand for our number

$$4 \times 60^2 + 2 \times 60^1 + 7 \times 60^0 = 14\,527.$$

This ancient Babylonian system was in essentials equivalent to our own. In some ways it was even better: there are advantages in using 60 as a base rather than 10, because 60 has many more integer factors and thus subdivisions are more easily made. Of course the Babylonians did not use our modern symbols to write their numbers: their number symbols were 'cuneiform' (wedge-shaped), with ⲩ standing for 1, ⲩⲩ for 2, ⟨ for 10 and ⟨⟨⟨ⲩⲩⲩ

for 59. The Babylonian system was well adapted to computation, especially because the place-value idea was extended to include (sexagesimal) fractions as well as integers; and the Babylonians were able to achieve remarkable accuracy in numerical approximation. Thus the square root of 2 was obtained (in modern symbols) as

$$1, 24, 51, 10 = 1 + \frac{24}{60} + \frac{51}{60^2} + \frac{10}{60^3} = 1.414\,212\,9\ldots$$

(correct value $1.414\,213\,5\ldots$). Such accuracy was not surpassed until the time of the Renaissance, over 3000 years later.[†] Powerful as the system was, the interpretation of Babylonian

† How did the Babylonians calculate square roots? They used the following powerful method – now known as 'Newton's algorithm'– to obtain their approximations: to find $\sqrt{a}$, suppose a_1 is a first approximation; form $b_1 = a/a_1$ and $a_2 = \frac{1}{2}(a_1 + b_1)$ (the second approximation); then form $b_2 = a/a_2$, $a_3 = \frac{1}{2}(a_2 + b_2)$ (the third approximation); and so on. (This is actually an infinite process, but was not recognised as such in ancient times.) If $a = \alpha^2 + \beta$ and $a_1 = \alpha$, this method gives $b_1 = \alpha + (\beta/\alpha)$ and $a_2 = \alpha + (\beta/2\alpha)$, the two-term approximation to the binomial series for $\sqrt{(\alpha^2 + \beta)}$.

numbers is not unambiguous, because there was no 'decimal point' to separate whole numbers from fractions, and (in the earlier periods) there was not yet a specific symbol denoting zero (so that an empty place *might* denote a zero): thus 4,2,7 could mean

$$4 \times 60^1 + 2 \times 60^0 + 7 \times 60^{-1}, \text{ or } 4 \times 60^2 + 2 \times 60^0 + 7 \times 60^{-1}.$$

The correct interpretation was presumably to be determined by the context in which the number appeared. The later Babylonians had a zero symbol for an empty space in the interior of a number, but not for a zero at the end.

In spite of much discussion the real reason for the Babylonians's introduction of a sexagesimal system is not definitely known. It appears to have arisen in response to the needs of their highly developed administrative and commercial activities which called for a convenient and accurate way of doing numerical calculations. Both the place-value principle and the sexagesimal system have remained with us permanently; the number base 60 appears in our own division of the hour into 60 minutes and 60^2 seconds, and of the circle into 6×60 degrees, each degree into 60 minutes and each minute into 60 seconds. In fact measurements of time intervals and angles were important for the later Babylonians (after 700 B.C.) who developed a scientific system of astronomy in which they kept systematic records of the positions of the sun, moon and planets.

The Greeks developed abstract pure mathematics to a high level but did not do much calculating with numbers. So perhaps we should not be surprised that they had a more primitive number system which had no place values. The early form of the Greek system was rather like the Roman and the Egyptian. Later, in Alexandrian times, a better system appears in which computation was not too difficult. This used 27 Greek letters (nine for $1, 2, \ldots, 9$; nine for $10, 20, \ldots, 90$; nine for 100, $200, \ldots, 900$); thus one could write any number less than 1000 with at most three symbols. Such a system was used by scientists, merchants and administrators for about 15 centuries.

Most of the Greek mathematical texts were in fact not written in Greece but in the Egyptian city of Alexandria during the period 350–200 B.C., well after the 'Golden Age' of Greece, around 430 B.C. Alexandria had become the centre of 'Hellenistic' Greek civilisation after the conquests of Alexander the Great. Euclid, the best-known Greek mathematician, probably lived in Alexandria at about 300 B.C. but nothing certain is known about his life. In fact we have virtually no direct sources to give us a picture of the development of Greek mathematics. We do have reliable editions of the work of the great Hellenistic mathematicians, Euclid, Archimedes and Apollonius. These give a very detailed account of Greek mathematics, but are texts systematically covering a highly developed mathematical science in which historical origins are hard to trace – much like most modern textbooks. So we have to reconstruct the formative period of Greek mathematics from various fragments transmitted by later authors, and from scattered remarks made by philosophers and others. Thus Plato, although not himself a mathematician, was very interested in mathematics and often talked about it and the achievements of mathematicians. A vast amount of research (see Heath 1921) has allowed us to construct a fairly consistent, but largely hypothetical, picture of the way Greek mathematics developed.

Under the Roman Empire Alexandrian mathematics combined the Greek tradition of pure abstract mathematics with the computational arithmetic and algebra of the Egyptians and Babylonians. For example, Ptolemy's famous treatise on astronomy, the *Almagest* (Arabic for 'Great Collection'), written about A.D. 150, contained a trigonometry, with tables of chords for different angles (equivalent to our sine tables). Chords were expressed as sexagesimal fractions, thus

$$\sin 1° \text{ was } 1,2,50 = \frac{1}{60} + \frac{2}{60^2} + \frac{50}{60^3} = 0.017\,453\,7\ldots$$

(actual value 0.017 452 4 . . .).

With the decline of the Roman Empire the focus of mathematical activity shifted eastwards to India, then back to Mesopotamia (now under the Arabs). It is the achievement of Indian mathematics to have combined the ancient notions of a decimal system and of a place-value (position) system into our modern method of writing numbers. Hindu astronomers, around A.D. 500, used words to represent digits ('moon' to denote 1, 'fire' or 'brothers' to denote 3, etc.); these were arranged in a positional system starting with units, then tens, hundreds, etc. Thus our number 365 would actually appear (in word form) as 563. Tables of sines could thus be prepared and memorised in verse form! Some time soon after A.D. 500 the Hindus changed to a digital notation which included the symbol o for zero (adopted from the Greeks), and switched to the Greek–Babylonian order for the numerals in which the largest units were written first. Hindu arithmetic then looked much like our own, but the Hindu numerals spread to Europe only very gradually, by way of the Arabs who translated the Indian texts.† Arab mathematics flourished in the centuries following the year 800. One of the best-known authors was Al-Khowarizmi (about 825) who wrote many books on mathematics and astronomy. A Latin translation of his arithmetic appeared about 1100 and served to popularise the Indian number system in Western Europe. Many modern mathematical terms are of Arab origin: thus 'algorithm' (meaning a systematic method for computation) is a latinisation of Al-Khowarizmi's name. His *Al-jabr wa'l-muqabalah* (science of reduction and cancellation) gave us the word 'algebra'; originally it meant the science of equations. The word 'zero' comes from the Latin 'zephirum' which is derived from the Arabic 'sifr' (sifra = empty); hence also the English word 'cipher'.

Over the period A.D. 1000–1500 the Hindu–Arab number system co-existed in Western Europe with the Greek and Roman numerals. Oriental science was brought to the West by Italian merchants who travelled in the East. One of them was Leonardo of Pisa (Fibonacci, 'son of Bonaccio') who wrote a famous mathematical treatise (in 1202), the *Liber Abaci*, which was influential in introducing Arabic numerals to the West. However, on the whole, people preferred the Roman numerals with which they were familiar; they had learned to do sums with them quite rapidly using an abacus (a counting board with

† The detailed circumstances of the introduction of Hindu–Arab numerals into Europe are still disputed among historians of mathematics.

movable counters, still in use in some parts of the world). The public disliked Hindu–Arab numerals because they were strange and difficult to read, and the authorities opposed them because they were too easily forged. In 1299 Florentine merchants were forbidden to use Arabic numerals in book-keeping; 200 years later Roman numerals had disappeared entirely from the books of the Medici.

Why should we use the Hindu–Arab system to represent numbers? Computation (addition and multiplication) is easy in this system; also we can tell at a glance whether one number is greater than another. (This is not true in the Roman system: compare C and LXX for example.) These advantages come from the place-value idea, but they do not depend on using the number 10 as a base. There is no particular mathematical reason for the use of this base. Earlier on, as we have noted, very accurate calculations had been made with the sexagesimal system (for example by Ptolemy). We can use any other base and still have the same advantages. In the seventeenth century the mathematician Weigel (who taught Leibniz; see Chapter 9) spent much of his life advocating the use of a number system with base 4 (nobody took much notice). Leibniz himself pointed out (in 1703) that in the *binary system*, with base 2, the digits 0 and 1 were sufficient to represent any number, but he did not recommend it for practical use as the expressions were too long. Nowadays the binary system is fundamental for modern computers.

How do we write the number 365 in binary form? We must express it as a sum of powers of 2. We have $2^1 = 2$, $2^2 = 4$, $2^3 = 8$, $2^4 = 16$, $2^5 = 32$, $2^6 = 64$, $2^7 = 128$, $2^8 = 256$, ... The largest power of 2 less than 365 is 2^8, and $365 - 2^8 = 109$; the largest power of 2 less than 109 is 2^6; and so on. Thus

$$365 = 2^8 + 109 = 2^8 + 2^6 + 45$$
$$= 2^8 + 2^6 + 2^5 + 13$$
$$= 1 \times 2^8 + 0 \times 2^7 + 1 \times 2^6 + 1 \times 2^5 + 0 \times 2^4$$
$$+ 1 \times 2^3 + 1 \times 2^2 + 0 \times 2^1 + 1 \times 2^0,$$

and the binary form of 365 is therefore 101 101 101. In practice,

to obtain the binary form of any number, we repeatedly divide
by 2 and note the remainders:

```
2)365
2)182   r. 1
2) 91   r. 0
2) 45   r. 1
2) 22   r. 1
2) 11   r. 0
2)  5   r. 1
2)  2   r. 1
2)  1   r. 0
    0   r. 1
```

The remainders in *ascending* order give 101 101 101, the correct
binary expression for 365. This systematic way of obtaining the
binary expression for any number always works (can you see
why?). Try it with a few other numbers.

It is true that the binary form of a number is much longer than
the decimal, but there are important advantages:

(i) we need only two digits 0, 1 to represent any number:
hence base 2 is suitable for electronic computers which work
with on/off circuit elements;

(ii) we have very simple addition and multiplication tables,
as follows:

+	0	1		×	0	1
0	0	1		0	0	0
1	1	10		1	0	1

Thus, to multiply 365 by 13, we convert 13 to its binary form
1101, and proceed by long multiplication:

```
        101101101
      ×      1101
      ───────────
        101101101
       101101101
      101101101
      ───────────
     1001010001001
```

(Notice the binary addition sums used here: $1+1+1=11$, $1+1+1+1=10+1+1=11+1=100$.) Check that the answer is the same as the decimal result: $365 \times 13 = 4745$. This arithmetic seems strange at first because it is unfamiliar, but it is in principle very easy. Multiplication involves only addition and 'moving to the left': a simple job for computers.

We have only considered whole numbers so far; let us now have a look at *fractions*. What do we mean when we represent a fraction such as $\frac{3}{8}$ by its decimal equivalent, 0.375? The decimal form 0.375 is an extension of our previous ideas on place values using base 10: 0.375 means

$$3 \times 10^{-1} + 7 \times 10^{-2} + 5 \times 10^{-3}.$$

This is another way of writing the fraction $\frac{3}{8}$. Notice that in order to obtain this decimal representation we need only divide 3 by 8:

```
      0.375
  8)3.0000
    2.4
     .60
     .56
     .040
     .040
      . . .
```

What happens, however, when we try to find the decimal form of the simple fraction $\frac{2}{3}$? Try it and see. You will find that this simple fraction produces an *infinite* (or 'periodic') decimal (one that never stops):

$$\frac{2}{3} = 0.6666\ldots = 6 \times 10^{-1} + 6 \times 10^{-2} + 6 \times 10^{-3} + \cdots$$

This is in fact an infinite series:

$$\frac{6}{10} + \frac{6}{100} + \frac{6}{1000} + \cdots$$

Does this make sense? If this infinite series is to represent the fraction $\frac{2}{3}$ then by adding up *all* its terms we should get $\frac{2}{3}$; thus $\frac{2}{3}$ should be equal to the *sum* of the infinite series. How do we find such a sum? We obtain it as the *limit*, as N tends to infinity (we write $N \to \infty$), of the sum s_N of the first N terms of the series. This limit indeed has the value $\frac{2}{3}$, i.e., as N gets larger and larger, s_N gets closer and closer to $\frac{2}{3}$. To check this statement we find the sum of N terms of our series (this is easy because we have a *geometric series*) and then let $N \to \infty$:

$$s_N = \frac{6}{10}\left(1 - \frac{1}{10^N}\right) \Big/ \left(1 - \frac{1}{10}\right)$$

$$= \frac{2}{3}\left(1 - \frac{1}{10^N}\right) \to \frac{2}{3} \text{ as } N \to \infty$$

(since $1/10^N$ tends to zero).

Are things better in another base? Try base 2. (A ruler divided into halves, quarters, eighths, ... of an inch uses base 2 for fractions.) Check that the fraction $\frac{2}{3}$ is still represented by an infinite decimal $(0.101\ 01\ldots)$. There is an interesting confirmatory proof to show that this binary expansion cannot be finite. If it were finite, we would have

$$\frac{2}{3} = \sum_{n=1}^{m} \frac{a_n}{2^n},$$

a finite sum terminating with $a_m/2^m$, say. Hence we would have $\frac{2}{3} = A/2^m$, with A some integer, or $2^{m+1} = 3A$: but we know that 2^{m+1} is not divisible by 3.

We get a simpler 'decimal' if we use base 3: $\frac{2}{3} = 0.2$; but now we find that $\frac{1}{2}$ in base 3 is an infinite 'decimal': $0.1111\ldots$. Thus no particular base is best for all fractions. We will however show in Chapter 3 that the 'decimal' form of all fractions, in base 10 or any other base, is either *finite* or *periodic*. A periodic (infinite) decimal has a group of digits which repeats. (See Rademacher & Toeplitz 1957, ch. 23, for a discussion of the length of the period and related matters.)

The Egyptians, about 4000 years ago, had a remarkable calculus of *unit fractions*. The idea was to write all fractions as sums of fractions with unit numerator and distinct denominators, for example

$$\frac{3}{23} = \frac{1}{10} + \frac{1}{46} + \frac{1}{115}.$$

This is quite ingenious but is very awkward for calculation. Also note that such a representation is not unique; thus

$$\frac{3}{5} = \frac{1}{2} + \frac{1}{10} = \frac{1}{3} + \frac{1}{5} + \frac{1}{15} = \frac{1}{3} + \frac{1}{4} + \frac{1}{60}.$$

It is thought that because of this cumbersome calculus Egyptian mathematics failed to progress beyond a primitive stage.

How can we construct this representation systematically? The following technique was described by Fibonacci in the *Liber Abaci*. Take the fraction $\frac{3}{13}$ as an example. Find the *largest* unit fraction $\leqslant \frac{3}{13}$: this can be done by increasing the denominator of the given fraction until it first reaches a multiple of the numerator. We obtain $\frac{3}{15} = \frac{1}{5}$. Subtract this from $\frac{3}{13}$:

$$\frac{3}{13} - \frac{1}{5} = \frac{15-13}{65} = \frac{2}{65}.$$

Now repeat the process: the largest unit fraction $\leqslant \frac{2}{65}$ is $\frac{2}{66} = \frac{1}{33}$. Subtract:

$$\frac{2}{65} - \frac{1}{33} = \frac{66-65}{2145} = \frac{1}{2145}.$$

At this stage we are left with a unit fraction, and thus

$$\frac{3}{13} = \frac{1}{5} + \frac{1}{33} + \frac{1}{2145}.$$

It is quite easy to show that this always works, that the process stops after a finite number of steps. Suppose A/B is a fraction between 0 and 1, with $A < B$, and $1/N$ is the largest unit fraction $\leqslant A/B$, then we are to form

$$\frac{A}{B} - \frac{1}{N} = \frac{NA-B}{BN},$$

and (if necessary) to repeat the process. (Of course, if A divides B, there is nothing to prove.) We need only show that the numerator of the new fraction, $NA - B$, is *less* than the original numerator: $NA - B < A$ (try to show this!) Then the numerators, which by construction are positive, diminish at each step, and must thus decrease to zero in a finite number of steps. Thus every positive fraction between 0 and 1 can be represented as a finite sum of unit fractions.

This process, however, is not the one used by the ancient Egyptians. The Rhind papyrus has tables listing decompositions into unit fractions, but $\frac{2}{15}$ for example is split into $\frac{1}{10} + \frac{1}{30}$, whereas our process gives $\frac{1}{8} + \frac{1}{120}$. There has been much speculation about the procedures used by the Egyptians to obtain their particular representations, but we do not really know what they were.

Egyptian unit fractions suggest more interesting (and harder) mathematical problems. Suppose for example that we limit ourselves to fractions with *odd* denominators only. Can such fractions always be written as sums of distinct unit fractions with odd denominators? (For example $\frac{2}{9} = \frac{1}{5} + \frac{1}{45}$.) The answer is yes, but the proof given above now fails because the numerators no longer necessarily decrease, and it is not known in this case whether Fibonacci's process of generating the unit fractions always stops after a finite number of steps.

The decimal fractions we use nowadays are much more suitable for numerical calculations. They were generally adopted in Europe around 1600: a book published by Simon Stevin, a Flemish engineer, in 1585 (*De Thiende*, meaning 'The Tenth') was influential in making them widely known. Interest in methods of computation was widespread at that time: engineers, astronomers, surveyors were all looking for better ways to do arithmetical calculations. Symptomatic of the search for greater accuracy was the effort to calculate π to as many decimal places as possible: in 1610 Ludolph van Ceulen computed 35 decimal places by Archimedes's method of inscribed and circumscribed polygons (see p. 97). He spent much of his life on the task and it was regarded as a great triumph of computation.

The introduction of logarithms soon after 1600 gave a powerful impetus to computational technique. In 1614 John Napier, the Laird of Murchiston in Scotland, published his famous work *Mirifici Logarithmorum Canonis Descriptio.*† ·(Jobst Bürgi in Switzerland had similar ideas at about the same time.) Napier's basic idea was to reduce multiplication to addition through the use of two series of numbers related in such a way that, when one grows in arithmetic progression, the other decreases in geometric progression. There is then a simple relation between the product of two numbers in the second

---

† 'A Description of the Marvellous Rule of Logarithms'. In the seventeenth century Latin was still, as it had been in the Middle Ages, the international language for scientific writing.

series and the sum of the corresponding numbers in the first series. This general idea was not new, but to put it into practice it was necessary to define a system of logarithms that was both convenient and accurate for numerical work. Napier's logarithm was defined as follows: $x = $ Naplog y if (in modern notation) $y = 10^7 e^{-x/10^7}$; thus Naplog $y = 10^7 (\log 10^7 - \log y)$, where log y is our 'natural logarithm' to base e. In this system, if Naplog $y = $ Naplog $y_1 + $ Naplog y_2, y is actually not $y_1 y_2$ but $y_1 y_2/10^7$.† Napier himself was not satisfied with his rather clumsy definition, and it was left to his admirer Henry Briggs, professor at Gresham College in London, to publish in 1624 (after Napier's death) the first tables of 'Briggsian logarithms' which are our common logarithms based on $y = 10^x$. The new technique was immediately recognised as a most important aid for simplifying complicated calculations, and tables of logarithms were soon produced which satisfied all practical requirements.

The discovery of logarithms stimulated the development of mechanical aids to calculation. The ancient abacus, useful enough for day-to-day commercial transactions, was too crude a tool for doing complicated scientific calculations. Napier himself invented a device of rectangular strips ('Napier's rods' or 'Napier's bones') which helped in carrying out long multiplications. This was popular in its time, but much more important was the invention of the slide rule by the Reverend William Oughtred in 1622. This was a device in which two pieces of wood marked with logarithm scales can slide relative to each other; by adding logarithmic distances one is multiplying the associated numbers. Up to the arrival, a few years ago, of pocket electronic calculators a slide rule was the standard calculating aid of every scientist and engineer. The inventor of the first widely known *calculating machine* was Blaise Pascal (see p. 117) who in 1642 designed and manufactured an instrument with interlocking dials which could perform the 'carrying'

---

† Napier's definitions were equivalent to these but he was not familiar with the concepts of the exponential function or of a basis for logarithms. Clarification of these ideas had to wait for the introduction of the calculus (see Chapter 9).

process in addition and could thus add numbers mechanically. Leibniz invented an improved machine which could also multiply and divide automatically. Later, in the early nineteenth century, the 'irascible genius' Charles Babbage spent his life designing much more elaborate calculating machines. His ambitious projects were never completed, but Babbage's 'analytical engine' contained many of the features (such as punched cards, a memory, input and output devices) of the modern electronic computer. The development of today's computers dates from the Second World War. As processors of information of all kinds they are revolutionising modern technology; as tremendously powerful calculating devices they are having a profound influence on mathematics. Goldstine (1972) gives an interesting account of the history of the computer.

A final remark: we have in this chapter considered only integers and fractions, i.e. *rational numbers*. Here, as we have noted, the decimal representation is either finite or, if infinite, is periodic. Numbers such as $\sqrt{2}$ or π, which we shall consider later, have no decimal representation of this simple type. They can be written as infinite decimals, but no pattern can be seen to generate all the digits. The non-mathematician may say π is 3.1416 (or 22/7, etc.). These rational numbers are certainly good numerical *approximations* for π, and this is usually sufficient for the practical scientist or engineer concerned with measuring. But for the mathematician π is quite a different sort of number which we shall consider in more detail in later chapters.

2

The integers

In this chapter we shall discuss a few of the properties of the *natural numbers* (positive integers) 1, 2, 3, ... As objects of mathematical study they have been of great interest since Greek times. In earlier days, number lore had been associated with magic and astrology: 'mathematici' in ancient terminology meant magicians or astrologers. The word 'mathematics' itself comes from a Greek root, and means 'something learned, science'. An example of number magic is 'gematria', a form of Hebrew cabbalistic mysticism in which each letter of the alphabet has a number value. Thus texts could be used to prophesy: in Isaiah (21:8) the lion proclaims the fall of Babylon because the letters in the Hebrew words for lion and Babylon add up to the same sum. While astrology has survived, mathematicians are no longer interested in such arguments.

The mathematical study of the integers is called the 'theory of numbers'. It is a branch of mathematics which has few practical uses. It is also fascinating, because many of the problems are both easy to formulate and very hard to answer. Gauss (1777–1855) – one of the greatest mathematicians – said 'Mathematics is the queen of the sciences, and the Theory of Numbers is the queen of mathematics'.

Let us consider the question of *divisibility*. A number which is composite can be written as a product of at least two other numbers different from 1, for example $6 = 2 \times 3$. (2, 3 are the *divisors* of 6.) *Prime numbers* have no divisors except 1 and the number itself. The first few primes are

$$2, 3, 5, 7, 11, 13, 17, 19, 23, 29, 31, 37, \ldots,$$

not counting 1 as a prime number. Clearly 2 is the only *even* prime. Prime numbers are the basic integers because every

15

composite integer can be written as a product of primes (thus $120 = 2 \times 2 \times 2 \times 3 \times 5 = 2^3 \times 3 \times 5$). The prime numbers are therefore the building bricks for the construction of all the integers. As mathematicians we are interested in general questions about the class of prime numbers, and not so much in the properties of any particular prime. Look at the list of prime numbers. There is no obvious regularity, but a few questions suggest themselves immediately. For example:

1. How many primes are there?
2. How big can the gaps be between successive primes?
3. How many pairs of primes differ by 2 ('twin primes', such as 5, 7; 17, 19)?
4. Can we find a *formula* $f(n)$ to represent the nth prime?

Some questions of this type are fairly easy to answer, others can be answered but are difficult, and yet others are so hard that we do not know the answer (and may not even know where to look for the answer). Many other interesting questions about the integers could be listed, and the theory of numbers, which has been studied since ancient times, is today a highly active field of research for many of the world's leading mathematicians. (See Dudley 1978 for a good elementary account of the subject.) Let us look at the above questions one by one.

1. *How many primes are there?* This was answered by the Greeks: *there is no end to the primes.* The proof given in Book 9 of Euclid is a classic example of a mathematical proof. Look at the following numbers:

$$2 \times 3 + 1 = 7,$$
$$2 \times 3 \times 5 + 1 = 31,$$
$$2 \times 3 \times 5 \times 7 + 1 = 211,$$
$$2 \times 3 \times 5 \times 7 \times 11 + 1 = 2311,$$
$$2 \times 3 \times 5 \times 7 \times 11 \times 13 + 1 = 30031, \text{ etc.}$$

(To form them we multiply together the first n primes, $n = 2, 3, 4, \ldots$, and add 1.) We see that none of these numbers is divisible by any of the primes used to form it, because there is always a remainder 1. This does *not* however mean that the numbers themselves are necessarily prime: what it *does* mean is that each number is *either* prime, *or*, if it is not, then its prime factors must be greater than the prime numbers used in the construction. In fact 7, 31, 211, 2311 are all primes, but $30\,031 = 59 \times 509$. Thus this process *generates new primes* from a collection of the first n primes. This shows that there is no 'last prime'. Why? Because, if p were to be the last prime, we form $2 \times 3 \times 5 \times 7 \times \cdots \times p + 1 = N$; then our argument shows that N is either prime or has prime factors bigger than p. Thus p cannot be the last prime.

This is an elegant proof, simple and tailored to the problem in hand. It does not attempt to do the 'obvious' thing, which would be to look for the *next* prime after p. That question presents a much harder problem because there is no simple law for the sequence of successive primes. Euclid's proof instead looks for *some* prime beyond p, and this is all that is needed for the purpose of the proof. Asking the question in the right way is often the secret of success in mathematics.

2. *How big can the gaps be between successive primes*? This question was not considered by the Greeks. We can show that the gaps between successive primes can be as large as we please; there is no upper limit. Given any number N, we can always find N consecutive composite numbers. For example to show that there are 99 consecutive composite numbers, we need only form the number $100! = 1 \times 2 \times 3 \times 4 \times \cdots \times 100$, and consider the 99 numbers

$$100! + 2, \quad 100! + 3, \quad 100! + 4, \ldots, \quad 100! + 100.$$

These are clearly all composite, since, for any number k from 2 to 100, $100!$ is divisible by k and therefore $100! + k$ is also divisible by k (note that $100! + 1$ might be prime). Of course these are very large numbers, so we have to go far along the sequence of primes to get large gaps, but evidently we can get gaps as large as we please by going far enough.

An interesting related question is: do arithmetical series of integers like 1, 4, 7, 10, ... or 3, 7, 11, 15, ... contain an infinity of primes? The answer is yes, but Euclid's type of proof works only for special sequences (try to construct a proof for 3, 7, 11, 15, ...). The general proof given by Dirichlet in 1837 is difficult and uses analytic (i.e. calculus) methods. (See Davenport 1970 for further details.)

3. *How many pairs of primes differ by 2?* This question looks innocent enough but is extremely hard to answer. It is believed that there are infinitely many twin primes but nobody knows how to prove it. The conjecture arose from looking at the sequence of primes and noting that twins such as 5, 7; 11, 13; 17, 19 keep occurring however long the list. Modern computers have immensely increased our ability to investigate properties of primes by this kind of 'experimental' approach.

A related and famous unsolved problem is the *Goldbach conjecture* (1742). Goldbach, who was the Prussian envoy to Russia, stated in a letter to the leading mathematician Euler that *every even number is the sum of two primes* (thus $8 = 5 + 3$, $16 = 13 + 3$, $48 = 29 + 19$, ...). The assertion that this is true for *every* even number was made without proof, and it is Goldbach's only claim to mathematical fame. (Nowadays interesting conjectures are still often made, but only a high-powered mathematician is likely to put forward a new conjecture which is worthy of serious attention.) No exceptions to the Goldbach conjecture are known, but it has never been proved. Properties such as this one which relate primes to *addition* are hard to prove since the primes are defined by multiplication. There was no progress with the Goldbach problem at all until 1931, when a young Russian mathematician showed that every positive integer can be represented as the sum of not more than N primes, where N was a large number around 300 000. Since then there has been more progress and it is now known that every *sufficiently large* even number can be written in the form $p + q$, where p is prime and q has at most 2 prime factors. It is often easier to demonstrate a result as a *limiting* property for numbers that are large enough than to give a proof which holds precisely for every number. The next question illustrates this strikingly.

4. *Can we find a formula $f(n)$ which, when we substitute in it the integer n, gives us the nth prime number?* People searched for such a formula in the seventeenth and eighteenth centuries but were unsuccessful. No simple formula exists; the distribu-

tion of primes is too irregular. Suppose we are less ambitious and look for a function $f(n)$ which produces *only* primes, but need not give them all. Fermat (1601–65), the chief originator of the modern theory of numbers, conjectured that all numbers of the form $f(n) = 2^{2^n} + 1$ ($n = 1, 2, 3, \ldots$) are prime. Check that

$$f(1) = 5, \quad f(2) = 17, \quad f(3) = 257, \quad f(4) = 65\,537;$$

all these numbers are indeed prime numbers. Clearly these 'Fermat numbers' increase very rapidly. It is not at all easy to determine whether any given very large number is prime or not, and it was a considerable feat of computation for his time when Euler showed in 1732 that $f(5)$ is composite: in fact

$$f(5) = 2^{32} + 1 = 4\,294\,967\,297 = 641 \times 6\,700\,417.$$

Thus, while a conjecture may seem plausible on the basis of a few examples, we must not believe it until a satisfactory mathematical *proof* has been given. With modern computers we can investigate numbers which are vastly larger than Euler's $f(5)$: at the time of writing (summer 1980) the largest number which is definitely *known* to be a prime number is the 'Mersenne number' $2^{44\,497} - 1$, a large number indeed!

But there are limits to what even the best present-day computers can do. Suppose we form a number of say 400 arabic digits by multiplying together two large primes, each of about 200 digits; then no computer, presented with such a product, could in practice disentangle the factorisation; the calculations required would simply take far too long. This fact underlies the recent invention of a system of coding messages called 'public-key cryptography'. The basic idea is to use the 400-digit number to encode the message, and to have a rule for decoding which can be operated only by someone who knows the prime factors. Since anyone who does not know the factors has no way of finding them within his lifetime, the code is effectively unbreakable. Thus prime numbers have their uses after all! But mathematicians are hard at work trying to discover more powerful 'factoring algorithms', so the security of the code may be short-lived. (For fuller details see Hellman 1979, Kolata 1980.)

Even if a formula for the nth prime can be written down, it will not necessarily be of any use for computation in practice. In recent years formulae have actually been given from which the $(n + 1)$th prime can be obtained when the first n primes are known; but they are very complicated. In the nineteenth century progress was made by formulating the problem in a different way. It was noticed that the law governing the *distribution* of primes appears to have a fairly simple form, at least for sufficiently large numbers. Thus, instead of searching for a formula for the nth prime, one looks for the *average* distribution of the primes among the integers.

Suppose $F(n)$ is the number of primes among the first n integers: thus $F(10) = 4$ (the primes $\leqslant 10$ are 2, 3, 5, 7). As n tends to infinity $F(n)$ increases also without limit, since there are infinitely many primes, but it increases more slowly than n. The *density* of primes among the first n integers is $F(n)/n$. This is also the *probability* that an integer picked at random from the first n integers is a prime number. When this number is computed it is found that it *decreases* as n increases, which means that the average *gap* between primes increases slowly (as we might expect):

n	$F(n)$	$F(n)/n$	$1/\log n$	$\dfrac{F(n)/n}{1/\log n}$
10^3	168	0.168	0.145	1.159
10^6	78 498	0.078	0.072	1.084
10^9	50 847 478	0.051	0.048	1.053

We now look for a function $f(n)$ which 'behaves similarly', at least for sufficiently large n. We want a function which decreases slowly with increasing n in much the same way as $F(n)/n$. Legendre and Gauss noticed (about 1800) that the simple function $1/\log_e n$ has the required behaviour. This is seen from the table above, where the ratio of $F(n)/n$ to $1/\log n$ appears to approach 1 as $n \to \infty$. The conjecture was thus made that the ratio indeed tends to the limit 1 as $n \to \infty$, or:

$$F(n) \sim \frac{n}{\log n} \left(\text{this means } \lim_{n \to \infty} \frac{F(n)}{n/\log n} = 1 \right).$$

It is a surprising relation because there is no obvious connection between the logarithmic function and the prime numbers. It took about 100 years before the first complete proofs of the conjecture were given (by Hadamard and de la Vallée Poussin in 1896); these proofs established the relation as the *prime number theorem*. The proofs used analytical methods, involving calculus and complex function theory. This was not the end of the story. Various refinements of the theorem were made giving better approximations, and it was also felt by many mathematicians that one should be able to derive results concerning only the integers by using proofs which operate *only* with integers and which do not use any 'foreign ideas' such as analysis. An 'elementary' proof of the prime number theorem was given by Selberg and Erdös in 1948; it succeeded in using only the integers, but it was by no means a *simple* proof. Very recently a much simpler proof has been given (see Newman 1980) which does however use some basic complex analysis. What constitutes a 'good' proof in mathematics is a matter open to argument and to changes in fashion.

Next we say something about the question of *unique factorisation* of a number into prime factors. It is easy to show that any integer can be written as a product of primes, but can this be done in only one way? Thus we can factorise the number 60 as $6 \times 10 = (3 \times 2) \times (2 \times 5) = 2^2 \times 3 \times 5$, or alternatively as $4 \times 15 = 2^2 \times 3 \times 5$, which gives the same factors. It may seem obvious that we should always get the same result, but suppose we take the Fermat number

$$2^{32} + 1 = 4\,294\,967\,297 = 641 \times 6\,700\,417;$$

is it really obvious that this is the *only* factorisation into primes? The unique factorisation property of the integers is a result that has to be proved; it is called the *fundamental theorem of arithmetic*. Euclid does not state it explicitly (hence many school books tend to assume the proof is unnecessary), but he does give a result which is essentially equivalent: if p (a prime) divides the product ab, then it must divide either a or b. The fundamental theorem is easily derived from this.

It becomes evident that unique factorisation is a property which needs proof when we construct other number systems for which the property does not hold. Consider, for example, the system which consists only of integers of the form $3n + 1$, i.e. the numbers $1, 4, 7, 10, 13, \ldots$. It is easy to check that the product of any two such numbers is also of the form $3n + 1$ and thus belongs to the system. Further, whilst the number 16 factorises as 4×4, the numbers 4, 10, 25 have no factors within the system and are thus primes in the system. Moreover, we have $100 = 4 \times 25 = 10 \times 10$, and thus we have two *different* representations of the number 100 as products of prime factors!

Another example where uniqueness fails is obtained when we consider all numbers of the form $a + b\sqrt{6}$, where a and b are positive or negative integers. Such generalisations of the integers are called *algebraic numbers* because they are roots of algebraic equations with integer coefficients: thus $2 + \sqrt{6}$ is a root of $x^2 - 4x - 2 = 0$. Algebraic numbers may be *complex*: $2 + \sqrt{(-6)}$ is a root of $x^2 - 4x + 10 = 0$. (Complex numbers are discussed in Chapter 3: here all we need to know is that $\sqrt{(-6)} \times \sqrt{(-6)} = -6$.) The numbers $a + b\sqrt{6}$ include the integers as the special case $b = 0$. Note that addition and multiplication of these numbers always gives numbers of the same class: thus

$$(3 + \sqrt{6}) + (-2 + \sqrt{6}) = 1 + 2\sqrt{6},$$
$$(3 + \sqrt{6})(-2 + \sqrt{6}) = -6 - 2\sqrt{6} + 3\sqrt{6} + 6$$
$$= \sqrt{6}, \text{ etc.}$$

It is not immediately clear which numbers are primes in this system. If we consider the factorisation of the number 6, there are apparently two different forms, since we can write $6 = 2 \times 3$, and also $6 = \sqrt{6} \times \sqrt{6}$. But the factors 2, 3, $\sqrt{6}$ are actually *not* primes in our system since we have

$$\sqrt{6} = (3 + \sqrt{6})(-2 + \sqrt{6}) = (2 + \sqrt{6})(3 - \sqrt{6}),$$
and
$$2 = (2 + \sqrt{6})(-2 + \sqrt{6}), \quad 3 = (3 + \sqrt{6})(3 - \sqrt{6}).$$

So in fact both the above factorisations of the number 6 lead to the same result:

$$6 = (2 + \sqrt{6})(-2 + \sqrt{6})(3 + \sqrt{6})(3 - \sqrt{6}),$$

and these four factors *are* the prime factors of the number 6 in our system. Thus it turns out that here unique factorisation still applies, although the result was hardly obvious. And, if we now consider the system of complex algebraic numbers $a + b\sqrt{(-6)}$, then we have the two factorisations $6 = 2 \times 3 = (-\sqrt{(-6)}) \times (\sqrt{(-6)})$, and now it turns out that 2, 3, $\sqrt{(-6)}$ *are* primes in the system and cannot be factorised. So here we again have two different factorisations into prime factors.

The theory of algebraic numbers is a large subject, developed intensively in the nineteenth century. A leading originator was Kummer (1810–93) who participated in the discussions on the validity (or otherwise) of unique factorisation. The question was of interest in the 1840s in connection with efforts to find a general proof of *Fermat's last theorem*. This arose as follows: the equation $a^2 + b^2 = c^2$ can be solved for a class of positive integers; the simplest example is $a = 3$, $b = 4$, $c = 5$, and in general all numbers of the form $a = u^2 - v^2, b = 2uv, c = u^2 + v^2$, with u, v positive integers and $u > v$, satisfy the equation. Such numbers are called *Pythagorean triples* because they represent (in accordance with the theorem of Pythagoras) the sides of a right-angled triangle in which the lengths of the sides are *commensurable* (i.e. the ratios of the lengths of the sides are ratios of whole numbers, see p. 33). The general method for constructing Pythagorean triples was given by the Greek mathematician Diophantos who lived about A.D. 250 in Alexandria; his *Arithmetica* contains the first systematic use of algebraic symbols (but a modern reader will not find it easy to follow his notation). In the margin of his copy of Diophantos's work Fermat wrote (in Latin): 'However, it is impossible to write a cube as the sum of two cubes, a 4th power as the sum of two 4th powers, and in general any power beyond the 2nd as the sum of two similar powers. For this I have discovered a truly wonderful proof, but the margin is too small to contain it.'

Thus Fermat's last theorem asserts that $a^n + b^n = c^n$ has no solution in positive integers a, b, c if n is an integer greater than 2. It is really a conjecture rather than a theorem because, despite all efforts over more than 300 years, it has never been proved as a general result valid for all n, though its truth has been demonstrated for every single value of n from 3 up to a few thousand. Some special cases are fairly easy to deal with; the proof for

$n = 4$ was given by Fermat himself. Fermat's theorem became a famous problem which, while not in itself very important, led to new developments in number theory and also attracted many amateurs. A prize of 100 000 marks was at one time offered in Germany for a proof, but its value was wiped out by the 1923 inflation. It is the arithmetical problem for which the greatest number of incorrect 'proofs' have been given!

Complex algebraic numbers arise when we factorise $a^n + b^n$ into linear factors:

$$a^n + b^n = (a+b)(a+rb)(a+r^2b) \cdots (a+r^{n-1}b),$$

where r is a complex number such that $r^n = 1$. (For example, when $n = 3$, $r = -\frac{1}{2} + \frac{1}{2}\sqrt{(-3)}$.) Attempts to prove Fermat's theorem in the 1840s failed because they assumed unique factorisation into primes for such complex numbers. This raises the question: can we define special kinds of algebraic numbers for which unique factorisation again holds? This *can* be done (they are called 'ideals'), and pursuit of this idea by Kummer and later mathematicians led to a powerful generalisation of the simple notion of arithmetic divisibility with many applications in number theory and modern algebra. The theory of ideals allowed Kummer to prove Fermat's last theorem for a large class of prime number exponents n called 'regular primes' (but not for all values of n).

Fermat's problem is an example of a *Diophantine equation*, an equation to be solved with integral values for the unknowns. Such equations lead to some very difficult problems in the theory of numbers. However, the simplest case, *the linear Diophantine equation in two unknowns,*

$$ax + by = c, \tag{1}$$

where a, b, c are given natural numbers and x, y are the unknowns, can be dealt with quite easily. Note that such an equation might have no solutions at all, or a finite number of solutions, or an infinite number. We shall derive the necessary and sufficient condition for equation (1) to have a solution in (positive or negative) integers.

For this purpose we introduce the number (a, b), the *greatest common divisor* of a and b, i.e. the largest integer which is a factor of both a and b. Then (a, b) has the interesting property that integers k, l always exist such that

$$(a, b) = ka + lb;\qquad(2)$$

we say that (a, b) is *linearly dependent* on a and b. This result follows from a systematic process, given by Euclid, for finding (a, b), the *Euclidean algorithm*. We illustrate it by means of an example. Let $a = 432$, $b = 156$; we are to express 432 as a multiple of 156 with a remainder:

$$432 = 2 \times 156 + 120.$$

(The idea is that any integer which divides 432 and 156 also divides 120; hence the common divisors of 432 and 156 are the same as the common divisors of the smaller pair 156 and 120.) Now we continue the process: we express 156 as a multiple of 120 and a remainder, and we carry on until the process terminates (as it must):

$$156 = 1 \times 120 + 36,$$
$$120 = 3 \times 36 + 12,$$
$$36 = 3 \times 12.$$

The greatest common divisor is the last remainder in the process, and thus $(432, 156) = 12$. The result (2) is implicit in the Euclidean algorithm; we need only work backwards as follows:

$$\begin{aligned}
12 &= 120 - 3 \times 36 \\
&= 120 - 3(156 - 120) \\
&= 4 \times 120 - 3 \times 156 \\
&= 4(432 - 2 \times 156) - 3 \times 156 \\
&= 4 \times 432 - 11 \times 156.
\end{aligned}$$

What can we say about equation (1), in the light of these results? Evidently, if c in equation (1) happens to be equal to (a, b), then the equation has the special solution $x = k$, $y = l$. More generally, if c is some multiple of (a, b), say $c = q(a, b)$ (with q an integer), then equation (2) gives $a(qk) + b(ql) = q(a, b) = c$, so the original equation (1) has a special solution $x = qk$, $y = ql$. *Conversely*, suppose equation (1) has integer solutions x, y for given c, then c must be a multiple of (a, b).

Proof: (a, b) divides both a and b (by definition), and therefore it also divides the linear combination $ax + by$, which equals c. Thus we have shown that the necessary and sufficient condition for the solubility of equation (1) is that c must be a multiple of (a, b). We consider two examples:

(i) $7x + 11y = 13$. $(7, 11) = 1$, and $1 = 2 \times 11 - 3 \times 7$ (by inspection, or by Euclid's algorithm); so we have $7 \times (-3) + 11 \times 2 = 1$, therefore $7 \times (-39) + 11 \times 26 = 13$. Thus one solution is $x = -39$, $y = 26$. (*Note*: there are other solutions. *Exercise*: find *all* solutions!)

(ii) $3x + 6y = 22$. $(3, 6) = 3$, and 22 is not a multiple of 3; hence there are no integer solutions in this case.

A rather harder example of a Diophantine equation is $x^3 + y^3 = z^3 + w^3$. Although $x^3 + y^3 = z^3$ is insoluble (by Fermat's last theorem for $n = 3$), this equation has infinitely many solutions in integers (apart from trivial solutions such as $x = z$, $y = w$; $x = -y$, $z = -w$). The formulae were given by Euler; see Davenport (1970). There is a story connected with this equation, relating to the brilliant Indian mathematician S. Ramanujan who had a deep intuitive feeling for the integers. When his friend G. H. Hardy visted Ramanujan who was ill in hospital, he said he had come in taxi no. 1729 and this seemed rather a dull number, whereupon Ramanujan immediately said: 'No Hardy, it is very interesting – it is the smallest number expressible as the sum of two positive cubes in two different ways'. And in fact $1729 = 1^3 + 12^3 = 9^3 + 10^3$. 'Every positive integer was one of Ramanujan's personal friends' (Littlewood).

How about $x^4 + y^4 = z^4 + w^4$? Even Ramanujan could see no 'obvious' solutions in this case but he felt sure that any number expressible as the sum of fourth powers must be large. In fact it was known to Euler that

$$158^4 + 59^4 = 134^4 + 133^4 = 635\,318\,657.$$

3

Types of numbers

We have seen that there are many interesting and difficult problems connected with the simplest numbers, the integers, but you will already have come across other kinds of numbers: fractions, 'irrational' numbers like √2, and perhaps complex or 'imaginary' numbers. Let us now have a more general look at the concept of number, and the way it has evolved over the ages.

The simplest numbers are the 'natural numbers' 1, 2, 3, . . . , required for the process of *counting* objects. It was quite an abstract idea when primitive man realised at some stage, long ago, that 3 apples, 3 men, 3 women, 3 stones, etc., all have something in common: the (abstract) *number* 3. Let us briefly review some of the rules for calculation with natural numbers. (It is not necessary for our purpose to present a logically complete set of rules.)

The basic operations are addition and multiplication. They arise in a simple and natural way when we combine sets of objects. Thus, to calculate $2 + 3$, we start with $2 = $ ⊙ objects and put next to them $3 = $ ⊙∙ objects; this gives us a collection of ⊙∙ ∙∙⊃ $= 5$ objects (by counting). We arrive at the same number by starting with 3 objects and putting next to them 2 objects: ⊙∙ ∙∙⊃ $=$ ⊙∙ ∙∙⊃ . Thus we adopt as a general rule of addition $a + b = b + a$ for any two natural numbers (we call this the *commutative law of addition*). Multiplication arises in the form of repeated addition. 2×3 tells us to combine 2 collections of 3 objects. This contains altogether 6 objects, so $2 \times 3 = 6$. We can clearly regard the combination also as consisting of 3 collections of 2 objects (Fig. 3.1), so $3 \times 2 = 6$, and generally $a \times b = b \times a$ (this is the *commutative law of multiplication*). The link between addition and

Fig. 3.1

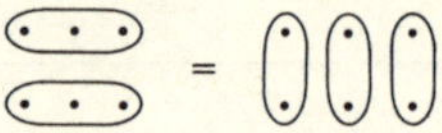

multiplication is important: $2 \times (3+4)$ appears as

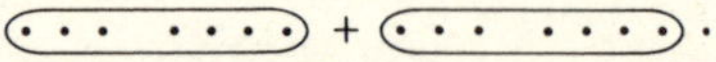

We can regard this collection as made up of two 3s and two

4s: 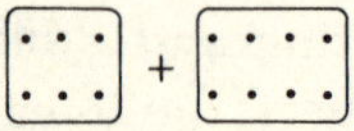 ; thus $2 \times (3+4) = 2 \times 3 + 2 \times 4$, and generally $a(b+c) = ab + ac$. This is the *distributive law*.

These rules for the natural numbers, established by practical experience in counting, seem 'obvious' and hardly worth so much fuss. However, one of the basic ideas of mathematics is to abstract and generalise, and the arithmetic of the natural numbers leads us to study other 'objects' which satisfy the same general rules but with which we may no longer be able to count.

Note that, if a and b are any two natural numbers, then $a+b$ and $a \times b$ are also natural numbers, so that we can add and multiply natural numbers without any restriction. So far so good, but we find that our number system is incomplete as soon as we want to carry out *subtraction*. We can define subtraction by an equation: given two natural numbers a and b, we wish to find a number x such that $a + x = b$. Such an x exists as a natural number *only* if a is not greater than b (there is no natural number x such that $5 + x = 3$).

To resolve this difficulty we can do one of two things: *either* we remark only that, within the set of natural numbers, the equation $a + x = b$ has *no* solution when $a > b$ (and go away and study something else, as there is then very little to do in mathematics); *or* we can say that we want always to be able to solve the equation, and that we must therefore *extend* the number system beyond the natural numbers. To achieve our end we introduce the *negative integers* $-1, -2, -3, \ldots$; -2 for example is *defined* to be the number which satisfies $5 + x = 3$. With these new objects $a + x = b$ always has a solution, and in fact a unique solution denoted by $b - a$. The natural numbers 1, 2, 3, ... are then called *positive integers*, and the positive and negative integers, together with 0, form the set of all *integers*. This extension of the number system is of course not just an abstract game, but is needed for all sorts of applications where *gain* and *loss* are involved, for example stock market movements or thermometer readings. At this stage we introduce the important *geometric* representation of the integers as points on a line:

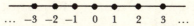

$$\ldots \quad -3 \quad -2 \quad -1 \quad 0 \quad 1 \quad 2 \quad 3 \quad \ldots$$

The positive integers then appear naturally as (evenly spaced) points to the *right* of zero, and the negative integers equally naturally as points to the *left* of 0. Evidently, if a, b are any two integers, then the point representing a on the number line is either to the right of the point representing b $(a > b)$, or coincident with b $(a = b)$, or to the left of b $(a < b)$: we say that the set of integers is *ordered*.

Having introduced a new type of number, we must establish rules for calculating with these new objects. The rules for negative numbers will be familiar, and we will not spend time developing them systematically. But let us take a moment to consider why (for example) we say that $(-1) \times (-1) = +1$. If a child asks you this, what do you say? 'Because it is'? (That is, in a sense, the right answer!) First, we agree that (for example) $2 \times (-3) = -6$ (i.e. two losses of 3 is a loss of 6), etc. Next, we postulate that our general laws, established for addition and multiplication of natural numbers, should still hold for the set of all integers. In particular, we postulate the continued validity of the distributive law: $a(b + c) = ab + ac$. Then, choosing the values $a = -1$, $b = 1$, $c = -1$, we obtain $(-1) \times (1 - 1) = (-1) \times (1) + (-1) \times (-1)$, or $0 = -1 + (-1) \times (-1)$, which holds only if we have $(-1) \times (-1) = +1$. Thus the rule for multiplication of two negative numbers follows from the postulate that the distributive law is valid. Why should we postulate this law? There is no *logical* need to do so: it just happens to be the most 'sensible'.procedure for many purposes. We get the most 'useful' number system by preserving the rules established for the simplest numbers when we generalize: 'useful' both in the sense that the number system is needed for developing mathematics itself to higher levels, and also that it is most useful in applications of mathematics to practical problems of many kinds.

This attitude: 'let us adopt some rules (which we call 'axioms'), let us make sure as far as we can that they involve no logical contradictions, and then let us see what we can do with our rules', is a modern one in mathematics which emerged gradually in the nineteenth century. Before that, people tended to look for some underlying reality: they asked, do negative numbers (or complex numbers, or square roots) 'really' exist? So there were controversies over what was 'really' allowed in mathematics and what was not. For example, it was thought that Euclid's geometry was the only 'really' possible one, and only in the nineteenth century was it realised that non-Euclidean geometries with different axioms could be developed which had the same status as Euclid's from a logical point of view.

The mathematician nowadays no longer looks for such an underlying external reality. This philosophical modesty is richly rewarding, since it has released mathematicians to develop new mathematical structures much more freely and to explore their consequences. We may still ask: why then do we do mathematics, and what's the use? There is no simple answer, and the question is worth debating; philosophical arguments about the nature and purpose of mathematics have by no means died out!† Most mathematicians would try to answer the question at two levels, not necessarily with equal emphasis on both. They would firstly stress the use and importance of mathematical ideas within mathematics itself (thus without the real numbers, see p. 37, most of the interesting branches of mathematics could not be developed); and they would secondly point to their use and importance in applications (thus complex numbers are needed in applied mathematics in the analysis of vibrations; non-Euclidean geometry is essential for the modern theory of gravitation; group theory is important for quantum

---

† And it must be admitted that arguments about what is 'really allowed' in mathematics have also continued, but at a more sophisticated level (see for example the reference to 'non-constructive proofs' in Chapter 11).

mechanics). It is worth remembering here that non-Euclidean geometry and group theory are branches of mathematics which were developed originally purely for their mathematical interest and whose important role in applications only became clear many years after their discovery. Thus one should not be too dogmatic in statements about which parts of mathematics are most 'relevant to the real world'.

The next generalisation of the number system arises when we want to do *division*. Given two integers a and b we wish to find x such that $ax = b$. Again, this equation has no solution among the integers except in the special case when b is a multiple of a (thus there is no integer x such that $3x = 5$). We deal with this problem by introducing the *rational numbers*. These are written in the form of fractions b/a, where a, b are integers. We exclude the case $a = 0$. (Division by zero must be excluded, since zero times any number is always zero, so there is no x such that $0 \times x = b$ if $b \neq 0$.) Such numbers must have originated very early on to deal with practical problems of subdivision such as sharing 5 sheep among 3 people; how much sheep for each person? A number of comments should be made. (1) The representation of rational numbers as fractions is not unique, since we want (for example) $2b/2a$ to be the same number as b/a (if you share 10 sheep among 6 people every person gets the same amount as when you share 5 among 3). We can obtain a unique representation by stipulating that a is positive and that a, b have no common factors; the fraction b/a is then 'in its lowest terms'. (2) A *field* in mathematics is essentially a collection of 'numbers' such that the sum, difference, product and quotient of any two numbers in the collection (excluding division by 0) are also in the collection. With the rationals we can perform these four operations, and the set of all rational numbers is the most familiar (but by no means the only) example of a field. (3) With the rationals we now have a wider class of numbers which includes the integers as a subset (they are rationals of the form $b/1$). (4) The rationals are an ordered field and can again be regarded as points on a line. They give us a subdivision of the line which we can make as fine as we like. To represent (for example) all rationals of the form $b/1\,000\,000$ as points on the line, we divide the interval $(0, 1)$

into a million equal pieces; similarly for all other intervals (1, 2), (2, 3), ... ; and the points of subdivision then correspond to fractions of the form $b/1\,000\,000$. We can make the denominator as large as we like (10^{100} or what you will) – so one would surely be inclined to think that one must in this way eventually catch *all* the points on the line; in other words, that every point on the line is described by *some* rational number. It is certainly true that rational numbers are sufficient for all practical purposes of measuring. What is more, the rational points are *dense* on the line; this means that we can never find an interval (a, b), however small, between any two given rational points which is entirely *free* from rational points. To verify this we merely observe that, if a and b are different rational numbers with $a < b$, the rational number $\frac{1}{2}(a + b)$ lies between a and b. (*Exercise*: demonstrate this.) The fact that any interval between rational points contains at least *one* other rational point immediately implies, remarkably enough, that any such interval must contain *infinitely many* rational points! For, if there were only a finite number, say m, we could mark them off as shown:

and then any interval between two adjacent points would be free of rational points; but we have just seen that this is impossible. Thus there *appear* to be no 'empty places' on the line.

It was one of the most remarkable discoveries in mathematics, made by the Pythagoreans about 2400 years ago, that this very natural conclusion is not correct: there *are* numbers which are not rational and which cannot be obtained by *any* subdivision of the line into an integral number of pieces. In fact 'most' numbers are not rational (in a sense to be discussed later on; see Chapter 11)! The discovery of irrational magnitudes may be regarded as the beginning of theoretical 'pure' mathematics. What exactly was the problem worrying the Greek mathematicians here? A rule for constructing a right angle (the 'carpenter's rule') had been known for a long time: take two arms, of lengths 3 and 4 units, and incline them so that the line joining the ends is of length 5 (Fig. 3.2). It is natural to try to find a common unit of measure for the sides of the even simpler triangle which has two *equal* sides inclined at a right angle. Suppose we divide these sides into 5 equal pieces; then the hypotenuse is found by measurement to contain just over 7 of these pieces. Try then dividing into 12 parts: the hypotenuse (to a much better approximation) will then contain 17 pieces, but the subdivision is still not exact. All efforts to find a 'common measure' for all the sides of such a triangle were fruitless, and eventually it was *proved* that no such common measure could ever be found. Thus the equal sides and the hypotenuse of the triangle are 'incommensurable'. Note that to the Greeks 'number' meant 'whole number' (they didn't even deal with fractional numbers, but always talked instead about *proportions* or *ratios* of two whole numbers): they did not conceive of the notion of an irrational quantity as a *number*, but thought of incommensurable *geometrical ratios.*

Given two lines of length 1, we construct a line, whose length x is not rational, as the hypotenuse of the right-angled triangle whose shorter sides are 1: the Pythagorean theorem then says $x^2 = 1^2 + 1^2 = 2$. Thus the problem is: find a number x such that $x \times x = 2$. (Note the difference from the *linear* equation $ax = b$ which defines the rationals.) The proof that no such rational number x exists can be given in many ways. The usual modern version, which is equivalent to a proof given by Aristotle, is as follows: suppose $x = p/q$, a rational number in its lowest terms (so that p, q are integers without common factor); then $p^2/q^2 = 2$, i.e. $p^2 = 2q^2$, hence p^2 is an even number, hence p is even, since the square of an odd number is always odd. So we can write $p = 2r$, where r is an integer, i.e. $4r^2 = p^2 = 2q^2$, so $q^2 = 2r^2$, so q^2 is even, hence q is even. Thus p and q are both even,

Fig. 3.2

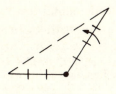
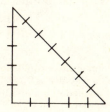

contradicting the assumption that p and q have no common factor. Denoting x by $\sqrt{2}$, we have shown that *no rational number is equal to* $\sqrt{2}$. The recognition that no common measure can be found for certain geometric magnitudes appears to be the first of many 'proofs of impossibility' which have played an important role in the development of mathematics.

It is not known for certain how incommensurability was first discovered, but it has been suggested that it could have arisen in connection with the method of subdivision of a regular pentagon, shown in Fig. 3.3, which was known to the Pythagoreans. If one starts with a regular pentagon $ABCDE$ and draws all five diagonals, then these diagonals intersect in points $A'B'C'D'E'$ which form another regular pentagon. The diagonals of this smaller pentagon form a still smaller regular pentagon, and so on. Clearly this process of subdivision never stops, and there is no 'smallest pentagon' whose side could serve as an ultimate unit of measure. It follows that the ratio of a side to a diagonal in a regular pentagon cannot be rational. (*Exercise*: show that the ratio is in fact $\frac{1}{2}(\sqrt{5}-1)$.)† This method of proof is called *infinite descent*: it was Fermat's favourite technique for demonstrating results in the theory of numbers.

Plato emphasised the importance of the discovery of incommensurability. He tells us that the mathematician Theodorus (born about 470 B.C.), a Pythagorean, had shown his pupils a proof that the side of a square of area 3 is incommensurable with the unit of measurement; similarly for squares of area 5, 6, 7, . . . up to 17 (excluding of course the squares 9 and 16).

To construct $\sqrt{2}$ as a length on the number axis we draw a right-angled triangle whose hypotenuse is $\sqrt{2}$ (Fig. 3.4) and use a compass to transfer the length $\sqrt{2}$ to the axis. This geometrical construction gives a point distinct from all rational points, so the set of rational points, although dense, does not cover the whole number line. This early and fundamental result shows that we must not trust 'first impressions' in mathematics. Care-

---

† To obtain this result, show first that the point D' divides AC in such a way that $AD'/D'C = D'C/AC$. Two thousand years later, this method of subdividing a line fascinated the painters of the Renaissance who called it the 'golden section'.

ful argument and subtle reasoning are needed and can lead to unexpected conclusions.

One can show, by extensions of the arguments used above, that other numbers formed by root extraction, such as $\sqrt{6}$, $\sqrt[3]{2}$ (these are solutions of the algebraic equations $x^2 = 6$, $x^3 = 2$), are also irrational. Further examples of irrational numbers are the familiar numbers π (the ratio of the circumference of a circle to its diameter) and e (the base of natural logarithms). These numbers can be defined in various equivalent ways, in particular by means of infinite series, but can they be obtained (like $\sqrt{2}$) as roots of algebraic equations with integer coefficients? We shall return to this interesting question later (see p. 67).

Fig. 3.3

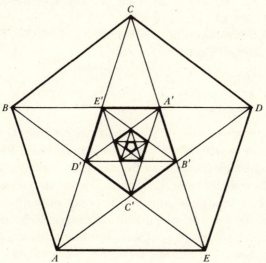

Fig. 3.4

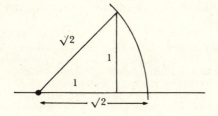

We now indicate another approach to irrational numbers which is not geometrical. This comes from the *decimal representation* of rational numbers. A decimal fraction represents a rational number if, and only if, it is periodic (or, as a special case, finite); e.g.

$$\tfrac{3}{4} = 0.75, \qquad \tfrac{2}{7} = 0.285\,714\,285\,714\,285\,714 \ldots$$

To prove this result generally we look at the usual long division of B into A which gives the decimal form of A/B. The only possible remainders at each stage of the division are $1, 2, \ldots,$ $B-1$ (i.e. there are $B-1$ different possibilities); if any remainder is zero the process stops and we have a finite decimal. But this means that, after *at most B* divisions, one of the remainders *must* repeat, and thereafter the decimal representation repeats itself (since subsequent remainders repeat). Clearly, also, the 'repeating block' can have *at most B* -1 digits. Conversely, if the decimal representation of a number is periodic, then the number is rational. Consider for example

$$x = 1.818\,181\,8\ldots$$

We can convert this into a *finite* decimal by writing down

$$100x = 181.818\,181\,8\ldots$$

and subtracting: we obtain $99x = 180$, so $x = 180/99 = 20/11$. This reduction is evidently possible for any periodic decimal: if the repeating block contains m digits we multiply by 10^m and subtract. Thus we can say that any *non-periodic* infinite decimal must be an irrational number. It is not difficult to invent simple rules for writing down infinite non-periodic decimals which therefore represent irrational numbers; for example the following decimal containing an increasing number of zeros:

$$0.101\,001\,000\,100\,001\ldots$$

No simple rule of this kind, however, exists for constructing the decimal representation of commonly occurring irrational numbers such as $\sqrt{2}$.†

---

† There is a (not very serious) difficulty over uniqueness, arising from the fact that $0.999\ldots$ (with the 9s recurring indefinitely) is the same number as 1. Thus the infinite recurring decimal $0.359\,99\ldots$ represents the same number as the finite decimal 0.36. If we wish every number to have a *unique* decimal representation, we can agree to write every finite decimal as an infinite decimal with recurring 9s.

We can thus now regard a 'number' as *any* finite or infinite decimal, and this definition will include both rational and irrational numbers. This gives us the set of *real numbers*. Our discussion shows that, if we regard the integers as the basic 'building bricks' to be used in constructing all other kinds of number, then a rational number can always be defined in terms of two integers only, but the definition of an irrational number necessarily involves in some way an infinite set of integers. Infinite processes are thus inevitably involved in any proper theory of the real number system.

Such a precise logical theory was first given in the nineteenth century, and it accompanied the rigorous formulation of the calculus in the same period. In fact the simple definition of a real number as an infinite decimal, while adequate for many purposes, is not altogether satisfactory, since there is no special merit in the decimal system and the use of the base 10, and one would prefer a definition which is not linked to any particular base. And, more important, the definition should bring out the fundamental property of the real numbers (not possessed by the rationals) of being *complete*, i.e. (in a geometrical sense) the property of representing *all* the points on the number line. It is this completeness property, the fact that there are no 'gaps' left on the line, which is needed to give precise definitions of *continuity* and of a *continuous function*, the key concepts needed to put the calculus on a rigorous basis. One way of formulating the completeness property precisely is by way of the property of the *least upper bound*: we require that, if a collection of elements of our set has an upper bound, then it must have a *least* upper bound belonging to the set. This property is not possessed by the rationals: the collection of all rationals whose squares are less than 2 has an upper bound (they are all less than, say, 3), but no rational number is a least upper bound (this is because we can find rational numbers arbitrarily close to the irrational number $\sqrt{2}$ which does not itself belong to the set). These observations suggest an alternative way of defining the real numbers. We use the fact that, while the real number $\sqrt{2}$ is itself not rational, its properties are completely determined by specification of the (infinite) set of *all* rationals less than $\sqrt{2}$. But this amounts to saying that the real number can be *defined* as a *set* of rational numbers (which will have as one of its properties that it contains no greatest element). This is essentially the approach to the construction of the real numbers adopted by Dedekind (in 1872); it is a modern version of ideas which go back to the time of Eudoxus (see p. 44). There are other, equivalent, ways of constructing the set of real numbers; the technical details of the construction are matters for a university course in analysis. The essential properties of the set are that it is a *field* (see p. 31) which is both *ordered* (see p. 29) and also *complete*, in the sense just discussed. It can be shown that these properties make the real numbers *unique*, in the sense that there is only one complete ordered field, or, more precisely, that any two fields which are both complete and ordered have the same properties and are, for mathematical purposes, identical.

We now introduce briefly a further extension of the number concept, and we can then in the next chapter review the historical development of the various generalisations we have met.

We have seen that, to solve a quadratic equation like $x^2 = 2$, we need irrational numbers, and that the rational and irrational numbers make up the real numbers. These numbers are ordered and correspond to points on a line. Now, since the square of a real number, whether positive or negative, is always positive, there is no real number x such that $x^2 = -1$. Thus real numbers are not sufficient to solve a quadratic equation as simple as $x^2 + 1 = 0$ (and many others). So we must generalise the number concept again by introducing the symbol i (not a real number!) with the property $i^2 = -1$ (the 'imaginary unit'). With this we form *complex numbers* like $2 + 3i$, $-5i$, ..., and generally $a + bi$, where a, b are real numbers; a is the 'real' and b the 'imaginary' part of the complex number $a + bi$. We assume that the usual laws for addition and multiplication hold for complex numbers as for reals. We can then calculate with complex numbers as with real numbers, always replacing i^2, whenever it occurs, by -1. So, for example, the product $(2 + 3i)(1 + 4i)$ is the complex number $-10 + 11i$, because

$$(2 + 3i)(1 + 4i) = 2 + 8i + 3i + 12i^2$$

$$= (2 - 12) + (8 + 3)i = -10 + 11i.$$

We can easily show that the processes of addition, multi-plication, subtraction and division of two complex numbers always lead to complex numbers of the form $a + bi$ (excluding division by 0), so the complex numbers form a *field*. This includes the field of real numbers as a subfield: real numbers are equivalent to complex numbers of the form $a + 0i$.

The equation $x^2 + 1 = 0$ now has the two solutions $x = i$ and $x = -i$. Of course we have gained much more: we can state, for example, that every quadratic equation $ax^2 + bx + c = 0$ (a, b, c real, $a \neq 0$) has precisely two roots, given by the well-known formula

$$x = \frac{-b \pm \sqrt{(b^2 - 4ac)}}{2a}.$$

The roots are real if $b^2 - 4ac \geq 0$, and complex if $b^2 - 4ac < 0$. In fact complex numbers do very much more than just this; they play a fundamental role in many branches of pure and applied mathematics.

There is no order relation among complex numbers of the kind that exists for real numbers, and we cannot represent them as points on a line. Nevertheless, a simple (and very important) geometric interpretation can be given; it was introduced in the early nineteenth century. This represents $x + yi$ as the point in a *plane* which has rectangular coordinates x, y. In this way any complex number is uniquely associated with a point in the 'complex plane' or 'Argand diagram', Fig. 3.5. Addition and multiplication of complex numbers also have simple geometric interpretations. For addition, we regard $x + yi$ as a displacement

Fig. 3.6

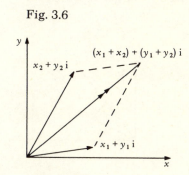

Fig. 3.5

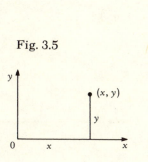

(a two-dimensional *vector*) from $(0, 0)$ to (x, y); then the sum

$$(x_1 + y_1 i) + (x_2 + y_2 i) = (x_1 + x_2) + (y_1 + y_2)i$$

is the point in the complex plane obtained by the vector (parallelogram) addition law (Fig. 3.6). This geometric interpretation shows that complex numbers are just as 'real' as 'real numbers'. We need only think in two dimensions instead of one. The names 'real' and 'imaginary' are historical, and remind us of earlier days when the 'square root of minus one' was regarded as something 'fictitious' or 'unreal', in fact 'imaginary'!

The geometric interpretation of multiplication by a complex number is also interesting. In particular, multiplication of $x + yi$ by a complex number of the form $\cos \theta + i \sin \theta$ is equivalent to a *rotation* of the vector represented by $x + yi$ through an anti-clockwise angle θ in the complex plane. To verify this we use *polar coordinates* in the plane (Fig. 3.7), and write

$$x + yi = r \cos \alpha + i\, r \sin \alpha.$$

Then

$$(x + yi)(\cos \theta + i \sin \theta)$$

$$= r\,(\cos \alpha \cos \theta - \sin \alpha \sin \theta)$$

$$+ ir\,(\cos \alpha \sin \theta + \sin \alpha \cos \theta)$$

$$= r \cos (\alpha + \theta) + ir \sin (\alpha + \theta),$$

and this is a vector of the same length r as $x + yi$, making an angle $\alpha + \theta$ with the x-axis. In particular, taking $\theta = \frac{1}{2}\pi$ (a right angle), we have $\cos \frac{1}{2}\pi + i \sin \frac{1}{2}\pi = i$, and we see that multiplication by i is equivalent to rotation through a right angle. What, then, about the product $i^2 = i.i$? Rotating the vector i through a right angle again, we get to the point -1 in the complex plane (Fig. 3.8).

Fig. 3.7

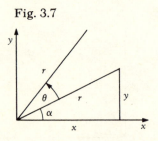

Fig. 3.8

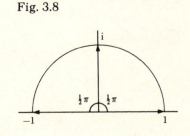

Thus we have a simple geometric interpretation of the fundamental rule $i^2 = -1$. The complex number $\cos \theta + i \sin \theta$ is a vector of unit length and corresponds to a point on the *unit circle* (with centre at the origin). It describes a rotation through an angle θ about the origin. Multiplication of two such complex numbers amounts to combining two rotations through θ_1 and θ_2, and gives a rotation through $\theta_1 + \theta_2$. This is a 'group operation', and the set of these complex numbers forms the *group of rotations* about the origin in two dimensions.

4

Historical development of the number concept I

The idea that we can freely create number systems to suit our requirements is a modern one, originating in the early nineteenth century. Let us now go back and review the situation in earlier periods.

We know that the Babylonians (about 2000 B.C.) had a well-developed system of mathematics which allowed them to solve quite tricky problems. It seems that they were not interested in general theory, only in computing answers (according to specified rules) to specific questions. They could deal with problems which gave rise to quadratic equations. For example: 'An area, consisting of the sum of two squares, is 1000. The side of one square is $\frac{2}{3}$ of the side of the other square, diminished by 10. What are the sides of the squares?' This leads to the equations $x^2 + y^2 = 1000$ and $y = \frac{2}{3}x - 10$, whence $13x^2 - 120x - 8100 = 0$, with positive root $x = 30$. The other (negative) root $x = -270/13$ was simply ignored. Were the Babylonians aware of the 'existence' of this second root? Probably not: they clearly wanted only to solve their practical problem of measurement and were happy to find a unique positive answer. Nowadays mathematicians are more interested in general properties such as the fact that quadratic equations always possess exactly two roots.

As we saw in Chapter 3 irrational magnitudes were discovered by the Pythagoreans. These people, a religious, scientific and philosophical brotherhood in Greece who lived in the period 600–400 B.C., were probably the first to recognise that mathematics deals with abstractions as distinct from physical objects or pictures. They dealt with whole numbers and their ratios only ('commensurable' ratios) and they assumed that all phenomena (in particular geometrical magnitudes) must be describable in terms of whole numbers. So the discovery that the two sides of a right-angled triangle can be incommensurable must have produced a serious crisis in Greek mathematics. (Legend ascribes the discovery to a certain Hippasus and says that he was thrown overboard as a punishment for shattering fundamental beliefs.) As the Pythagoreans did not accept irrational numbers the identification of number with geometry was destroyed.

Just why was this discovery such a serious matter? It demolished most of the Greek geometry of the time. Consider for example the theorem that for two triangles of the same height the areas are in the ratio of their bases, area A : area $B = a : b$ (Fig. 4.1). Let us assume that we have proved that the areas are equal

Fig. 4.1

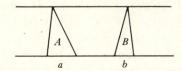

when the bases are equal $(a = b)$. We can then easily prove our more general result when a and b are commensurable. For example let $a : b = 3 : 2$, then $2a = 3b$, so we can construct *equal* triangles by comparing 2 As and 3 Bs (Fig. 4.2). These have equal bases and therefore equal areas, so $2A = 3B$, i.e. $A:B = 3:2$. For incommensurable lengths all such proofs (i.e. all the theory of *proportion* and *similarity*) fail, and it is not clear how we can compare two areas at all in such cases. Here the problem of *continuity* appeared. Number to the Greeks is a discontinuous concept, but for geometry we need to deal with continuously variable magnitudes. The general problem of

Fig. 4.2

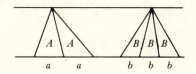

calculating areas and volumes of all kinds of figures (particularly those with curved boundaries) led on to the *calculus*, for which one needs properly formulated concepts of *continuity* and *limits*. We deal with these questions nowadays by starting with a generalised concept of number. Our modern ideas had their roots in the Greek approach to the problem of comparing incommensurable magnitudes. They invented the following special rule for dealing with magnitudes which have incommensurable ratios: suppose p, q are any two whole numbers and we want to compare a and b with A and B. Since it may not be possible to choose p and q such that $qa = pb$, we distinguish three cases: either $qa < pb$, or $qa = pb$, or $qa > pb$. Then if, *whenever* $qa < pb$, we have also $qA < pB$; *whenever* $qa = pb$ we have $qA = pB$; and *whenever* $qa > pb$ we have $qA > pB$, we say that $a : b = A : B$. This postulate forms the basis of Eudoxus's *theory of proportions*, given by Euclid. It contains the case of commensurable magnitudes (the middle possibility) as a special case, and it allows us once again to compare (for example) the areas of triangles when the bases are incommensurable. Consider q triangles with base a and p with base b, then we shall have *one* of the cases $qa < pb$, $qa = pb$ or $qa > pb$; suppose the first. But suppose two triangles with areas U, V have the same height and have bases u, v with $u < v$, then also $U < V$ (see Fig. 4.3). It follows that, whenever $qa < pb$, we have also $qA < pB$, and similarly in the other two cases. Thus, in accordance with Eudoxus's postulate, we can conclude that $a : b = A : B$. The nineteenth-century theory of irrational numbers follows this mode of thought quite closely, translated into modern language. Eudoxus's theory superseded the arithmetical theory

Fig. 4.3

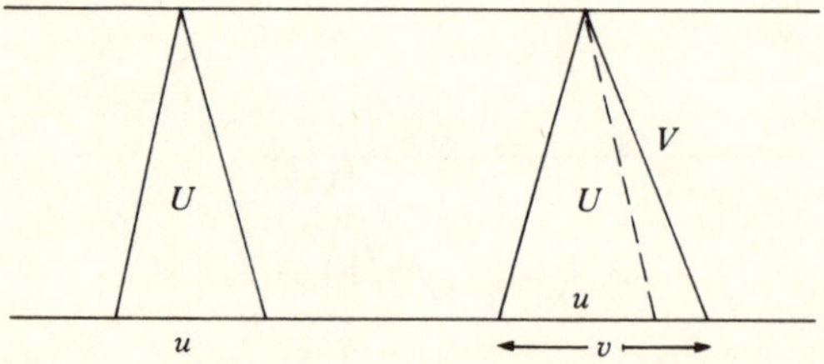

of the Pythagoreans which applied to commensurable quantities only. It cast algebraic reasoning into geometric form ($\sqrt{A}$ is the side of a square of area A, and so on), and it is presented by Euclid in strict axiomatic form.

Geometrical thinking thus became the basis for almost all rigorous mathematics for about 2000 years. We still call x^2 'x squared', x^3 'x cubed', because these symbols had only geometrical meaning for the Greeks. The intellectuals of classical Greece were philosophers with little interest in the requirements of commerce and trade. Computation played little part in their science which tended to be qualitative in character. Euclid's *Elements*, which present an organised account of the mathematical work of classical Greece, consist of geometry and theory of numbers: the 'purest' branches of the subject. In the later stages of the Alexandrian period educated men became more interested again in practical affairs and the emphasis shifted to quantitative knowledge and the development of arithmetic and algebra. In particular Archimedes (287–212 B.C.) was not only a highly original pure mathematician, but also a master of calculating technique and a prolific inventor of mechanical devices. In Chapter 8 we shall discuss his contributions to the early calculus.

Throughout the Hindu–Arab–Medieval period and well into the nineteenth century people worried about the meaning of negative and complex numbers. Such entities kept on making an appearance in calculations, for example as unwelcome 'extra' roots in the solution of quadratic equations, but what did they *mean*? Diophantos, already in the third century A.D., was prepared to multiply together algebraic expressions like $(x-1)$ and $(x-2)$, and to say that one must replace $(-1) \times (-2)$ by $+2$ in the expansion. But he took it for granted that x had always to be such that $x-1$ and $x-2$ were both positive; there was at that time no suggestion that negative numbers could have any meaning standing by themselves. Also quadratic equations could have only positive roots. The assumption that mathematics dealt with positive numbers only was commonly held until A.D. 1600 and later. The Indian mathematician Bhaskara (about A.D. 1150) went so far as to give the roots of $x^2 - 45x = 250$ as

$x = 50$ and $x = -5$, but said: 'the second value is in this case not to be taken, for it is inadequate; people do not approve of negative roots'.

During the sixteenth and seventeenth centuries mathematicians began to operate with complex numbers, but without any real understanding of their nature. Thus Cardan (in 1545) considers the problem of dividing 10 into two parts whose product is 40. He obtains the answer $5 + \sqrt{(-15)}, 5 - \sqrt{(-15)}$ and says: 'putting aside the mental tortures involved, multiply these numbers together; the product is $25 - (-15) = 40$. So progresses arithmetic subtlety the end of which, as is said, is as refined as it is useless'. (See also Chapter 5.) Descartes, who laid the foundation of coordinate geometry in his *Geométrie* (in 1637), also rejected complex roots and coined the term 'imaginary'. Even Newton did not regard complex roots as significant, presumably because in his day they lacked physical meaning. Leibniz wrote: 'The Divine Spirit found a sublime outlet in that wonder of analysis, that portent of the ideal world, that amphibian between being and not-being, which we call the imaginary root of negative unity'. (Should we regret that such colourful language is no longer used by mathematicians?)

By 1700 all the familiar members of our number system were known, but opposition to the newer types of numbers continued throughout the eighteenth century, and it was considered mathematically respectable to formulate problems so as to avoid them if possible. This could not always be done. Thus, for example, there was confusion in the early part of the century about the correct values of logarithms of negative numbers.†
Johann Bernoulli argued as follows: since $(-x)^2 = x^2$ it follows that $2 \log(-x) = 2 \log x$, hence $\log(-x) = \log x$, and in particular $\log(-1) = \log 1 = 0$. Leibniz disagreed. He pointed out that, if

---

† Logarithms of negative and complex numbers made their appearance in the evaluation of simple real integrals by 'partial fractions'. Thus

$$\int \frac{dx}{x^2+1} = \frac{1}{2i} \int \left(\frac{1}{x-i} - \frac{1}{x+i} \right) dx = \frac{1}{2i} \log \frac{x-i}{x+i}.$$

Without understanding logarithms of complex numbers one could not show that this strange-looking result was the same as $\tan^{-1} x$.

$y = \log x$, then

$$x = e^y = 1 + y + \frac{y^2}{2!} + \cdots$$

If $\log(-1) = 0$, this equation would have to hold when $x = -1$ and $y = 0$. This is clearly not the case, and Leibniz maintained that logarithms of negative numbers had to be imaginary. Such a fundamental disagreement between two leading mathematicians of the period was disturbing. The matter was clearly resolved by Euler (about 1747) with the aid of the fundamental formula $e^{i\theta} = \cos\theta + i\sin\theta$. When $\theta = \pi$ this gives $e^{i\pi} = -1$, so $\log(-1)$ has the purely imaginary value $i\pi$: Leibniz was right! Euler showed furthermore that the disagreements about the correct value for the logarithm arose from its *multivalued* character. In modern form his argument amounts to saying that $e^y = e^{y + 2in\pi}$ for all integral n and therefore, if $\log x = y$, then $y + 2in\pi$ is also a natural logarithm of x for every n. (*Exercise*: find the error in Johann Bernoulli's argument.) Although Euler's reasoning was remarkably clear, the idea of a 'multivalued function' was one that his contemporaries found hard to accept. The mathematicians of the eighteenth century were concerned primarily to *use* mathematics, following the creation of the calculus as a powerful tool for scientific problems. In their quest for results they were usually content to apply intuitively known rules of operation, but – as the example of the logarithm shows – reliance on crude intuition could lead to confusion and contradictions, and towards the end of the eighteenth century it became increasingly apparent that better logical foundations were needed for the calculus and for the number systems used in mathematics.

Mathematicians began to feel much happier about complex numbers when their geometric interpretation became familiar in the years after 1800. Important new mathematical concepts do not usually have a single discoverer, and the *idea* of complex numbers as points in a plane was already 'in the air' in Euler's time.† The main credit for the earliest clear recognition of the

---

† Indeed the idea occurs in rudimentary form already in John Wallis's *Treatise of Algebra* (1685). It was however ignored by his contemporaries.

correspondence between complex numbers and points in a plane is nowadays given to three men: C. Wessel, a Norwegian-born surveyor, who in 1797 emphasised the picture of a complex number as a two-dimensional vector (his paper, published in the transactions of the Danish Academy, remained unnoticed for 100 years); J. R. Argand, a Swiss self-taught bookkeeper, whose publication (in 1806) emphasised the interpretation of multiplication by i as a rotation through 90°; and Gauss, who indeed anticipated many of the most important nineteenth-century mathematical discoveries (for example elliptic functions and non-Euclidean geometry) without publishing them, and who seems to have been in full possession of the geometric theory of complex numbers by 1815. Nevertheless, as late as 1831 the distinguished mathematician Augustus de Morgan (one of the originators of modern mathematical logic) could say, in his book *On the Study and Difficulties of Mathematics*, 'The imaginary expression $\sqrt{(-a)}$ and the negative expression $-b$ have this resemblance, that either of them occurring as the solution of a problem indicates some inconsistency or absurdity. As far as real meaning is concerned, both are equally imaginary, since $0-a$ is as inconceivable as $\sqrt{(-a)}$.' Even some twentieth-century textbooks on trigonometry were still trying to avoid the use of $\sqrt{(-1)}$.

Complex numbers

5

The cubic equation

One particular development which occurred in the sixteenth century is worth discussing in more detail. Throughout the period from about 1200, the time of Fibonacci, to about 1500, the revival of mathematics in Western Europe had consisted of a rediscovery, by way of translations of the ancient works, of the mathematics of the Greeks and Arabs. It was an exciting surprise when Italian mathematicians discovered, early in the sixteenth century, a new mathematical theory which the Ancients and the Arabs had missed. This was the *general algebraic solution of the cubic equation*, and it has a curious history.

The rich commercial life of the Italian cities of the fifteenth century, and their traffic with the Orient, led to the development of improved methods of calculation for practical purposes, needed as aids for book-keeping and navigation. Several of the great painters and architects of the early Renaissance were good mathematicians: their intense interest in the use of *perspective* for the plane representation of three-dimensional objects led them to study the laws of solid geometry. The state of knowledge in the late fifteenth century in arithmetic, algebra and trigonometry is summed up in Pacioli's *Summa di Arithmetica*, printed in 1494 (it was one of the first mathematical books to appear in print). Pacioli says at the end of this book that the solution of cubic equations like $x^3 + mx = n$ is 'as impossible at the present state of science as squaring the circle'.

Here began the work of the mathematicians of the University of Bologna. This university was, around 1500, one of the largest and most famous in Europe. Let us discuss what is involved in the problem of the cubic equation.

We all know how to solve a *quadratic equation*: $x^2 + bx + c = 0$. We suppose for the present, with the Middle Ages in mind, that b and c are positive numbers, and we look for real roots. How is the solution expressed by the standard 'quadratic formula' obtained? We first note that we can *remove* the term bx which is linear in x by making the substitution $x = y - \frac{1}{2}b$: then $x^2 = y^2 - by + \frac{1}{4}b^2$, and the equation for the new unknown y is

$$y^2 - by + \tfrac{1}{4}b^2 + b(y - \tfrac{1}{2}b) + c = 0, \qquad \text{i.e. } y^2 = \tfrac{1}{4}b^2 - c.$$

This contains no term linear in y, and we obtain y by simply taking the square roots of the number on the right-hand side (assuming they exist!):

$$y = \pm \sqrt{(\tfrac{1}{4}b^2 - c)}, \qquad \text{giving } x = -\tfrac{1}{2}b \pm \sqrt{(\tfrac{1}{4}b^2 - c)}.$$

Taking a modern view, we note that this process always gives two (real or complex) roots for any two (real or complex) numbers b and c (the roots may be coincident). Historically this method of solution had been known from the time of the Babylonians and had been used to obtain the (real) roots of interest in specific problems. Whenever $\frac{1}{4}b^2 \geqslant c$ the formula gives two real roots without any trouble (provided that negative roots are allowed); in other cases it would have been said that there are no roots.

The mathematicians of Bologna showed that a similar, but more complicated, formula can be derived for the general cubic equation $x^3 + ax^2 + bx + c = 0$. (Note that this was not an achievement of any *practical* significance. People knew quite well at that time how to obtain *approximate* numerical solutions of cubic equations which were sufficiently accurate for all practical purposes. The problem, a purely theoretical one, was to derive an exact algebraic *formula* expressing the roots of the cubic equation in terms of the coefficients a, b, c appearing in the equation.) The method of solution goes as follows: we first remove the quadratic term ax^2 by putting $x = y - \frac{1}{3}a$ (the coefficient of y^2 in the new equation is then $-3(\frac{1}{3}a) + a = 0$). The new equation is thus of the form $y^3 + py + q = 0$, where the coefficients p and q are easily expressible in terms of the original coefficients *a*, *b* and *c*. Now put $y = u + v$, then

$$y^3 = u^3 + 3u^2v + 3uv^2 + v^3 = u^3 + v^3 + 3uv(u+v)$$
$$= u^3 + v^3 + 3uvy.$$

Hence the equation becomes

$$u^3 + v^3 + (3uv + p)y + q = 0.$$

Now *choose* *u* and *v* to satisfy

$$3uv + p = 0.$$

Then we have

$$u^3 + v^3 = -q, \qquad u^3v^3 = -p^3/27.$$

These are two simultaneous equations for the two unknowns u^3 and v^3. If we eliminate one of these, we find that the other satisfies the *quadratic equation*

$$t^2 + qt - \frac{p^3}{27} = 0.$$

The two roots of this equation are u^3, v^3 and thus, using the quadratic formula to write down these roots, we have

$$u^3 = -\tfrac{1}{2}q + \sqrt{\left(\frac{q^2}{4} + \frac{p^3}{27}\right)}, \qquad v^3 = -\tfrac{1}{2}q - \sqrt{\left(\frac{q^2}{4} + \frac{p^3}{27}\right)},$$

and finally

$$y = u + v = \left[-\tfrac{1}{2}q + \sqrt{\left(\frac{q^2}{4} + \frac{p^3}{27}\right)}\right]^{1/3}$$
$$+ \left[-\tfrac{1}{2}q - \sqrt{\left(\frac{q^2}{4} + \frac{p^3}{27}\right)}\right]^{1/3}.$$

Thus we have derived a formula for the roots of the cubic equation. Let us leave the mathematics for the moment to have a look at the tortuous history of this discovery.

The solution is called 'Cardan's solution', but the first man to find it was Scipione del Ferro (about 1500). He was a professor of mathematics at Bologna who told a pupil of his discovery but did not publish the result. Nowadays a mathematician with an important new result is only too anxious to see it in print, but at that time it was usual to keep one's discoveries secret, so as to secure an advantage over one's rivals by proposing problems for solution which were beyond their reach. Hence disputes over priority were common. It is believed that the result was discovered independently (about 1530) by Nicolo of Brescia (called Tartaglia, the stammerer) who was a powerful self-taught mathematician. He challenged del Ferro's pupil to a public discussion (1535), in which each contestant gave thirty problems to the other. Such contests aroused great interest, like football matches today, and Tartaglia, who won easily, became famous. He kept his method for the cubic equation secret, saying he would publish it eventually. But a certain Cardano from Milan ('a singular mixture of genius, folly, self-conceit and mysticism', Cajori 1924, p. 134) persuaded Tartaglia to reveal the method, giving a solemn promise of secrecy. He then proceeded to publish the solution (in 1545) in his *Ars Magna* (giving, it is true, the credit for the discovery to Tartaglia). This betrayal shattered Tartaglia (to quote Cajori again: 'his most cherished hope, of giving to the world an immortal work which should be the monument of his deep learning and power for original research, was suddenly destroyed; for the crown intended for his work had been snatched away'). Bitter disputes, and hectic problem-solving contests, ensued between Tartaglia and Cardan (and the latter's pupil Ferrari). Finally Tartaglia started writing his great work after all, but he died before he reached the topic of cubic equations. Thus the method became known as Cardan's solution of the cubic, although Cardan was not the first discoverer. The complete details of the discovery are not known, nor are they very important; and we need not feel too sorry for Tartaglia, who was himself guilty of publishing works without giving due credit.

Our algebraic method of solution looks simple enough, and you may wonder why the discovery should have caused so much excitement. One must remember that for Cardan and his contemporaries the task was long and difficult: where we use a simple binomial expansion he used geometrical theorems which were much harder to handle, and he also had to consider separately the cases $x^3 = mx + n$, $x^3 + mx + n = 0$, $x^3 + n = mx$, $x^3 + mx = n$, because only positive numbers were allowed to appear in the equations, and a separate geometrical demonstration was needed for each type. Our account of the mathematics is given in modern notation, and it must not be thought that Cardan wrote down symbols such as are used here. Where we write $x^3 + mx = n$, Cardan would use geometrical language, with specific numerical coefficients, and say 'let the cube and five times the side be equal to eighteen' (he regarded the equation $x^3 + 5x = 18$ as typical of all those 'having a cube and a multiple of a side equal to a number'). Advances in mathematics often followed rapidly upon the invention of improved notation; in the calculus this was the achievement of Leibniz (see p. 123), and in elementary algebra much of the transition towards our modern forms took place in the hundred years or so between Cardan and Descartes.

How does Cardan's method of solution work in practice? Consider say the equation $x^3 - 2x^2 + 2x - 1 = 0$. Putting $x = y + \frac{2}{3}$ this becomes $y^3 + \frac{2}{3}y - \frac{7}{27} = 0$, so $p = \frac{2}{3}$, $q = -\frac{7}{27}$, and

$$\frac{q^2}{4} + \frac{p^3}{27} = \frac{49 + 32}{4.27^2} = \frac{81}{54^2},$$

thus

$$\pm \sqrt{\left(\frac{q^2}{4} + \frac{p^3}{27}\right)} = \pm \frac{9}{54},$$

and the Cardan formula gives

$$y = \left(\frac{7}{54} + \frac{9}{54}\right)^{1/3} + \left(\frac{7}{54} - \frac{9}{54}\right)^{1/3} = \left(\frac{8}{27}\right)^{1/3} + \left(-\frac{1}{27}\right)^{1/3}$$

$$= \frac{2}{3} - \frac{1}{3} = \frac{1}{3}$$

(taking real cube roots!); hence $x = y + \frac{2}{3} = 1$.

In fact $x^3 - 2x^2 + 2x - 1 = (x - 1)(x^2 - x + 1)$, so we can see without using Cardan's formula that there is just one real root $x = 1$ (but of course the formula can be used also when there is no such simple factorisation). Also the graph of $x^3 - 2x^2 + 2x - 1$ (Fig. 5.1) shows that there is *one* real root in this case. However, the cubic equation $x^3 + ax^2 + bx + c = 0$ with real coefficients a, b, c may have either *one* or *three* real roots, and Cardan's formula leads to trouble when there are three real roots (this is the so-called 'irreducible' case). To see what happens we consider as an example the equation $x^3 - 2x^2 - x + 2 = 0$. The left-hand side factorises as $(x + 1)(x - 1)(x - 2)$, so the equation has the three real roots -1, 1, 2. What does Cardan's formula give us? Putting $x = y + \frac{2}{3}$ gives

$$y^3 - \frac{7}{3}y + \frac{20}{27} = 0, \quad \text{so} \quad p = -\frac{7}{3}, \quad q = \frac{20}{27},$$

and now

$$\frac{q^2}{4} + \frac{p^3}{27} = \frac{400 - 1372}{4.27^2} = -\frac{972}{54^2} = -\frac{1}{3},$$

and Cardan's formula tells us to take the square root of this number which is unfortunately negative! Thus, although the roots of the original cubic equation are known to be real, Cardan's method fails to produce the solution if we are not prepared to use complex numbers. The formula gives

$$y = \left[-\frac{10}{27} + \sqrt{\left(-\frac{1}{3}\right)} \right]^{1/3} + \left[-\frac{10}{27} - \sqrt{\left(-\frac{1}{3}\right)} \right]^{1/3}$$

$$= \left(-\frac{10}{27} + \frac{i}{\sqrt{3}} \right)^{1/3} + \left(-\frac{10}{27} - \frac{i}{\sqrt{3}} \right)^{1/3}.$$

How can this complicated-looking expression give a real result? In fact it does do so because, while the cube roots in this formula are all (individually) complex, their *sum* turns out to be real! Every complex number has exactly three cube roots; the cube

Fig. 5.1

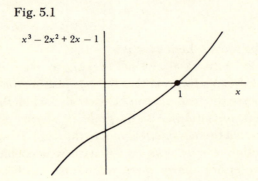

$x^3 - 2x^2 + 2x - 1$

roots in the expression for y turn out to be

$$u = \tfrac{1}{6}(-5+\sqrt{3}\mathrm{i}), \qquad v = \tfrac{1}{6}(-5-\sqrt{3}\mathrm{i}),$$
$$\tfrac{1}{6}(1-3\sqrt{3}\mathrm{i}), \qquad \tfrac{1}{6}(1+3\sqrt{3}\mathrm{i}),$$
$$\tfrac{1}{6}(4+2\sqrt{3}\mathrm{i}), \qquad \tfrac{1}{6}(4-2\sqrt{3}\mathrm{i}).$$

(You can check that this is correct by cubing these expressions and using $\mathrm{i}^2 = -1$.) Why does this not give *nine* values of y ($y = u + v$)? We must combine u and v here to produce a real y (in general, u and v must satisfy $3uv + p = 0$, see p. 51); and this condition restricts us to the three values $y = -\tfrac{5}{3}$ or $\tfrac{1}{3}$ or $\tfrac{4}{3}$; therefore $x = y + \tfrac{2}{3} = -1$ or 1 or 2, as required.

This problem of complex numbers appears whenever the cubic equation has three real roots. Cardan noted the difficulty but did not know what to do about it. Some progress in recognising the nature of the problem was made by a later sixteenth-century Bologna mathematician, R. Bombelli (his *Algebra* appeared in 1572). He *guessed* that, if (say) the real root $y = \tfrac{1}{3}$ is to come from

$$\left(-\frac{10}{27}+\frac{\mathrm{i}}{\sqrt{3}}\right)^{1/3} + \left(-\frac{10}{27}-\frac{\mathrm{i}}{\sqrt{3}}\right)^{1/3},$$

then the cube roots are presumably of the form $\tfrac{1}{6}+\lambda\sqrt{(-1)}$ and $\tfrac{1}{6}-\lambda\sqrt{(-1)}$ (i.e. they are what we call 'conjugate complex numbers'); it is then easy to verify that λ must be $-\tfrac{1}{2}\sqrt{3}$. But this approach succeeds only if the answer is already known: if one tries to find the cube roots of complex numbers algebraically (i.e. given a and b, tries to find x and y such that $(x+\mathrm{i}y)^3 = a + \mathrm{i}b$), then one merely returns to the original cubic equation (that's why this is called the 'irreducible' case). It was only much later, about 1730, that it was clearly recognised (by Euler) that Cardan's solution always gives precisely three roots (possibly repeated); and it was only then that a systematic method of calculating the roots of complex numbers was given.

Another way of dealing with the irreducible case is to make use of the trigonometric identity $\cos^3 A - \tfrac{3}{4}\cos A - \tfrac{1}{4}\cos 3A = 0$. This can be identified, after a slight transformation, with a given cubic equation in the form $x^3 + 3px + q = 0$. Put $x = \cos A / m$, then the cubic equation becomes

$$\cos^3 A + 3m^2 p \cos A + m^3 q = 0.$$

So, in order to satisfy the equation, we put $3m^2 p = -\frac{3}{4}$ and $m^3 q = -\frac{1}{4} \cos 3A$. We can then calculate m and hence $\cos 3A$ in terms of the coefficients p and q. We now obtain the angle $3A$ from a table of cosines. We thus have A, and hence the root $\cos A/m$ of the original equation. There are two additional roots $\cos (A + 120°)/m$, $\cos (A + 240°)/m$, which correspond to the same value of $\cos 3A$. (*Exercise*: why are there precisely *three* roots?) This method is due to Francis Vieta who was the foremost French mathematician of the sixteenth century (he was a lawyer who did mathematics in his spare time). Vieta's approach avoids the use of complex numbers in the irreducible case.

Vieta in fact knew the general formulae which express $\cos nx$ and $\sin nx$ in powers of $\cos x$ and $\sin x$. These enabled him to solve a fearsome-looking problem, characteristic of the age, proposed as a challenge by the Belgian A. van Roomen (in 1593): solve the equation

$$x^{45} - 45x^{43} + 945x^{41} - 12300x^{39} + \cdots - 3795x^3 + 45x = K.$$

Vieta, noting that the equation arises in the expansion of $\sin 45\theta$ in terms of $\sin \theta$, found all the positive roots and vindicated the honour of French mathematics.

It is curious that the first use of imaginary numbers was in the theory of *cubic* equations, and not in the theory of quadratic equations where we usually introduce them now. In the case of the cubic equation it was clear that real solutions existed, though in a strange form, and the appearance of imaginary quantities could not be avoided by saying that the solution did not exist. From this time on, complex numbers began to lose their mystery, though they were not fully accepted until the nineteenth century.

After the solution of the cubic equation it was natural to try to deal similarly with equations of order 4 (*quartic* or *biquadratic* equations). Cardan had himself considered some special cases, and the general solution was soon found by Cardan's pupil and secretary Ferrari. Let us see how it goes.

There are various equivalent methods: all of them reduce the problem to the solution of cubic and quadratic equations. One version proceeds as follows. Consider

$$x^4 + ax^3 + bx^2 + cx + d = 0;$$

add $(ex + f)^2$ to both sides, obtaining

$$x^4 + ax^3 + (b + e^2)x^2 + (c + 2ef)x + (d + f^2) = (ex + f)^2. \quad (*)$$

Choose e and f to get a perfect square on the left; suppose the left-hand side is $(x^2 + px + q)^2$. Squaring this and comparing, we have

$$2p = a, \quad p^2 + 2q = b + e^2, \quad 2pq = c + 2ef, \quad q^2 = d + f^2.$$

This fixes p. Rewrite the other equations as

$$e^2 = p^2 + 2q - b, \quad 4e^2f^2 = (2pq - c)^2, \quad f^2 = q^2 - d.$$

Substitute the first and third of these equations into the second:

$$(2pq - c)^2 = 4(p^2 + 2q - b)(q^2 - d),$$

or (using $p = \tfrac{1}{2}a$)

$$(aq - c)^2 = (a^2 + 8q - 4b)(q^2 - d).$$

This is a *cubic* equation for q and can be solved for q in terms of a, b, c, d. Any root will do; then e and f can be obtained from the above equations. (*) becomes

$$(x^2 + px + q)^2 = (ex + f)^2,$$

or

$$[x^2 + (p + e)x + (q + f)][x^2 + (p - e)x + (q - f)] = 0,$$

i.e. we have the two *quadratic* equations

$$x^2 + (p + e)x + (q + f) = 0,$$
$$x^2 + (p - e)x + (q - f) = 0,$$

whose roots are the four roots of the original equation.

As an example we use the method to solve

$$x^4 - 2x^2 + 8x - 3 = 0.$$

Here $a = 0$, $b = -2$, $c = 8$, $d = -3$. Thus $p = 0$, and the cubic equation for q is $64 = (8q + 8)(q^2 + 3)$, which reduces to $q^3 + q^2 + 3q - 5 = 0$, or $(q - 1)(q^2 + 2q + 5) = 0$. We choose as solution $q = 1$ (the only real solution!), and have

$$e^2 = 2 + 2 = 4, \quad e = 2; \quad f^2 = 1 + 3 = 4, \quad f = -2$$

(we must be careful here to choose the signs so that the equation $2pq = c + 2ef$ is satisfied). The two quadratic equations are

$$x^2 + 2x - 1 = 0, \qquad x^2 - 2x + 3 = 0,$$

with solutions

$$x = -1 \pm \sqrt{2}, \qquad 1 \pm \sqrt{2}i.$$

The details of this process are not very important; what *is* theoretically significant is that there are general methods, involving only operations in the field of complex numbers (addition, subtraction, multiplication and division), together with extraction of roots, which enable us to express the roots of any polynomial equation of degree up to 4 in terms of the coefficients in the equation. This, then, was in essence known before 1600.

6

Historical development of the number concept II

The algebraic solution of the cubic and quartic equations which we discussed in the last chapter suggests a number of questions, of general significance, which were not properly answered for another 200 years or more.

Firstly: we have seen that, within the field of real numbers, a simple equation like $x^2 + 1 = 0$ has no solution, but in the field $\mathbb{C}$ of complex numbers it has exactly two roots ($\pm i$). Consider then the *general* algebraic equation of degree n

$$x^n + a_1 x^{n-1} + a_2 x^{n-2} + \cdots + a_{n-1} x + a_n = 0, \tag{1}$$

where the as are any (real or complex) numbers. We ask: (i) does this equation always have a root (in the field $\mathbb{C}$)? And (ii), if *yes*, just how many roots are there? Once question (i) has been answered with 'yes', it is relatively easy to answer question (ii). For the cubic equation, as we have noted, it was Euler who first clearly recognised (1732) that there are always exactly three roots. For the general equation (1) the fundamental result is that the equation *always has a solution in* $\mathbb{C}$. From this it is easy to show, by successive applications of the fundamental result, that (1) can be *factorised* into an expression of the form

$$(x - c_1)(x - c_2) \cdots (x - c_n) = 0 \tag{2}$$

(the theory of factorisation of polynomials is very similar to the theory of factorisation of whole numbers); this result shows that equation (1) has exactly n *roots* in $\mathbb{C}$. This conclusion is remarkable. It means that, with the introduction of complex numbers, we have 'finished the job' as far as the solution of algebraic equations is concerned. The field $\mathbb{C}$ suffices to solve all algebraic equations and we do not have to invent any further kinds of numbers. We say that the field is *algebraically closed*.

The first more or less satisfactory proof of the fundamental result was given by Gauss in his doctoral thesis (in 1799). Gauss's great insight led him to formulate the problem in the 'correct' way which allowed a simple general result to be derived. Before his time, when complex numbers had not been fully accepted, people studied instead the factorisation of polynomials with real coefficients and found of course that these could not always be factorised, as in (2), into linear factors with real coefficients.†

Gauss was very fond of this theorem and later gave two further demonstrations. His first proof used geometrical arguments, not entirely rigorous by modern standards. But Gauss's proof was very original for its time, and helped to inaugurate a new approach to the question of *mathematical existence*. The Greeks had already recognised that the existence of mathematical entities must be established before one can try to prove theorems about them. Their test for existence was (geometrical) constructibility. In later work on equations, existence was established by obtaining a *formula* displaying the quantity in question: for example Cardan's formula actually exhibits the quantity which satisfies the cubic equation. From 1600 to 1800 people (very naturally) tried to obtain analogous formulae for the solutions of algebraic equations of degree greater than 4. It was assumed without question that, if a solution exists, then it must be displayable as a formula; and it was very puzzling that, in spite of all the efforts over such a long period, no such formula could be found. Gauss realised that, in order to show that a root *exists*, we do not in fact have to be able to give a formula for computing it. He argued (more or less) as

---

† They found, instead, that a factorisation into *linear* and *quadratic* factors was always possible. This result follows at once from (2) and the fact that, if the as in (1) are real and $c_1 = \alpha + i\beta$ is a root of (1), then $\bar{c}_1 = \alpha - i\beta$ is also a root. Two linear factors thus combine into a quadratic factor with real coefficients:

$$[x - (\alpha + i\beta)][x - (\alpha - i\beta)] = x^2 - 2\alpha x + (\alpha^2 + \beta^2).$$

Examples:

$$x^4 + 1 = (x^2 + x\sqrt{2} + 1)(x^2 - x\sqrt{2} + 1),$$
$$x^4 + x^2 + 1 = (x^2 + x + 1)(x^2 - x + 1).$$

follows: for complex z $(z = x + iy)$ equation (1) is

$$(x + iy)^n + a_1(x + iy)^{n-1} + \cdots + a_{n-1}(x + iy) + a_n = 0. \quad (3)$$

Write each a_i as $\alpha_i + i\beta_i$, multiply out and collect real and imaginary parts. This leads to an equation of the form $u(x, y) + iv(x, y) = 0$, where $u(x, y)$, $v(x, y)$ are polynomials in the real variables x, y with real coefficients; and this implies that $u(x, y) = 0$ and $v(x, y) = 0$. These are the equations of two *curves* in the x, y-plane. Gauss, by studying the general form of these curves, was able to show that they must always *intersect* at least once. To do this he looked at the form of the curves *far from the origin* (where only the highest powers in the polynomials matter); he found that the curve $u(x, y) = 0$ has a branch with asymptotic directions defined by lines making angles $\theta = \pi/2n$ and $\theta = 3\pi/2n$ with the x-axis, and the curve $v(x, y) = 0$ has a branch with asymptotic directions defined by $\theta = 0$ and $2\pi/2n$ (Fig. 6.1). Since the curves are continuous it is clear from the figure that they must intersect *somewhere*, and the point of intersection defines a complex number $x + iy$ which satisfies equation (3).

As an example consider $z^3 - 2i = 0$. Here $n = 3$, $u(x, y) = x^3 - 3xy^2$, $v(x, y) = 3x^2 y - y^3 - 2$ and $\pi/2n = \pi/6$. In the positive quadrant the curve $u = 0$ consists of the y-axis and the straight line $y = x/\sqrt{3}$ which makes an angle $\pi/6$ with the x-axis, and the curve $v = 0$ consists of a single branch with asymptotic directions 0 and $\pi/3$. Clearly $u = 0$ and $v = 0$ must intersect somewhere in the angular interval $(0, \pi/3)$. Fig. 6.2 shows all the

Fig. 6.1

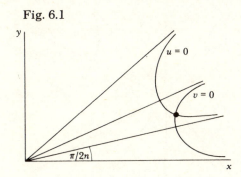

curves $u = 0$ and $v = 0$. There are exactly *three* points of intersection, one of which lies on the negative imaginary axis. (In
this simple case formulae can of course be obtained for the
roots.)

The general argument we have outlined shows that a root
exists but it does not give us a formula for it, and an existence
proof may not help us actually to *compute* the object whose
existence is proved (in the present problem a computer would
always do it by numerical methods). For a modern version of
Gauss's proof see Courant & Robbins (1941).

This result leads us on to the second question: having
established their existence, can we not after all derive *formulae*
for the roots of equations of degree greater than 4, which would
allow us to calculate these roots by algebraic processes (i.e. by
using the operations of addition, subtraction, multiplication,
division and root extraction, as in Cardan's formula)? Or we
might instead ask: *why* had no one been able to find such
formulae? (After all, for equations of degrees 3 and 4 the process
is fairly simple.) The answer to this question was found about
1820–30 and is interesting and important. Note that there are of
course many special cases of higher-degree equations where
formulae can be given for the roots (thus $x^n - a = 0$ has the n
roots $x = a^{1/n}$; $x^6 - 2x^3 + 4 = 0$ is a quadratic equation in x^3, and
we find $x^3 = 1 \pm \sqrt{(-3)}$, $x = [1 \pm \sqrt{(-3)}]^{1/3}$). But by about 1800

Fig. 6.2

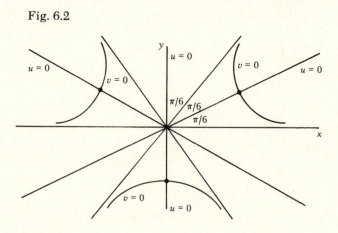

leading mathematicians such as Lagrange and Gauss suspected that it might be *in principle* impossible to solve the *general* equation of degree greater than 4 algebraically, i.e. that in the general case there is *no formula* which gives the roots algebraically in terms of the coefficients in the equation. But can one prove this, once and for all? Ruffini attempted such a proof (in 1799) but it was not conclusive. The matter was finally cleared up by two remarkable young geniuses, Abel and Galois.

N. H. Abel (1802–29) was the son of a Norwegian pastor who studied in Christiania (now Oslo) and Copenhagen and won a scholarship which took him to Paris. There he met the famous mathematicians of the age, but he was very shy and they ignored him. Eventually Abel returned to Norway, where he struggled to earn money to keep his family by giving lessons to young students. Just as his brilliant mathematical work began to attract attention he died of tuberculosis. Abel thought at one time that he had solved the equation of the fifth degree algebraically, but he corrected this claim in a paper which proved (in 1824) the *impossibility* of solving the general equation of the fifth degree by radicals. This celebrated theorem marked a great advance, but left open the question: just which equations are, and which are not, solvable by radicals; what exactly are the criteria for solubility? This and many related questions were answered by E. Galois (1811–32), the most romantic figure in the history of mathematics. He, also, made no impression on his mathematical contemporaries. Cauchy and Fourier lost the papers Galois submitted to them, and Poisson found them incomprehensible. He was also in trouble because of his political activities, and he died from wounds received in a duel. On the eve of the duel he jotted down his latest discoveries in a letter to a friend: 'you will publicly ask Jacobi or Gauss to give their opinion, not on the truth, but on the importance of the theorems. After this there will be, I hope, some people who will find it to their advantage to decipher all this mess.' (In fact Galois's last manuscripts were eventually published in 1846, but his work was not fully appreciated until 1870 or so.) The 'mess' was essentially the *theory of groups*; although earlier mathematicians had been aware, in a rudimentary way, of the concept of a group, it was

Galois who recognised its fundamental importance. In 1770 Lagrange, studying the solubility of algebraic equations by radicals, had found an important clue: he noted that the special tricks which work for equations of degree less than or equal to 4 all depend on finding functions of the roots of the equation which are unchanged under *permutations* of the roots, and he observed that this invariance property did not hold for $n = 5$. Galois associated with any polynomial a group of permutations of its zeros, now called the *Galois group*, and he showed that the problem of solubility by radicals can be reduced to a theorem on the structure of this group. Galois theory has many interesting applications in mathematics. In particular, it can be used to demonstrate the impossibility of trisecting an angle, or of 'duplicating a cube', by ruler-and-compass constructions, and thus it finally settles two of the 'three famous mathematical problems of antiquity' (see Chapter 8). For a modern account of Galois theory, with historical sections, see Stewart (1973).

We should not be surprised that Galois's work was not recognised in his own lifetime. Not only was he an impatient genius, unwilling to express himself in ways intelligible to more conventional mortals, but the emphasis on algebraic *structure* in his work only became part of the common way of mathematical thinking much later in the nineteenth century. All those who find the 'new mathematics' unfamiliar and strange will sympathise!

With the work of Gauss, Abel and Galois we know that an algebraic equation of degree n has n roots (in the field of complex numbers), and that in general no algebraic formula exists for the roots of an equation of degree greater than 4. Now let us recall the Greek discovery that the number $\sqrt{2}$ is irrational, i.e. that it cannot be written as the ratio of two integers. The number is nevertheless in a sense very closely related to the integers since it is the (positive) root of a simple algebraic equation (namely $x^2 - 2 = 0$) which has been formed from a polynomial with integer coefficients. The question arises: does *every* irrational number have this property, i.e. can irrational numbers always be obtained as the root of *some* equation of the form of equation (1)

$$x^n + a_1 x^{n-1} + a_2 x^{n-2} + \cdots + a_{n-1} x + a_n = 0,$$

where the as are integers? The roots of such an equation (real or complex) are *algebraic numbers*, so we ask: are there irrational numbers which are not algebraic? If such numbers exist, they must belong to a class with special and unusual properties.

In what ways, other than as solutions of algebraic equations, can irrational numbers arise? They often occur as sums of convergent infinite series; for example the famous number e ('Euler's number', the base of natural logarithms) is defined by

$$e = 1 + \frac{1}{1!} + \frac{1}{2!} + \frac{1}{3!} + \cdots.$$

Again, the number π, representing the ratio of the circumference of a circle to its diameter, can be defined by

$$\frac{\pi}{4} = \frac{1}{1} - \frac{1}{3} + \frac{1}{5} - \frac{1}{7} + \cdots,$$

or by a definite integral:

$$\tfrac{1}{2}\pi = \int_0^\infty \frac{dx}{1+x^2},$$

or by an (infinite) 'continued fraction':

$$\frac{4}{\pi} = 1 + 1 \over \displaystyle 2 + 9 \over \displaystyle 2 + 25 \over \displaystyle 2 + 49 \over \displaystyle 2 + \cdots$$

(many other representations are possible). Note that in all these definitions an infinite process of some kind is involved.

It is quite easy to show that e is irrational (Euler, in 1737). Since

$$\frac{1}{2!} + \frac{1}{3!} + \frac{1}{4!} + \cdots < \frac{1}{2} + \frac{1}{2^2} + \frac{1}{2^3} + \cdots = 1,$$

we see from the series defining e that $2 < e < 3$. Now suppose that e is rational and hence equal to p/q, where p and q are integers and q must be greater than or equal to 2 (since e is not an integer). Then we must have

$$\frac{p}{q} = 1 + \frac{1}{1!} + \frac{1}{2!} + \cdots + \frac{1}{(q-1)!} + \frac{1}{q!} + \frac{1}{(q+1)!} + \cdots ,$$

so, multiplying by $q!$,

$$p(q-1)! = \left(q! + q! + \frac{q!}{2!} + \cdots + q + 1 \right) + \frac{1}{q+1}$$

$$+ \frac{1}{(q+1)(q+2)} + \cdots \qquad (4)$$

The sum in brackets on the right-hand side is an integer, and

$$\frac{1}{q+1} + \frac{1}{(q+1)(q+2)} + \cdots < \frac{1}{3} + \frac{1}{3^2} + \frac{1}{3^3} + \cdots \text{ (since } q \geq 2),$$

and the sum of the geometric series on the right is $\frac{1}{3}/(1-\frac{1}{3}) = \frac{1}{2}$. Thus, in (4), the left-hand side is an integer but the right-hand side is not an integer, and we have a contradiction.

The number π is also irrational, but this is not so easy to prove. The proof was given by Lambert (in 1761) who showed that, if x is rational, then $\tan x$ *must* be irrational. Since $\tan \frac{1}{4}\pi = 1$, which is rational, $\frac{1}{4}\pi$ cannot be rational. It is often extremely difficult to decide whether any given number is rational or irrational. It has only very recently been shown that the number defined by the infinite series

$$\frac{1}{1^3} + \frac{1}{2^3} + \frac{1}{3^3} + \frac{1}{4^3} + \cdots$$

is irrational, and at the time of writing no one knows whether

$$\frac{1}{1^5} + \frac{1}{2^5} + \frac{1}{3^5} + \frac{1}{4^5} + \cdots$$

is rational or irrational.

Obviously all 'surds' formed by root extraction from whole number are algebraic numbers, for example $\sqrt[3]{(1+\sqrt{2})}$ is a root of the equation $x^6 - 2x^3 - 1 = 0$, and so on. But not all algebraic numbers are surds: the roots of the general polynomial equation (with integer coefficients) of degree greater than 4 are algebraic numbers, although, as we have seen, they are not in general expressible in terms of radicals. A number x is called an *algebraic number of degree n* if it satisfies an equation of the form (1), but no equation of lower degree: thus $\sqrt[3]{2}$ is an algebraic number of degree 3.

The existence of irrational numbers which are not algebraic was first demonstrated by Liouville (in 1844). Such numbers are called *transcendental*, because they 'transcend the power of algebraic methods' (Euler). Liouville actually *constructed* numbers which can be shown to be non-algebraic, for example

$$z = \frac{1}{10^{1!}} + \frac{1}{10^{2!}} + \frac{1}{10^{3!}} + \cdots.$$

This is a number defined by a series with extremely rapidly decreasing terms. Why is such a number not algebraic? The reason is, essentially, that an algebraic number can not be approximated by a rational number 'too closely'; specifically, if p/q is any rational approximation to an algebraic number x of degree n, with q a large positive integer, then it is not difficult to show (see Davenport 1970, p. 164) that the difference between x and p/q must satisfy the inequality

$$|x - p/q| > K/q^n,$$

where K is a constant for given x. Thus, for a given denominator q, the approximation p/q can never be closer than is permitted by this inequality. This result was proved by Liouville. Now, if we break off the infinite series which defines z after a sufficiently large number of terms, we have a rational approximation for z which is 'too close', i.e. the above inequality is violated. So transcendental numbers exist![†] But, although this argument allows us to construct examples of such numbers, it is much more difficult to show that any particular *given* real number is transcendental. Liouville could not answer the question for e or π; the proof that e is transcendental was given by Hermite in 1873, and the proof for π was given by Lindemann in 1882. This last result, incidentally, finally and conclusively

---

[†] In Chapter 11 we mention another proof of the existence of transcendental numbers. It is more abstract but is perhaps easier to follow.

proved the impossibility of 'squaring the circle' with ruler and compass (since for this to be possible π would have to be an algebraic number).

It has also been shown that Liouville's inequality on the approximation of algebraic numbers by rationals can be strengthened considerably. This is a problem on which much work was done in the first half of this century, culminating in K. F. Roth's proof (in 1955) that

$$|x - p/q| > 1/q^{\nu}$$

for all but a finite number of approximations p/q, where ν can be any number greater than 2. This is the 'best possible' result, since the inequality does not hold for $\nu = 2$ (see Davenport 1970, p. 164).

The question of establishing the nature of numbers like $2^{\sqrt{2}}$ was posed in Hilbert's famous collection of outstanding unsolved problems in mathematics (in 1900). It was answered by Gelfond and Schneider in 1934 when they demonstrated the transcendence of α^{β}, where α is any algebraic number different from 0 and 1 and β is any irrational algebraic number. But what (for example) about α^{β} when α and β are both transcendental? The number $e^{\pi} = (-1)^{-i}$ is known to be transcendental (Gelfond), but at the time of writing the nature of the numbers e^{e} and π^{π} has not been definitely established. There are many other deep problems, too technical to be described here, in 'transcendental number theory' which is a highly active field of present-day research (see Baker 1975). The study of different types of numbers, with its long history going back to the Greeks, has not lost its fascination nor the ability to throw up very difficult mathematical problems.

7

Complex numbers, quaternions and vectors

Let us finally, in our discussion of the development of the number system, look again at the question of generalising the concept of number beyond the real numbers. We recall that, to solve an algebraic equation with real coefficients such as $x^2 + 1 = 0$, it was necessary to introduce the complex numbers $x + iy$, but the set of complex numbers is 'algebraically closed'. Every algebraic equation with real or complex coefficients has solutions in the field of complex numbers. This implies, in particular, that roots and powers of complex numbers always exist within the field of complex numbers. So, as far as the solution of algebraic equations of all kinds is concerned, our search is finished – no further generalisation of number is needed. But in another, more geometrical, sense the search is not finished. We discussed in Chapter 3 the interpretation of complex numbers as displacements, or vectors, in a space of two dimensions (the complex plane), and we noted that multiplication by a complex number of unit magnitude could be regarded as a rotation in this space. In classical applied mathematics we usually deal with displacements and vectors in 'physical' space which is three-dimensional. It is therefore a natural question, and one likely to be of practical importance, to ask whether one can define 'complex numbers' in spaces of dimension greater than two which, one would hope, could represent displacements and rotations in such spaces. In particular, we want to know whether we can invent a 'hypercomplex number' which can represent a vector in three dimensions and which is such that multiplication by it is equivalent to a rotation in three-dimensional space. Such an entity would be extremely useful for the formulation of the laws of physics, and in particular for the description of the motion of rigid bodies in space. Also, quite apart from its physical applications, the search for generalisations of the notion of complex number to spaces of many dimensions is a question of intrinsic mathematical interest.†

The answer to this question is less simple than one might at first sight suppose. Once an understanding of the two-dimensional geometrical representation of complex numbers had been achieved in the early nineteenth century, the search for a generalisation to three and more dimensions was taken up by many mathematicians. A key step forward was taken by William Rowan Hamilton (1805–65), who did brilliant work both as a mathematician and as a physicist. Hamilton was an infant prodigy (at the age of 13 he was said to have been familiar with as many languages as he had lived years). At Trinity College Dublin he was appointed professor of astronomy while still an undergraduate. His early work included a highly original general reformulation of the laws of optics and mechanics. The 'Hamiltonian function' plays a fundamental role in modern quantum theory. Not all of Hamilton's ideas have stood the test of time, however. One of his favourite themes was that 'space and time are indissolubly connected'; much later on this notion was indeed incorporated in the theory of relativity, but Hamilton argued that, since geometry is the 'science of space', algebra must be the 'science of pure time'; such an idea does not have any meaning for us.

In 1833 Hamilton wrote a paper in which complex numbers were regarded as *ordered pairs* (a, b) of real numbers, with the rules for addition and multiplication given by

$$(a, b) + (c, d) = (a + c, b + d),$$
$$(a, b)(c, d) = (ac - bd, ad + bc);$$

and he recognised that these algebraic rules implied the interpretation of addition as (parallelogram) addition of vectors, and

† We give no formal definitions here of notions such as 'space', 'rotation' and 'dimension'; it will be sufficient for the present to regard an n-dimensional space as a generalisation of 'physical' (Euclidean) three-dimensional space, with the coordinates of a 'point' given by n real numbers $x_1, x_2, \ldots, x_n$. The notion of 'dimension' in fact contains subtleties which are discussed in Chapters 10 and 11.

of multiplication by $(\cos\theta, \sin\theta)$ as a rotation. In this formulation a complex number was for the first time explicitly recognised as equivalent to an ordered pair of real numbers, and such a pair was seen to be equivalent to a two-dimensional vector.

This point of view led Hamilton to consider, as the natural generalisation to three dimensions, *ordered triples* (a, b, c) of real numbers. Or, equivalently, a complex number written as $a + bi$ would be replaced by something of the form $a + bi + cj$, containing now *two* non-real 'units' i and j replacing the 'imaginary unit' i. Such a generalised complex number will certainly represent a vector in three-dimensional space, with rectangular components a, b, c, and there is no difficulty over defining *addition* for these entities: the rule is

$$(a + bi + cj) + (a' + b'i + c'j)$$
$$= a + a' + (b + b')i + (c + c')j,$$

and this is just the general parallelogram law of addition for forces, which had been known from ancient times. However, Hamilton was held up for ten years in following up this idea because of difficulties with the definition of *multiplication* for these generalised complex numbers and its relation to rotations in three-dimensional space. It is said that in 1843, when he was walking with his wife along the Royal Canal in Dublin, Hamilton suddenly saw what had to be done: to represent rotations in three dimensions he must use *quadruples* of real numbers, not triples, and he must also abandon the *commutative law of multiplication*!

It is in fact clear on geometrical grounds that four real numbers, not three, are needed. In two dimensions we need two numbers, because multiplication by a complex number must in general specify both an angle of rotation and the ratio by which the length of the vector is changed. In three dimensions, if multiplication by our 'hypercomplex number' is to transform the vector A into some other vector B (Fig. 7.1), we must specify first the *direction* in space of the axis OO' about which the vector A is to be rotated: specification of a direction in space needs two numbers (for example the latitude and longitude angles). Then we need another two numbers to specify the angle of rotation about the axis and the 'stretch' of the vector, making four in all. Thus our numbers must be of the form $a + bj + ck + d\ell$, where a, b, c, d are four real numbers and j, k, ℓ are new 'unit elements' analogous to i for ordinary complex numbers. Hamilton called these new entities *quaternions*.

What rules must be adopted for calculating with j, k, ℓ (replacing the rule $i^2 = -1$)? At first Hamilton assumed that the 'ordinary' rules of traditional algebra must apply (we would say nowadays that the new numbers must form a field); we must remember that it had not really occurred to anyone before his time that there *could* be any other rules in algebra. In fact the notion that, in the search for generalisation, the 'familiar' rules of calculation must continue to apply had been elevated into a mathematical principle, the *principle of continuity* (or *permanence*): its formulation was vague, but it was a serious hindrance to progress.

Hamilton found that application of the familiar rules of addition and multiplication to his quaternions invariably led to a contradiction somewhere. It was his inspiration to see that these rules, derived from experience in calculating with 'ordinary' numbers, were not the only ones possible, and that in calculating with quaternions 'something' must be given up. Of course the step from real to complex numbers had already been a

Fig. 7.1

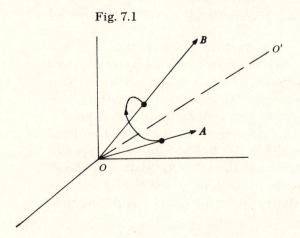

move towards abstraction, but now a much bolder innovation was needed. Hamilton realised that, if his quaternions were to follow rules 'as similar as possible' to the familiar ones, it was the *commutative law* of multiplication which must be abandoned. This becomes clear when we try to define *division* by a quaternion.† To do this we require that, given any non-zero quaternion w, the equation $ww_1 = 1$ (where '1' is the *unit quaternion* $1 + 0j + 0k + 0\ell$) should have a unique quaternion solution w_1 (then we can write $w_1 = w^{-1}$ and define division by w as multiplication by w_1). How does such an approach work for ordinary complex numbers? Since $a^2 + b^2 = (a + ib)(a - ib)$, every non-zero complex number $a + ib$ has a unique complex number as its inverse:

$$(a + ib)^{-1} = \frac{1}{a + ib} = \frac{a - ib}{a^2 + b^2}$$

$$= \left(\frac{a}{a^2 + b^2}\right) - i\left(\frac{b}{a^2 + b^2}\right).$$

($a - ib$ is the complex number *conjugate* to $a + ib$, and the positive real number $a^2 + b^2$ is the *norm* of the complex number $a + ib$.)

To do the same thing for the quaternion $w = a + bj + ck + d\ell$ we need similarly to factorise the norm $N(w)$, now defined as the positive real number $a^2 + b^2 + c^2 + d^2$, into a product of two linear quaternion factors. To achieve this let us try

$$a^2 + b^2 + c^2 + d^2 = (a + bj + ck + d\ell)(a - bj - ck - d\ell),$$

where we regard $a - bj - ck - d\ell$ as the conjugate of $a + bj + ck + d\ell$. If we multiply out the right-hand side, using the 'ordinary' rules, we obtain terms like $-b^2 j^2$ (showing that $j^2 = -1$), but also 'cross terms' like $-2bc jk$; thus the factorisation fails (since clearly j, k are both non-zero). But, if the commutative law of multiplication does not hold for j, k, ℓ, so that $jk \neq kj$, etc., then the *order* in which the terms appear in the multiplication matters, and a typical cross term must be written $-bc(jk + kj)$; it

---

† We are not following here precisely Hamilton's own train of reasoning. He explains this himself in the preface to his *Lectures on Quaternions* (see Hamilton 1967).

will now be zero if $jk = -kj$. Clearly we achieve the desired factorisation by taking

$$j^2 = k^2 = \ell^2 = -1$$

and

$$jk = -kj, \qquad k\ell = -\ell k, \qquad \ell j = -j\ell.$$

To ensure that the product of any two quaternions will again be a quaternion we require in addition that a product such as jk should be a linear combination of j, k and ℓ. In fact Hamilton postulated that

$$jk = -kj = \ell, \qquad k\ell = -\ell k = j, \qquad \ell j = -j\ell = k.$$

With these rules we now have

$$(a + bj + ck + d\ell)^{-1} = \frac{a}{r} - \frac{b}{r}j - \frac{c}{r}k - \frac{d}{r}\ell,$$

where

$$r = a^2 + b^2 + c^2 + d^2,$$

and the quaternions satisfy all the axioms for a field *except* that multiplication is in general not commutative. (Such a set is nowadays called a *skew field* or *division algebra*.) So, for a product of any two quaternions, $w_1w_2 \neq w_2w_1$ in general. But note that our argument implies that the norm of the product, $N(w_1w_2)$, is equal to the product of the norms $N(w_1)N(w_2)$ (you can verify this by direct calculation of the norms). We say that the division algebra is *normed*.

To finish the story about Hamilton: it seems that he was so excited by his discovery that he took out a knife and cut the fundamental formulae $j^2 = k^2 = \ell^2 = jk\ell = -1$ into the stone of the bridge. Hamilton's invention of quaternions (the first non-commutative algebra) was a revolutionary step, as it shattered preconceived notions as to how numbers 'must' behave. It was at about the same time that people such as George Peacock in Cambridge first tried to formulate systematically the fundamental laws of arithmetic and algebra in axiomatic form. The early attempts at identifying these laws were not very satisfactory, since intuitive notions and preconceived habits of thought about the way mathematical entities 'must' behave were still too strong (we have already mentioned the 'principle of continuity', a blind alley). After the work of Hamilton, and others at about the same time, it began to be realised that the *rules* of algebra could be formulated independently of the *objects* to which they were applied; this discovery set algebra free to invent and study new structures, and a very rapid development set in around the middle of the nineteenth century. One of the most original contributions was Grassmann's *Lineale Ausdehnungslehre* (Theory of Linear Extension, published in 1844), a very general vector algebra, highly abstract and written in rather obscure form and therefore slow to be recognised. Another important development was the axiomatic formulation of the laws of formal logic by George Boole in his famous books, *The Mathematical Analysis of Logic* (1847) and *Investigation of the Laws of Thought* (1854). Boolean algebra is a general algebra of sets which is of wide application to modern problems, in particular to probability problems arising in business and insurance and to the switching system of a large digital computer.

Returning to quaternions, let us now examine how they in fact describe rotations of vectors in three-dimensional space. Note first that the need for a non-commutative multiplication law again becomes evident when we think about rotations, because the combination of two rotations about different axes, carried out in succession, is a non-commuting process: the result depends on the order in which the rotations are carried out. To convince yourself of this, let Ox, Oy, Oz be three mutually perpendicular axes. Take a pencil oriented along Oz, rotate it through a right angle about Ox so that it lies along Oy, and then rotate it through a right angle about Oz so that it finishes along Ox. If you rotate *first* about Oz and *then* about Ox, the pencil will finish up along Oy!

We represent a three-dimensional vector v, with components b, c, d along Ox, Oy, Oz, by the quaternion $bj + ck + d\ell$ (this is sometimes called a 'pure quaternion'; it has no 'real part'). We want to rotate this vector through a given angle θ about a given axis whose direction can be specified by its *direction cosines* α, β, γ (these are the cosines of the angles between the axis and

Ox, Oy, Oz; they satisfy $\alpha^2 + \beta^2 + \gamma^2 = 1$). The rule is that the new vector $v' = b'j + c'k + d'\ell$ is obtained by forming the quaternion product

$$v' = \{\cos \tfrac{1}{2}\theta + \sin \tfrac{1}{2}\theta(\alpha j + \beta k + \gamma \ell)\}$$
$$\times v\{\cos \tfrac{1}{2}\theta - \sin \tfrac{1}{2}\theta(\alpha j + \beta k + \gamma \ell)\}.$$

(To make the rule quite unambiguous we must also specify the *sense* of the rotation about the axis. θ is *positive* if the rotation is seen as *anticlockwise* by someone observing it from the 'positive end' of the axis of rotation; see Fig. 7.2.)

We will not give a general derivation of this formula, but let us check it for the special composition of two rotations mentioned above. Suppose the original vector lying along Oz was of unit length; then $v = \ell$. Rotate v about the x-axis through $+\tfrac{1}{2}\pi$: then $\theta = \tfrac{1}{2}\pi$, $\alpha = 1$, $\beta = \gamma = 0$, and the rotated vector is

$$(\cos \tfrac{1}{4}\pi + j \sin \tfrac{1}{4}\pi)\ell(\cos \tfrac{1}{4}\pi - j \sin \tfrac{1}{4}\pi) = \tfrac{1}{2}(1+j)\ell(1-j),$$

since $\cos \tfrac{1}{4}\pi = \sin \tfrac{1}{4}\pi = 1/\sqrt{2}$. Using the quaternion multiplication laws we find that this becomes $\tfrac{1}{2}(\ell - k)(1-j) = \tfrac{1}{2}(\ell - k - k - \ell) = -k$. Now rotate about the z-axis through $\tfrac{1}{2}\pi$: we obtain

$$(\cos \tfrac{1}{4}\pi + \ell \sin \tfrac{1}{4}\pi)(-k)(\cos \tfrac{1}{4}\pi - \ell \sin \tfrac{1}{4}\pi) = -\tfrac{1}{2}(1+\ell)k(1-\ell)$$
$$= -\tfrac{1}{2}(k-j)(1-\ell) = -\tfrac{1}{2}(k-j-j-k) = j;$$

thus we finish with a vector along Ox. Now reverse the order of rotation, and we obtain first

$$(\cos \tfrac{1}{4}\pi + \ell \sin \tfrac{1}{4}\pi)\ell(\cos \tfrac{1}{4}\pi - \ell \sin \tfrac{1}{4}\pi) = \ell,$$

and then

$$(\cos \tfrac{1}{4}\pi + j \sin \tfrac{1}{4}\pi)\ell(\cos \tfrac{1}{4}\pi - j \sin \tfrac{1}{4}\pi) = -k.$$

Fig. 7.2

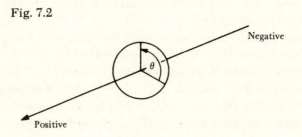

We see that the different end positions in the two cases are a consequence of the non-commutative multiplication law for quaternions. We can deal similarly with any sequence of rotations in three-dimensional space.

Our quaternion rule for rotating vectors in three dimensions looks quite different from the simple multiplication of complex numbers which does the trick in two dimensions. The reasons for this difference are of considerable mathematical interest. A full exploration would lead us into advanced theory, but we may note the following. Our rotations are constructed with the use of the quaternion $\cos \frac{1}{2}\theta + \sin \frac{1}{2}\theta(\alpha j + \beta k + \gamma \ell)$ and its conjugate. This quaternion, like the complex number $\cos \theta + i \sin \theta$, has *unit norm* (since $\cos^2 \frac{1}{2}\theta + \sin^2 \frac{1}{2}\theta(\alpha^2 + \beta^2 + \gamma^2) = 1$). It corresponds to a point on the surface of the *unit sphere S^3* in a space of *four* dimensions. A continuous rotation in three dimensions can thus be recorded by plotting the (continuous) path on S^3 traced out by the corresponding quaternion. But, because of the appearance of the half-angles $\frac{1}{2}\theta$ in the rotation quaternion, a given rotation through θ corresponds, not to one, but to *two* points on S^3 lying at opposite ends of a diameter (the angles θ, $\theta + 2\pi$ give the same rotation in three dimensions, but the quaternion changes sign when we replace θ by $\theta + 2\pi$). Thus we need *two* rotations through 2π in three dimensions in order to return to our starting point on S^3. This curious behaviour is connected with the fact that the path of the rotation on S^3 (a great circle) can be *continuously deformed* into a point on the sphere; this is something that has no analogue in the two-dimensional case where our paths are confined to the unit circle S^1, and a great circle on S^1 always coincides with S^1 itself and cannot be deformed. The study of such continuous deformations belongs to the subject of *topology*, a vast and highly active branch of modern mathematics which is becoming increasingly important in many applications to science.

Hamilton had an exaggerated enthusiasm for his quaternions and spent the rest of his life working on them. He thought that his discovery was as important as that of the infinitesimal calculus, and he regarded it as the key to all of geometry and mathematical physics. A few scientists in England (particularly

P. G. Tait) shared Hamilton's enthusiasm and did their best to propagate the use of quaternions, but on the whole the concept was ignored by physicists who went on using Cartesian coordinates in their theories. In fact quaternions were not what physicists really wanted; they were looking for a concept more directly associated with the three Cartesian coordinates representing a three-dimensional vector. For mathematicians nowadays quaternions represent just one example of an algebraic system, and there are very many other systems all with their own interesting properties. Quaternions, and other hypercomplex number systems, owe their continued mathematical interest chiefly to their connection with topology to which we have alluded above.

We mention briefly some developments in algebra in the second half of the nineteenth century which followed Hamilton's discovery of quaternions.

Pursuing the argument which led to quaternions we may ask whether we can generalise the concept of number further, by inventing new hypercomplex numbers in a greater number of dimensions. In 1845 Cayley (and independently Hamilton's friend J. T. Graves) showed that there is an *eight-dimensional* generalisation of number ('octonions', constructed from pairs of quaternions) which satisfies the rules for a field except that for these entities multiplication is in general *neither* commutative *nor* associative (so that $(ab)c \neq a(bc)$ in general). We have here again a 'normed division algebra' in which every non-zero 'number' has an inverse. These 'Cayley numbers' are little more than mathematical curiosities. But are there any other 'division algebras'? This question poses a very difficult problem which required the full resources of modern algebraic topology for its solution. It was finally answered (with *no*) in 1958, when J. F. Adams and others showed that there are no division algebras constructed from the real numbers other than those of dimension 1, 2, 4 or 8. This shows again that quaternions and octonions are of only restricted significance in algebra.

But suppose we ask about the description of *rotations* in general spaces. (Note that in the nineteenth century the idea that geometry might make sense in more than three dimensions was, once again, a strange new concept, at first treated with suspicion and disbelief, and slow to be generally accepted. The same was true, of course, of *non-Euclidean geometry*, in which Euclid's 'parallel postulate' was replaced by a different axiom about the number of lines that could be drawn through a given point parallel to a given line. Non-Euclidean geometry dates from about 1830 and was thus historically the earliest break away from 'traditional' assumptions about the proper concerns of mathematics.) In four dimensions we can again use quaternions to carry out rotations: the general quaternion $a + b\mathrm{j} + c\mathrm{k} + d\ell$ constructed from four real numbers can be regarded as a vector in four dimensions, and a generalisation of our earlier rule for rotating vectors in three dimensions describes rotations of such vectors in four-dimensional space. An extension of the quaternion calculus to the general case of n dimensions which can be used to describe rotations of n-dimensional vectors was given by W. K. Clifford in 1878. The *Clifford algebras*, again, play a significant role in modern differential topology. Rotations in four dimensions are important in the theory of relativity (see below, p. 85).

To define the 'algebra' of vectors in n dimensions one needs to know the 'multiplication table' (analogous to $\mathrm{jk} = -\mathrm{kj} = \ell$, etc., for quaternions) of all possible products $e_j e_k = \sum_{i=1}^{n} c_{ijk} e_i$ which can be formed from the n unit vectors e_i $(i = 1, 2, \ldots, n)$ in the space considered. If we require in addition that, always, $(e_i e_j)e_k = e_i(e_j e_k)$, we have a *linear associative algebra*. The general theory of such algebras was investigated in the 1860s by the American mathematician Benjamin Peirce and his son Charles. Benjamin Peirce worked out the multiplication tables for 162 different algebras, a far cry from the assumption in the early nineteenth century that there could be only *one* set of rules for 'algebra'!

Our topic is the concept of 'number'. With algebra's new-found freedom to invent its own rules it became largely a matter of definition and language to decide which entities should be called 'numbers' (clearly one would expect them to have some, at least, of the traditional properties of numbers). It is important to realise that the new freedom also led, from around 1850 onwards, to increasing interest in mathematical structures obeying less restrictive laws than those traditionally associated with numbers. It gradually became clear to mathematicians that they could obtain structures of very great mathematical interest by imposing *fewer* rules on the elements of their collection (or *set*) than the full array of arithmetical operations. Next to the general theory of sets, perhaps the most fundamental concept to emerge was that of the *group*, already mentioned in Chapter 6, in which one has only one binary operation which assigns to any pair of elements in the set another element in the same set.† In a modern mathematics course non-commutative multiplication is often first encountered in connection with the arrays of numbers called *matrices*. They arise when one is studying the linear transformations which change a vector into another, and it was Cayley again who first studied matrices systematically (1858) in the context of linear transformations in geometry. In the calculus of square matrices one has two laws of combination (addition and multiplication) and multiplication is associative, but matrices have a fundamentally new property not possessed by numbers (elements of a field): the relation $AB = 0$ (where '0' is the zero matrix) can hold for two matrices even when A and B are both non-zero.‡ Non-zero matrices whose product is zero do not possess inverses: for a matrix A of this type one cannot find a matrix A_1 such that AA_1 is equal to the unit matrix. They are called *singular* matrices.

Since matrices and quaternions are both associated with rotations, one might expect a connection between them. This exists, and in fact the algebra of Hamilton's quaternion units j, k, ℓ is precisely the same as that of the following special 2×2

† We emphasise again that we are not attempting here to give full definitions; these will be found in any textbook of algebra. It should also be realised that concepts such as *group, ring, field* etc. emerged gradually during the nineteenth century, and their general significance was only slowly recognised: general abstract definitions (with which modern treatments usually start) only came later.

‡ An example (for those familiar with matrix multiplication):

$$\begin{pmatrix} 1 & 2 \\ 2 & 4 \end{pmatrix}\begin{pmatrix} -2 & -4 \\ 1 & 2 \end{pmatrix} = \begin{pmatrix} 0 & 0 \\ 0 & 0 \end{pmatrix}.$$

The set of all 2×2 matrices is said to form a *ring*.

matrices built from complex numbers:

$$\sigma_1 = \begin{pmatrix} 0 & i \\ i & 0 \end{pmatrix}, \qquad \sigma_2 = \begin{pmatrix} 0 & 1 \\ -1 & 0 \end{pmatrix}, \qquad \sigma_3 = \begin{pmatrix} -i & 0 \\ 0 & i \end{pmatrix},$$

with $i^2 = -1$. Using the rules of matrix multiplication you will quickly verify that $\sigma_1^2 = \sigma_1 \times \sigma_1 = -I$

$$\left(\text{where } -I \text{ is the matrix } \begin{pmatrix} -1 & 0 \\ 0 & -1 \end{pmatrix} \right),$$

and that $\sigma_1 \sigma_2 = -\sigma_2 \sigma_1 = \sigma_3$, etc.; these are precisely the rules for j, k and ℓ. We say that the general non-zero quaternion $a + bj + ck + d\ell$ is *isomorphic* with the 2×2 complex matrix defined by

$$a 1 + b\sigma_1 + c\sigma_2 + d\sigma_3 = \begin{pmatrix} a - id & c + ib \\ -c + ib & a + id \end{pmatrix}.$$

(A non-zero matrix of this particular form is non-singular and has an inverse, so there is no contradiction with what was said about quaternions.) These 2×2 complex matrices (or the corresponding quaternions) can be regarded as describing rotations of two-dimensional complex vectors called *spinors*, and the matrices $\sigma_1, \sigma_2, \sigma_3$ (multiplied by $-i$) are the *Pauli spin matrices*. These names derive from the use of spinors in modern quantum theory to describe the state of an electron, a particle with *spin* (intrinsic angular momentum). The appearance of the half-angles in the quaternions which describe the rotations of spinors, and the resulting peculiar double-valued property which we discussed earlier, here acquires physical significance; it is connected with the fact (a quantum-theoretical property) that the electron's spin is half-integral. The theory of the electron spin was put forward in the 1920s, and this application of his quaternions could not have been foreseen by Hamilton!

But, as we have already noted, Hamilton's quaternions did not provide the all-purpose vector calculus needed for classical physics. Hamilton himself and some later nineteenth-century physicists, in particular Clerk Maxwell (famous for his theory of the electromagnetic field), tried to overcome the difficulty by treating the 'real' and the 'pure quaternion' parts of a quaternion separately (see p. 75): these were then called the *scalar* and *vector* parts of the quaternion. For instance Hamilton had noted that, if $\alpha = b\mathrm{j} + c\mathrm{k} + d\ell$, $\alpha' = b'\mathrm{j} + c'\mathrm{k} + d'\ell$ are two pure quaternions, the 'scalar part' of the product $\alpha\alpha'$ is $-(bb' + cc' + dd')$ and the 'vector part' is

$$(cd' - dc')\mathrm{j} + (db' - bd')\mathrm{k} + (bc' - cb')\ell,$$

and he had discussed the geometrical implications of these formulae; he had thus already in the 1840s exhibited the structure of the scalar and vector products in modern vector algebra. In such ways the algebra of quaternions can be developed so as to exhibit many of the results of modern vector analysis, but it was eventually recognised that the quaternion formalism is unnecessarily cumbersome. The modern algebra of three-dimensional vectors which has become a standard mathematical language in physics and geometry was created in the 1880s by two people: J. W. Gibbs in the USA, a physicist, and Oliver Heaviside in England, an electrical engineer. They broke away completely from the concept of quaternions and treated the 'vector part' as an entirely separate entity. The 'vector algebra' which was then created for calculating with these objects is a branch of mathematics originally developed for use in science. Vectors have a more complex algebraic structure than do quaternions and other hypercomplex numbers. For example we define two kinds of product (useful in three dimensions): the 'vector product' which is non-commutative and analogous to the quaternion multiplication rule $\mathrm{jk} = -\mathrm{kj} = \ell$; and the 'inner product' (or 'scalar product') which is a number, not a vector. The concept of a product which does not belong to the original collection is a new idea, not contained in the structure of a field.

This work on vectors led to bitter controversy with the adherents of quaternions over the relative merits of the two algebras. In 1895 two colleagues of Gibbs at Yale University felt it necessary to organise an 'International Association for Promoting the Study of Quaternions and Allied Systems of Mathematics'. This published its own bulletin for a while (but, it seems, did not in fact spend much time in 'promoting' quaternions). Nowadays we no longer get heated about the matter, and we know that both vectors and quaternions have their recognised place in science and mathematics. In a way the vectors have won the argument, because vector algebra embodies an idea, that of *linearity* and *linear superposition*, which has turned out to be of very general significance in mathematics and many of its applications. Thus vectors are nowadays widely used throughout mathematical science. The basic laws of mechanics and electromagnetism are relations between three-dimensional vector quantities: forces, accelerations, electric and magnetic fields. In physics these vectors now form part of the more general mathematics of *tensors* (quantities with special linear transformation properties). The tensor calculus was originally developed for geometry by Riemann and later by Ricci and Levi-Civita (Italy). It is the formalism required for studying *symmetry* and *invariance* properties of geometric and physical magnitudes under various kinds of transformation. Tensors thus find applications in the study of crystal lattices, in elasticity (hence their name), and above all in Einstein's general theory of relativity (1915) which underlies our present-day efforts to understand gravitation and many of the large-scale properties of the universe. Modern analysis and geometry in n dimensions also make extensive use of the tensor concept.

The basic idea of linear superposition has given rise to the modern mathematical concept of a *linear vector space*, where 'space' and 'vector' are defined as abstract mathematical entities. The idea derives from the physicist's vector addition of forces to give a resultant force. The mathematician conceives a linear vector space L (over a field K) to be a set of abstract elements $a, b, c, \ldots$ (the 'vectors') for which addition is defined, together with elements $\alpha, \beta, \ldots$ of a field K (the 'scalars', for example the field $\mathbb{C}$ of complex numbers). Multiplication of vectors by scalars is defined and gives new vectors such as αa, βb and the linear combination $\alpha a + \beta b$: the key idea is then that $\alpha a + \beta b$ also belongs to the set L. This has become an important unifying idea in mathematics. Thus in analysis the set of all twice-differentiable functions $f(x)$ of the real variable x forms a linear vector space (a *function space*) over the real or complex numbers. This realisation leads to a theory of linear differential equations in which functions are treated as vectors. Function spaces have an infinite number of dimensions, and a full investigation of their mathematical properties is difficult, but function-vectors in such spaces have many important applications: for example they are the fundamental ingredients in the mathematical formulation of quantum theory. In such ways, as always in the past, mathematical and scientific ideas continued to influence each other, backwards and forwards.

It is thus not surprising that the modern mathematics student hears a lot about vectors in various parts of his course. He should perhaps bear in mind that the emphasis and the motivation for the study of these objects are not always the same. In algebra it is the general properties which are of chief interest, and the theory is formulated with the least possible restrictions. Therefore the basic axioms do not include any products of two vectors: these are not part of the basic idea of the linear combination of objects. When we are doing physics and analytic geometry in three dimensions we want our vectors to represent physical magnitudes and displacements, and we would like them to have both a *length* (a positive real number, not a vector) and a *direction* in space (so that we can ask for the *angle* between two vectors). Therefore we make additional postulates which allow us to define these attributes. We then have a *Euclidean* vector space in which the length of a vector is defined in terms of the scalar product of two vectors. In three-dimensional Euclidean space the square of the length of the displacement vector which joins the origin to the point P with coordinates (x, y, z) relative to a set of mutually perpendicular axes is $x^2 + y^2 + z^2$, in accordance with the ancient theorem of Pythagoras. This quantity (equivalent to what we earlier called a 'norm') remains invariant when we rotate the coordinate axes about the origin.† Although this definition of the length (or magnitude) of a vector is the most familiar, other definitions are possible and may be of interest in applications. An important

---

† This means that $x^2 + y^2 + z^2 = x'^2 + y'^2 + z'^2$, where (x', y', z') are the coordinates of the point P referred to a rotated set of perpendicular axes. Instead of considering a given *vector* and rotating the axes, we can consider the rotation of a vector in a given *coordinate system*, as described for example by the quaternion multiplication rule on p. 76. The reader may verify that, under this rule, $b^2 + c^2 + d^2 = b'^2 + c'^2 + d'^2$, so that the length of the vector is invariant.

generalisation occurs in the special theory of relativity where we are interested in *events*, characterised by their coordinates (x, y, z, t) in both space and time, and thus represented by points in a *four-dimensional* mathematical space (the 'space–time world'). Transformations of axes in this space (called *Lorentz transformations*) connect the space and time coordinates of an event as seen by observers in uniform motion relative to each other; and the fundamental fact that the velocity of light c is the same for all such observers is expressed by the mathematical requirement that the quadratic form $x^2 + y^2 + z^2 - c^2 t^2$ must be invariant under Lorentz transformations. This 'space–time norm' can be either positive or negative for real x, y, z, t (we say that it is 'indefinite'), and the Lorentz transformations of special relativity leave such an *indefinite* quadratic form invariant. There is a close connection between the 'four-vectors' of special relativity and the two-dimensional spinors mentioned on p. 81: it was Dirac's great discovery (in 1928) that the relativistic quantum theory of the electron automatically describes a particle possessing half-integral spin.

8

Greek ideas about infinity

The concept of infinity lies at the core of mathematics. We have
already met it many times in our discussion of the idea of
number. Even in the very simplest case, the collection of natural
numbers 1, 2, 3, . . . , the series does not end and we have an
infinitely large collection.

The Babylonians must have encountered infinite processes,
but they avoided coming to grips with them. For example, when
working out their sexagesimal fractions, they made a table of
reciprocals which gives the reciprocal of 10 as the finite fraction
6/60, the reciprocal of 12 as the finite fraction 5/60, but the
reciprocal of 11, which is an infinite series, is simply omitted
from the table.

Not only the idea of infinitely large collections, but also that
of infinitely small subdivisions, created difficulty from early
days. The infinitely small arose in two questions of great
concern to the Greeks: the problem of finding the areas of
figures bounded by curved lines, and the problem of understanding motion, in particular the motions of the heavenly
bodies studied by the astronomers. Why do such questions
involve the infinitely small? In the case of areas there is no
difficulty so long as we are dealing with plane figures bounded
by straight lines. Thus, for a square, since *area* is itself defined
as *rectilinear* area, i.e. the number of squares of unit size
contained in the figure, we need only subdivide the area into
unit squares and count their number, provided always that we
have a unit of length in terms of which we can express the length
of a side (Fig. 8.1). And this notion is easily extended to
rectangles, triangles and polygons. But what happens when the
boundary is 'continuously turning'? Take the area of a circle; we
may draw an inscribed polygon to give us an approximate

estimate of the area (Fig. 8.2), and we may then increase the number of sides of the polygon to improve the approximation. But does this process continue indefinitely? Or can we stop at some stage and say that our polygon now coincides with the circle? If so, how far must we go? If not, we, must presumably continue until we have 'infinitely many, infinitely small' sides; what does this mean? We would now call this puzzle a problem in *integral calculus*, in contrast to the differential calculus which deals with problems of rates of change and tangents to curves. The integral calculus is in fact the older branch of the 'infinitesimal calculus', although the differential calculus is usually taught first nowadays. Again, when we come to the study of motion, a body is continuously changing its position with time; how does this happen? Can we think of time as infinitely subdivisible, or is there a smallest unit of time, so that time jumps 'discontinuously' from one instant to the next? The problem of infinite subdivisibility troubled the Greeks very much, and there were two main philosophic schools of thought: ⟩ ?school the school which believed in infinite subdivisibility and denied the existence of any smallest units, and the school of *atomism* which held that everything in our experience (in particular matter, time and space) was ultimately made up of smallest basic units. The problem of ultimate constituents is the most fundamental one in science. It is far from finally decided at the present time, although in the case of the constitution of matter

Fig. 8.1   Fig. 8.2

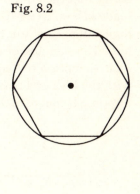

Area = a^2 units

we nowadays hold with atomism, while in our notions of (physical) space and time we believe in continuity and infinite subdivisibility. Since both atomism and continuity are *models* of empirical reality there is no final certainty possible on this question. While the basic philosophic problems must remain unresolved, we can at least claim that we have much more powerful ways these days of formulating these old questions mathematically.

The Pythagoreans reduced all problems to whole numbers and thus believed in numerical atomism! The *Eleatics* were a rival school of philosophers who believed in the so-called 'permanence of being'; for them all change was only apparent. Zeno (about 450 B.C.), their best-known member, propounded the famous 'paradoxes on motion'. These propositions were designed to show that motion was impossible under both types of assumption. Thus the 'Achilles paradox', which assumes infinite subdivisibility of space and time intervals, claims to show that the fast Achilles can never overtake the slow tortoise in a race in which the tortoise has a start and both start running simultaneously (Fig. 8.3): if A runs twice as fast as T, then, when A has reached A_2 (level with T_1), T will be at T_2, where $T_1 T_2 = \frac{1}{2} A_1 A_2$; when A is at A_3 (level with T_2), T will be at T_3 where $T_2 T_3 = \frac{1}{2} A_2 A_3$; and so on indefinitely. Thus T is always ahead of A. Zeno did not really believe that in practice Achilles would never overtake: his argument challenged the common belief that the sum of an infinite number of quantities can be made as large as we like, and showed in a vivid way that a proper logical theory of infinite series was needed to resolve the problem. The paradox of the 'Stade' (stadium) uses the concept of relative motion to demonstrate that we also get into difficulties with the idea of a smallest unit of time (see Boyer 1968, p. 83). Suppose B moves to the right relative to A with a speed such that

Fig. 8.3

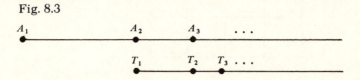

one unit of B (such as b_4) passes one unit of A (such as a_4) in the time unit τ (Fig. 8.4). Similarly C moves to the left with the same speed. Starting in configuration (a) we reach configuration (b) in time τ. But now c_1, originally opposite b_3, is opposite b_1, having passed *two* B units; hence τ cannot be the smallest possible time interval, since we can take as a new (and smaller) time unit the time taken by c_1 to pass *one* of the B units.

Although Zeno could hardly have grasped the full mathematical implication of his arguments, they served to worry the contemporary mathematicians – as did the discovery of the irrational discussed in Chapter 3 – and they made them aware of the subtlety of reasoning about the infinite. The paradox of the Stade employs what has remained one of the most powerful methods of reasoning in mathematics ('reductio ad absurdum'), in which the truth of a proposition is postulated and it is shown by logical argument that the postulate eventually leads to a contradiction.

We turn to the problem of areas, in particular the problem of 'squaring the circle'. This was one of the 'three famous mathematical problems of antiquity': (i) *the trisection of the angle*: to divide a given angle into three equal parts; (ii) *the duplication of the cube*: to find the side of a cube whose volume is twice that of a given cube; (iii) *the quadrature of the circle*: to find a square of area equal to that of a given circle. The second problem is the so-called 'Delian' problem: the story goes that an Athenian delegation, sent to ask the oracle of Apollo at Delos how to avert the plague, was told that 'the cubical altar to Apollo must be doubled'. However, construction of an altar with a side twice that of the old one did not cure the plague! These problems are

Fig. 8.4

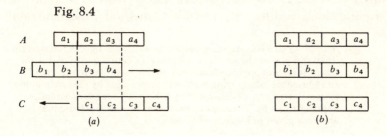

important in the history of mathematics because they cannot be solved, except approximately, by construction of a finite number of straight lines and circles, i.e. solution is impossible by ruler-and-compass construction.† In their efforts to deal with this challenge mathematicians were led to try new methods which opened up new fields of mathematics. The Greeks were led to the discovery of the conic sections and of higher-order curves such as the Archimedean spiral (Boyer 1968, p. 140); and in modern times the ancient Greek problems have found their full resolution within the context of Galois theory and transcendental number theory (see pp. 64, 68), quite abstract branches of mathematics.

An early contribution to the problem of the quadrature of the circle was made by Hippocrates of Chios (a contemporary of Zeno). It is the only complete mathematical fragment surviving from the Golden Age of Greece, and is interesting because it indicates that Euclid's strict axiomatic approach to geometrical problems existed more than a hundred years before Euclid's time. The fragment deals with a typically useless, but theoretically interesting, problem: that of determining the areas of circular 'lunes' which are crescents bounded by two circular arcs. Hippocrates shows the following (Fig. 8.5): suppose circle 1 has centre M and diameter AB. Let MC be a radius perpendicular to AB and draw circle 2 with centre C passing through A and B. This defines the shaded lune: Hippocrates proves that its area is equal to that of the square on the radius MB. The proof assumes as known the result that the areas of two circles are in the same ratio as the squares on their radii (and hence also that two circular segments, like the shaded areas in Fig. 8.6, which subtend the same angle at the centre, are in the ratio of the squares on the radii). The Greeks had a rigorous method for proving such results, the so-called 'method of exhaustion'

---

† According to Plato the only perfect geometrical figures are straight lines and circles; hence the preference in Greek geometry for the use of ruler and compass only (where the 'ruler' is an unmarked straight edge). Many constructions are possible by these methods: thus a line can be divided into an arbitrary number of equal parts, any angle can be bisected, a square can be constructed equal in area to a given polygon, and so on.

which we describe below; but its discovery is usually ascribed to Eudoxus who lived later than Hippocrates (around 370 B.C.), and we do not know how Hippocrates proved this result.

We subdivide the lune by drawing two tangents to circle 2, at A and at B (Fig. 8.7). Then α is a segment of circle 1 subtending a right angle at M, and δ is a segment of circle 2 subtending a right angle at C. Hence

$$\alpha : \delta = AM^2 : AC^2 = 1 : 2 \text{ (by the theorem of Pythagoras)},$$

and clearly $\alpha = \beta$; hence $\alpha + \beta = \delta$, and thus the area of the lune, which is $\alpha + \beta + \gamma$, is equal to $\delta + \gamma$, i.e. the area of the triangle ABD, and this is BM^2 as required.

Hippocrates's result is important, for it is the first demonstration in the history of mathematics that a curvilinear area *can* be commensurable with a straight-sided figure. Surely this should also be possible for the simplest curvilinear area, the full circle. It seems natural to suppose that Hippocrates must have tried to divide the whole circle into lunes which could all be 'squared' as above, and in this way to achieve the quadrature of the circle. This seems a very natural thing to try; unfortunately

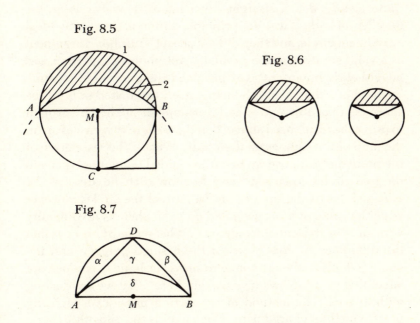

Fig. 8.5

Fig. 8.6

Fig. 8.7

the trick does not work for the whole circle! As we noted on p.
67, the final proof that this was not possible was not given until
more than 2000 years later.

The *Sophists* were a group of professional teachers in Athens,
active towards the end of the fifth century B.C. They were quite
unlike the Pythagoreans: while the latter were forbidden to
accept payment for their teaching, the Sophists supported
themselves by tutoring, not only in honest study, but also in the
art of 'making the worse appear the better'. (We have to remember that our descriptions of the Sophists are due to Plato,
Socrates and others who opposed their philosophy in general
and who, when they described a Sophist as 'vain, boastful and
acquisitive', were unlikely to be unprejudiced observers.) One
of the Sophists, Antiphon, claimed to have squared the circle by
the method, mentioned at the beginning of this chapter, of
inscribing a regular polygon, doubling the number of sides, and
continuing this process until the polygon became indistinguishable from the circle. While they realised that one can, in
this way, *estimate* the area of a circle with an accuracy sufficient
for all practical purposes, the Greek mathematicians also saw
quite clearly that a straight-sided figure, however large the
number of sides, was in principle different from the ideal
curvilinear circle, and they did not accept Antiphon's argument
as a valid solution of the problem. Antiphon's suggestion was
nevertheless important as it provided the germ of Eudoxus's
'method of exhaustion' (the name itself originated only in the
seventeenth century). We shall illustrate the method by using it
to prove the result used above, that the areas of two circles are in
the ratio of the squares on their radii. What is the real nature of
the problem? Suppose we inscribe n-sided regular polygons in
the two circles; then it is easy to show that the areas of the
polygons are as the squares on the radii of the circles however
large the value of n (as we noted on p. 86, there is no difficulty
with areas of straight-sided figures). What we must *prove* is that
the difference in area between the n-sided polygon and the
circle (which is always non-zero however large n is) does not
affect this result. Nowadays we would say that we are dealing
with a *limit*. The method of exhaustion provides a logically
precise method of argument which avoids the difficulties asso-

ciated with arguing about 'infinitely many' 'infinitely small' quantities. It is in fact a primitive form of integral calculus.

The method rests on the 'axiom of continuity' (given in Euclid, and sometimes called the 'axiom of Archimedes'), which says essentially that, if A and B are magnitudes of the same kind, and A is less than B, then one can always find a multiple of A which is greater than B. (This seems 'obvious' and is certainly valid for finite non-zero real numbers. It excludes from consideration vaguely conceived 'infinitesimally small' quantities. Nowadays (see also Chapter 10) we know how to construct 'non-Archimedean' fields which allow us, if we wish, to give precise definitions of both 'infinitely large' and 'infinitely small' numbers.) From the axiom of continuity the Greeks deduced the equivalent proposition: if α is greater than ε, and if one subtracts from α at least one-half of α, then from the rest at least one-half again, and so on, one will eventually be left with a magnitude which is less than ε. (*Proof*: given ε, we can find n such that $n\varepsilon > \alpha$. Now $2\varepsilon = 2\varepsilon$, $3\varepsilon < 2^2\varepsilon$, $4\varepsilon < 2^3\varepsilon$, and so on; finally $\alpha < n\varepsilon < 2^{n-1}\varepsilon$. Thus we can go on *doubling* ε until it is greater than α; or, equivalently, we can go on *halving* α until it is less than ε.) Now we can formulate our proof. We start the process of 'exhausting' the area of the circle with straight-sided figures by inscribing a square $ABCD$ in the circle (Fig. 8.8); this

Fig. 8.8

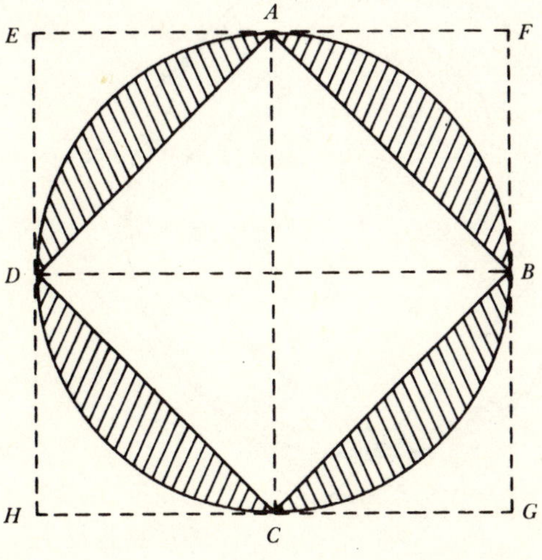

differs from the circle by the shaded region (S). Add to the figure four triangles *ABF, BCG, CDH, DAE* as shown; their total area equals the area of the inscribed square. The area S is less than the area of the four triangles, hence S is less than the area of the inscribed square, which equals the area of the circle minus S; thus we see that S is less than *half* the area of the circle. We continue by removing four triangular areas *ABW, BCX, CDY, DAZ* from S (Fig. 8.9), giving us an inscribed *octagon AWBXCYDZ*. The four triangles clearly have half the area of the four rectangular boxes such as *ABPQ*. We see from the figure that the (shaded) difference in area (S') between the octagon and the circle is less than the sum of the areas of the four triangles. Thus we have shown that, if one cuts from the circle the inscribed square, one removes more than half the area; if one now cuts out the four triangles (thus removing an octagon), one again removes more than half of the remaining area. And so the exhaustion process continues; the next step is to erect eight triangles on the sides of the octagon to give a 16-gon, and this removes more than half the area S'.

Fig. 8.9

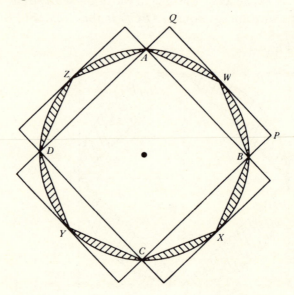

How does one clinch the argument? At this stage the axiom of continuity is used. Suppose ε is an arbitrary area greater than zero. Eventually (see above) we must get to a stage where the difference in area between the inscribed polygon and the circle is less than ε. Suppose the circles we wish to compare have areas A, A' and radii r, r'; we want to prove that $A : A' = r^2 : r'^2$. Suppose B is the area of a polygon inscribed in A for which $A - B < \varepsilon$, (or $A - \varepsilon < B$). Now suppose the result is wrong because A is 'too big'; then (for *some* positive δ) we must have

$$\frac{A - \delta}{A'} = \frac{r^2}{r'^2}.$$

Choose ε (which is arbitrary) to be not greater than δ, then $A - \delta < B$. Suppose B' is the area of the corresponding polygon in A', so that $B' < A'$, then we have the inequalities

$$B > A - \delta, \qquad B' < A'.$$

Hence

$$\frac{B}{B'} \text{ is certainly greater than } \frac{A - \delta}{A'} = \frac{r^2}{r'^2}.$$

But we *know* that $B/B' = r^2/r'^2$ (since our result is known to be true for polygons), and thus we have a contradiction. In the same way (try this for yourself) we can dispose of the assumption that A is 'too small', and our result is thus proved. This is a logically rigorous proof (given by Euclid): all the mystery of the infinite process lies in the axiom of continuity!

Of the ancients it was Archimedes who made the most beautiful use of the method of exhaustion and who came nearest to integration in the modern sense. (For fuller details on Archimedes's works, see Dijksterhuis 1957.) Archimedes, who lived approximately 287–212 B.C., was the leading mathematician of the Hellenistic age. He lived and died in Syracuse in Sicily. Many picturesque legends about him are related by the Roman historians, but we have little hard fact concerning his life. He was a great pure mathematician who also dealt with practical matters; he was an inventor of ingenious war machines and one of the founders of the science of mechanics. Archimedes is an early example of the conflicts that arise between 'pure' and 'applied' mathematics. According to Plutarch: 'he regarded as sordid and ignoble the construction of instruments, and in general every art directed to use and profit, and he only strove after those things which, in their beauty and excellence, remain beyond all contact with the common needs of life'. So he did pure mathematics: 'continually bewitched by a siren who always accompanied him, he forgot to nourish himself and omitted to care for his body; and when, as would often happen, he was urged by force to bathe and anoint himself, he would still be drawing geometrical figures in the ashes or with his finger would draw lines on his anointed body, being possessed by a great ecstasy and in truth a thrall to the Muses'. But (as happens these days too) he was told to make himself useful: 'most of [his technical inventions] were the diversions of a geometry at play which he had practised formerly, when King Hieron had emphatically requested and persuaded him to direct his art a little away from the abstract and towards the concrete, and to reveal his mind to the ordinary man by occupying himself in some tangible manner with the demands of reality'.

The story of how the works of Archimedes have come down to us is interesting; in order to learn how the historian of science actually gets his material, read Chapter 2 of Dijksterhuis (1957). We are fortunate that a large part of Archimedes's extensive writings have been preserved, but we also know from these writings that there are other works (in particular one on the centres of gravity of solids) which are lost.

Archimedes's results include the formulation of the 'law of the lever' in statics and of 'Archimedes's principle' in hydrostatics. He was fascinated by very large numbers, and in *The Sand-Reckoner* he estimated the number of grains of sand which would fill the universe. (His answer, about 10^{63} in our notation, is not too far from modern estimates of the number of atoms in the universe.) The 'spiral of Archimedes' is defined as the plane locus of a point which moves uniformly outwards along a line from the origin, while the line itself rotates uniformly about the origin (the polar equation is $r = k\theta$). With this curve, as Archimedes showed, the trisection of the angle and the quadrature of the circle are easily accomplished (see Boyer 1968, p. 141).

Archimedes also obtained an excellent estimate of π. Given a circle, he calculated the perimeter of inscribed and circumscribed regular polygons (Fig. 8.10), thus obtaining upper and lower bounds for the circumference. Archimedes gives a rule for going systematically from any polygon with n sides to one with $2n$ sides (this only requires bisection of angles); thus he had a systematic method of calculating the irrational number π to any desired accuracy. Note that this was not an attempt to 'square the circle' in the sense of Hippocrates, but to find (in modern terms) a good 'rational approximation' for the ratio of the circumference of a circle to its diameter. The details of the calculation are elaborate and cunning. Archimedes goes as far as a polygon with 96 sides, and he needs rational approximations for square roots like $\sqrt{3}$. He takes, in fact, $\sqrt{3} \approx 1351/780$, a very close estimate ($\sqrt{3} = 1.732\,050\,8\ldots$, $1351/780 = 1.732\,051\,2\ldots$), but he does not say how he got this result, and

Fig. 8.10

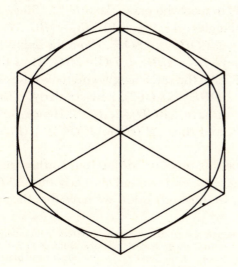

there has been much speculation on this question.† Archimedes's final result, in modern notation, is that $3\frac{10}{71} < \pi < 3\frac{1}{7}$.

Our chief interest, from the point of view of the early calculus, is in Archimedes's famous *quadrature of the parabola*. This was a sensational achievement: the conic sections (ellipse, hyperbola, parabola) were quite well known at the time of Archimedes, and the quadrature of circle, ellipse and hyperbola had all been tried by many Greek mathematicians, always in vain; then the young Archimedes had the idea to try the parabola and was successful! Archimedes in fact gives two different proofs, both of which contain ideas which were taken up again much later. We therefore outline both of them. We define the parabola (Fig. 8.11) as the locus of a point C such that $BC/EF = BO^2/EO^2$ (this is equivalent to the modern equation $y = x^2$), and we want to *prove* that the area of the segment FOF' is two-thirds the area of the rectangle $FF'E'E$, thus showing that the parabolic segment is commensurable with a rectangle.

First proof. We 'exhaust' the parabolic area by means of triangles (Fig. 8.12). The first triangle is FOF'; we denote its area by $\triangle FOF'$. The second stage is to add the triangles FOC, $F'OC'$, where C, C' are defined by dividing the line $E'OE$ at B, B' such that $BO = \frac{1}{2}EO$, $B'O = \frac{1}{2}E'O$, and drawing vertical lines through B, B' to meet the parabola at C, C'. Since $BO = \frac{1}{2}EO$, by similar triangles (see Fig. 8.12), $BG = \frac{1}{2}BD$. We shall show that $\triangle FOC + \triangle F'OC' = \frac{1}{4}\triangle FOF'$. From the definition of the parabola we have $BC = \frac{1}{4}BD$, so $DG = 2GC$. Thus the triangles DGF, GCF have the same height and have bases in the ratio $2:1$. Hence $\triangle DGF = 2\triangle GCF$, and similarly $\triangle DGO = 2\triangle GCO$. Adding, we have $\triangle FOD = 2\triangle FOC$, Hence $\triangle FOA = 2\triangle FOD = 4\triangle FOC$, and thus $\triangle FOC + \triangle F'OC' = \frac{1}{4}\triangle FOF'$, as required.

We now continue this process, adding four further triangles as indicated in Fig. 8.13, and we find similarly that $\triangle FCC_1 + \triangle OCC_2 = \frac{1}{4}\triangle FOC$, so (for both sides) we have that the area of

† Because of the use of a primitive number system, Archimedes had trouble with handling complicated fractions. But (see p. 3) the Babylonians, already about 2000 B.C., knew how to calculate square roots with considerable accuracy.

Fig. 8.11

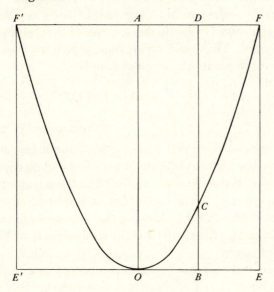

Fig. 8.12

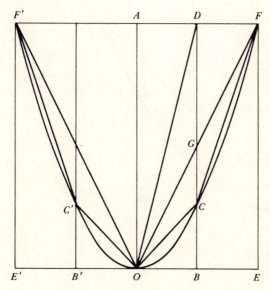

the added triangles equals $(1/4^2)\triangle FOF'$. Removing more and more triangles from the parabolic segment in this way, the area removed at each stage is exactly one-quarter of that removed at the previous stage. Thus, adding all these areas, we conclude that the area of the parabolic segment equals

$$\triangle FOF' \times \left[1 + \frac{1}{4} + \frac{1}{4^2} + \frac{1}{4^3} + \cdots \right] = \tfrac{4}{3}\triangle FOF'$$

$$= \tfrac{2}{3} \times \text{rectangle } FF'E'E,$$

as was to be proved. Note that Archimedes did not say, at this final stage, 'we now sum an infinite series'; that had no rigorous meaning for him. But he knew very well that the required sum was $\tfrac{4}{3}$, and he proved it rigorously by an application of the method of exhaustion, i.e. by showing that the assumptions (i) that the sum is greater than $\tfrac{4}{3}$, (ii) that the sum is less than $\tfrac{4}{3}$, both lead to contradictions.

Second proof (this is close to modern integration, as defined by Riemann). We wish to find the area R *under* the parabolic arc lying above OE, where we take $OE = 1$ (Fig. 8.14). We divide

Fig. 8.13

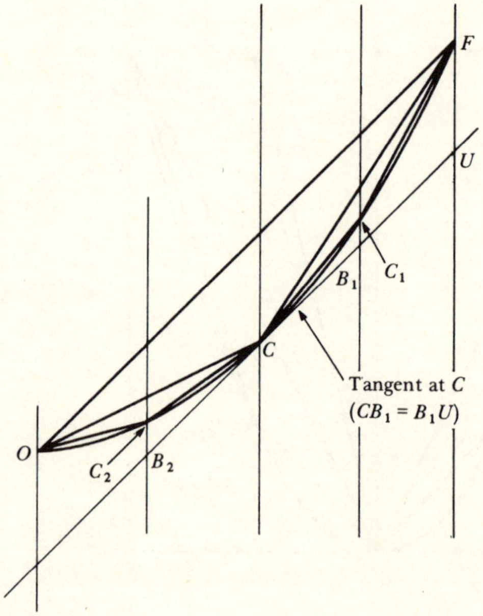

OE into four equal parts and erect rectangles of width $\frac{1}{4}$ as shown. The area R then clearly lies between S_4 and T_4, where the 'lower sum' S_4 is the sum of the areas of the rectangles lying under the parabola,

$$S_4 = \frac{1}{4}0^2 + \frac{1}{4}\left(\frac{1}{4}\right)^2 + \frac{1}{4}\left(\frac{2}{4}\right)^2 + \frac{1}{4}\left(\frac{3}{4}\right)^2,$$

and the 'upper sum' is clearly

$$T_4 = \frac{1}{4}\left(\frac{1}{4}\right)^2 + \frac{1}{4}\left(\frac{2}{4}\right)^2 + \frac{1}{4}\left(\frac{3}{4}\right)^2 + \frac{1}{4}\left(\frac{4}{4}\right)^2.$$

If we now divide the interval *OE* into n equal parts, then we have, similarly, $S_n < R < T_n$, with

$$S_n = \frac{1}{n}0^2 + \frac{1}{n}\left(\frac{1}{n}\right)^2 + \frac{1}{n}\left(\frac{2}{n}\right)^2 + \cdots + \frac{1}{n}\left(\frac{n-1}{n}\right)^2,$$

and

$$T_n = \frac{1}{n}\left(\frac{1}{n}\right)^2 + \frac{1}{n}\left(\frac{2}{n}\right)^2 + \cdots + \frac{1}{n}\left(\frac{n}{n}\right)^2.$$

This holds for any n. We see that the difference $T_n - S_n = (1/n)(n/n)^2$ which tends to zero as n increases. Also $T_n = (1/n^3)(1^2 + 2^2 + \cdots + n^2)$. Thus we do not now have a geometric series to sum, but Archimedes knew that $1^2 + 2^2 + \cdots + n^2 = \frac{1}{6}n(n+1)(2n+1)$. Hence

$$T_n = \frac{1}{6}\left(1+\frac{1}{n}\right)\left(2+\frac{1}{n}\right) \to \frac{1}{3} \quad \text{as } n \to \infty.$$

Fig. 8.14

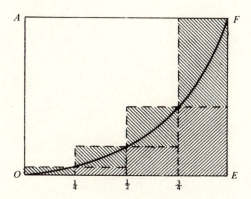

(Again the limits were established using the method of exhaustion.) Thus we have shown that the area R under the parabola is one-third the area of the (unit) square $OEFA$. The area of the parabolic segement OFA therefore equals two-thirds the area of the square $OEFA$, which is our previous result.

Archimedes could calculate volumes and centres of gravity of many solids. How did he get his results? Most of his treatises are highly rigorous and logically precise, like modern papers in pure mathematics, and give little hint of the actual way the results were obtained. And in fact the method of exhaustion, although rigorous, is essentially a way of proving a result once it is already known, since one must show that any assumption *other* than the known result leads to a contradiction; thus the method is not a technique for discovering new and unexpected results.

We now know something of Archimedes's way of thought through a remarkable discovery, made as recently as 1906, of a previously unknown work by Archimedes. J. L. Heiberg, a Danish historian of science, heard of the existence in Constantinople of a palimpsest with mathematical content (a palimpsest is a parchment where the original text has been covered by a different one). He found that, underneath a collection of prayers for the Eastern Orthodox Church, there was a mathematical text which had been copied in the tenth century. This text consisted of several well-known works by Archimedes, together with a new one called simply *The Method*. It was in the form of a letter

Fig. 8.15

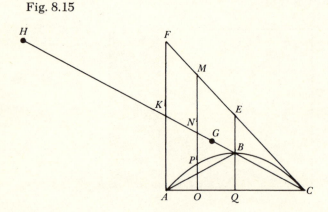

to Eratosthenes, a mathematician and librarian at the University of Alexandria (remembered for originating the so-called 'sieve method' for obtaining prime numbers). The letter describes a non-rigorous 'mechanical' approach which Archimedes used as his guide to discovery. It involves an 'atomistic' way of thinking, in which areas are thought of as the totality of a very large number of constituent lines, and volumes as the totality of the constituent areas. (This is similar to the way a 'naive' scientist nowadays tends to think when he applies calculus methods.) But Archimedes, in his refusal to use this approach in his published works, was well aware of its tentative nature (how many lines are needed, and are they of zero, or 'very small', thickness?).

We illustrate the ingenious use made by Archimedes of the 'Method' by deriving (once more) the result on the area of a parabolic segment (Fig. 8.15). Archimedes thought of the segment $ABCA$ as the sum of all parallel lines such as OP, and he wanted to compare this area with the area of the triangle AFC (FC is the tangent to the parabola at C). To do this he balanced the constituent lines like weights in mechanics, using the 'law of the lever'. In Fig. 8.15, CK is a median of the triangle AFC, and $HK = KC$. Archimedes placed a weight equal to the length of the line OP at H, and noted that this exactly balances the line OM placed at its centre of gravity N, with the point K as fulcrum.† If we do this balancing for *all* parallel lines such as OP, then we see that the whole parabolic area placed at H balances the whole triangle AFC, and thus balances the area of the triangle placed at its centre of gravity G, where $KG = \frac{1}{3}KC$. Hence the parabolic area must be $\frac{1}{3}\triangle AFC = \frac{4}{3}\triangle ABC$, the previous result. Boyer (1968) says about the discovery of the 'Method': 'In a sense the palimpsest is symbolic of the contribution of the Medieval Age. Intense preoccupation with religious concerns nearly wiped out one of the most important works of the greatest mathematician of antiquity; yet in the end it was medieval scholarship that inadvertently preserved this, and much besides, which might otherwise have been lost.'

† From the geometry of the parabola we have $OM/OP = AC/AO$ (check this); hence $OM/OP = KC/KN = HK/KN$, i.e. $OP.HK = OM.KN$, as required by the law of the lever.

9

The calculus in the seventeenth century

After Archimedes 1900 years elapsed before further significant advances were made in the calculus, but then things happened fast. The hundred-year span of the seventeenth century was a 'heroic age' during which the infinitesimal calculus grew from rudimentary beginnings into a highly developed mathematical discipline. The discovery of the calculus is usually attributed to Newton and Leibniz, and associated with the period 1665–75. There is no reason to dispute this attribution, but it would be wrong to imagine that these two men invented the calculus more or less 'out of the blue'. On the contrary, 'infinitesimal methods' were very much 'in the air' in their time, and virtually every mathematician of note in the seventeenth century contributed to their development. In this period it makes even less sense than usual to argue about who discovered what, and when a result is associated with a particular author all one can really say with any certainty is that the result was known to that author at the date in question.

Why should such a tremendous advance have occurred in the seventeenth century, after such a long period of stagnation? It was undoubtedly part of the new spirit in art and science associated with the Renaissance. Editions of the works of Archimedes and other Greek mathematicians had been published during the sixteenth century, so the Greek methods for finding areas, volumes and centres of gravity were known to scholars. Strong stimuli for the development of theoretical mechanics, and thus for the elaboration of computational methods and the application of infinitesimal methods to the study of motion and change, came from sources such as the increasing use of machines in early forms of industry, for example pumps and lifts in mining; the 'new astronomy' associated with Copernicus, Tycho Brahe and Kepler which gave hope that the science of mechanics might account for celestial as well as earthly phenomena; the perfection of clocks leading to accurate measurement of time and demonstrating the occurrence of order and regularity in natural events.

Characteristic of all the new work on the calculus was the abandonment of Archimedean standards of rigour. People wanted to get results, and they sensed that the methods under study could be powerful aids for making new discoveries; they therefore pushed ahead without worrying too much about logical deficiencies in the argument, though they usually realised quite well that the rigorous foundation was lacking. Each author tended to set his own standard of rigour. This attitude persisted throughout the seventeenth and eighteenth centuries, and it was only after 1800 that Greek standards were reintroduced to put the whole subject on a logically sound basis, turning it from 'calculus' into 'analysis'.

We have space to mention only a few of the more important contributions to the calculus in the period immediately preceding the time of Newton and Leibniz. Cavalieri, a disciple of Galileo and professor at Bologna, published in 1635 his *Geometria Indivisibilibus Continuorum*, a systematic account of infinitesimal methods which did much to stimulate interest in such problems. Cavalieri's calculus is related to Archimedes's *Method* with which Cavalieri was, however, presumably not acquainted. It regards a plane area as made up of lines ('indivisibles'), and a solid volume as composed of areas. The 'indivisibles' were not so much the small but finite 'atoms' of the Greeks, but were derived from medieval scholastic philosophy which considered every continuum to be indefinitely subdivisible. A typical result obtained by Cavalieri is the following: consider the areas F, G under two curves f, g (Fig. 9.1). Draw the curve h which is such that the ordinate h' of any point is the sum of the corresponding ordinates of points on f and g: $h' = f' + g'$. The method of indivisibles deduces from this that the sum of all ordinates f' (i.e. the area F) plus the sum of all ordinates g' equals the sum of all ordinates h'; hence the area H under the curve h equals $F + G$. This conclusion is correct, but it was soon realised that this type of argument can also give results which are obviously wrong: applied to two circles regarded as the sums of all their radii one would conclude (Fig. 9.2) that, if $OQ = 2OP$, then the area of the larger circle must be twice that of the smaller, and this of course is incorrect. Again, suppose we divide a triangle into two parts A and B as shown in Fig. 9.3. With each constituent line of part A we can associate an equal line of part B and *vice versa*, as shown; thus the area of A should be equal to the area of B (this difficulty was pointed out by Torricelli, another disciple of Galileo). Thus it was clear that the method of indivisibles, in Cavalieri's form, could not provide a satisfactory general definition of areas and volumes.

Cavalieri's most enduring contribution was his generalisation of Archimedes's quadrature of the parabola. He considered

Fig. 9.1

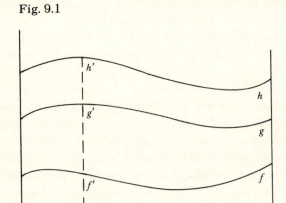

Fig. 9.2

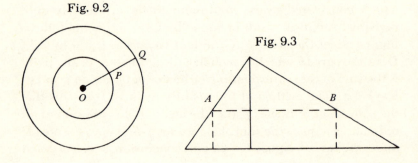

Fig. 9.3

the area under the cubic curve $y = x^3$ between $x = 0$ and $x = 1$ and obtained, summing rectangular areas in the manner of Archimedes's second proof (p. 101).

$$T_n = \frac{1}{n^4}(1^3 + 2^3 + \cdots + n^3).$$

He thus needed to be able to sum the first n *cubes* of the integers. A closed formula for this sum had been known from ancient times. The Arabs had the following elegant construction: take a square of side $1 + 2 + 3 + \cdots + n$ and subdivide it in the manner shown in Fig. 9.4. Since

$$1 + 2 + 3 + \cdots + n = \tfrac{1}{2}n(n + 1),$$

the area of the square is $[\tfrac{1}{2}n(n+1)]^2$. But we can also evaluate the area as the sum of the areas of the L-shaped pieces: the area of the nth piece consists of two rectangles and is clearly

$$n[\tfrac{1}{2}n(n+1)] + n[\tfrac{1}{2}(n-1)n] = n(\tfrac{1}{2}n^2 + \tfrac{1}{2}n + \tfrac{1}{2}n^2 - \tfrac{1}{2}n) = n^3.$$

Hence

$$1^3 + 2^3 + \cdots + n^3 = [\tfrac{1}{2}n(n+1)]^2,$$

and therefore

$$T_n = \frac{1}{4}\frac{n^2(n+1)^2}{n^4} = \frac{1}{4}\left(1 + \frac{1}{n}\right)^2 \to \frac{1}{4} \quad \text{as } n \to \infty.$$

As in the case of the parabola the result is a rational number, so

Fig. 9.4

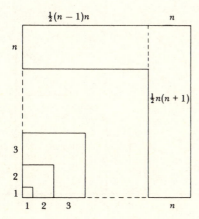

the area in question is commensurable with a rectangle. Cavalieri went on to work out the corresponding area for $y = x^4$ (result $\frac{1}{5}$), $y = x^5$ (result $\frac{1}{6}$), and so on. Each case had to be considered separately, and the labour involved increased at each step! When he had reached $y = x^9$ (with result $\frac{1}{10}$) Cavalieri gave up, and he could not see how to deal with the case $y = x^k$ for general integral k. The difficulty was overcome by Fermat, around 1650. He realised that in order to approximate the area with rectangles it was not necessary to divide the interval $(0, 1)$ into *equal* parts, in the manner of Archimedes's second proof, and that a clever choice of subdivision could lead to a simpler summation. This was a brilliant idea, fundamental for the further development of the integral calculus; it was really a new form of Archimedes's *first* proof for the parabola. Fermat's subdivision is shown in Fig. 9.5; ρ is some number between 0 and 1. The total area of the rectangles under the curve is the infinite sum

$$S_\rho = (1-\rho)\rho^k + (\rho - \rho^2)(\rho^2)^k + (\rho^2 - \rho^3)(\rho^3)^k + \cdots$$
$$= (1-\rho)\rho^k + (1-\rho)\rho^{2k+1} + (1-\rho)\rho^{3k+2} + \cdots$$
$$= (1-\rho)\rho^k[1 + \rho^{k+1} + \rho^{2k+2} + \cdots].$$

Summing the infinite geometric series we have

$$S_\rho = (1-\rho)\rho^k/(1-\rho^{k+1}),$$

Fig. 9.5

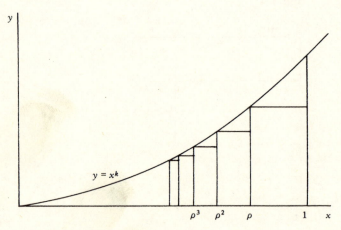

$y = x^k$

and, since

$$1-\rho^{k+1} = (1-\rho)(1+\rho+\rho^2+\cdots+\rho^k),$$
$$S_\rho = \rho^k/(1+\rho+\rho^2+\cdots+\rho^k).$$

At this stage we let ρ approach 1; the width of each of the rectangles then tends to zero, and their total area tends to the area R under the curve. Thus $R = S_{\rho=1} = 1/(k+1)$, the general result suggested by Cavalieri's calculations. Fermat noted that this argument is easily extended to the case when k is a fraction, say $k = p/q$ with p, q positive integers. It is in fact only in the last step, the factorisation of $1-\rho^{k+1}$, that we assumed k to be integral; we now obtain instead (with $t^q = \rho$)

$$S_\rho = \frac{(1-\rho)\rho^{p/q}}{1-\rho^{(p+q)/q}} = \frac{(1-t^q)t^p}{1-t^{p+q}}$$
$$= \frac{t^p(1-t)(1+t+t^2+\cdots+t^{q-1})}{(1-t)(1+t+t^2+\cdots+t^{p+q-1})}.$$

As ρ and t approach 1, this tends to

$$\frac{q}{p+q} = \frac{1}{(p/q)+1} = \frac{1}{k+1}$$

as before. Negative k can also be dealt with, and Fermat was thus able to integrate x^k for all rational k except $k = -1$; for this special value the method does not give a geometric series and fails. This special case is the problem of the area under the *hyperbola*, $y = 1/x$.

A method of subdivision for finding the area under this curve was, it seems, first given by a Belgian Jesuit scholar, Gregory of Saint-Vincent, in 1647. It appears at the end of an enormous and useless work on squaring the circle and brought its author little credit; presumably he was not aware of the importance of his discovery. Gregory's idea is to fill the area under the curve $y = 1/x$ between (say) $x = 1$ and $x = 2$ with a certain number of rectangles (Fig. 9.6); then to fill the area between 2 and 4 with the *same* number of rectangles (which therefore have double the width); then the area between 4 and 8 with the same number again (again doubling the width); and so on. Since $y = 1/x$, *doubling* the value of x means *halving* the value of y; hence a rectangle of doubled width also has its height halved, so that its area is unchanged. Thus the total area of the rectangles between $x = 1$ and $x = 2$ is equal to the total area of the rectangles between $x = 2$ and $x = 4$, and so on. This conclusion remains unchanged if we increase the number of rectangles used in each segment of the x-axis, and so it follows, on increasing the number indefinitely, that the property of the rectangles must also hold for the *area $J_{a,b}$ under the curve* between $x = a$ and $x = b$: $J_{1,2} = J_{2,4} = J_{4,8} = J_{3,6} = \cdots$. The general conclusion is that $J_{a,b} = J_{ka,kb}$, where k is any positive integer, and it is easy to generalise to the case where k is any positive fraction (try to show this yourself). It follows that the area under the curve between 1 and xy is

$$J_{1,xy} = J_{1,x} + J_{x,xy} \text{ (since areas add)} = J_{1,x} + J_{1,y}.$$

This shows that the *area function $J_{1,x}$* has the basic property of a *logarithm*, $\log xy = \log x + \log y$.

Does this mean that Gregory *discovered* the formula $\int dx/x = \log x$ which we find nowadays in tables of integrals? We have already suggested that questions like this can hardly be answered; there is no single discoverer. We do know that the formula in its familiar form was given by Leibniz. We must be

Fig. 9.6

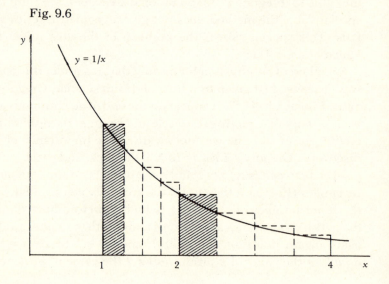

careful not to attribute our modern way of thinking to the people who were groping their way towards the calculus in the early seventeenth century. Nowadays the definition of an integral is given in analysis as the limit of a certain sum, and intuitive geometrical concepts play no part in the definition. We can then *define* the area under the curve $y = 1/x$ as a certain definite integral. Gregory on the other hand was concerned with the *geometrical* problem of areas; others at his time had become familiar with logarithms as *numbers* which were useful aids to calculation (see Chapter 1). The two concepts were quite distinct, and $\log x$ was not yet regarded as a *function* worth studying for its mathematical significance. What Gregory showed – and it was a key step – was that the area under the hyperbola between a fixed and a variable abscissa *behaves like a logarithm*, increasing 'arithmetically' as the abscissa increases 'geometrically'.

Thus by about 1650 a fair amount of progress had been made with the ancient *quadrature problem* of finding areas under curves. It was also found that related geometrical problems, such as the 'rectification' of various curves (i.e. finding a straight line of the same *length*), and determining areas of surfaces of revolution, could all be reduced to quadratures. At first problems were classified in accordance with the geometrical (or mechanical) situation from which they arose, but it was gradually realised that different problems, whatever their origin, were mathematically equivalent if they led to the same quadrature problem; in this way the integral calculus came into being as a separate mathematical discipline in its own right.

How about the other basic concept of the calculus, the *derivative*? It is implicit in several classes of problems dating back to antiquity: the geometrical problem of finding the directions of *tangents* to curves; the *maximum/minimum* problem of finding the greatest and least values of variable magnitudes; and the kinematical problem of the *speed* of a moving object, i.e. the rate at which its position changes with time. Progress with all these questions contributed to the creation of the differential calculus in the seventeenth century. The Greeks had no differential calculus analogous to the method of exhaustion for finding areas. They determined tangents to simple curves by geometrical construction: for the circle as the line perpendicular to the radius, and for the ellipse as the line making equal angles with the lines to the foci (Fig. 9.7). (Note that for both these curves the Greeks found the *area problem* insoluble!) Indeed the properties of tangents and normals to all the conic sections had been thoroughly studied in Apollonius's famous *Conics*. But the Greeks had no satisfactory general definition of the tangent to an *arbitrary* curve; they had only the vague notion of it as a line such that no other line could be drawn through the point of contact to lie 'between' the tangent and the curve. The only hint of differential-calculus ideas comes in an observation of Archimedes who determined the direction of the tangent to his spiral $r = k\theta$ (see p. 96) by thinking in terms of the instantaneous direction of motion of a moving point, the motion being the resultant of a uniform radial motion away from the origin and a circular motion about the origin. This was however an isolated result.

It seems that Fermat, around 1630, first clearly knew how to differentiate a simple function. (Pierre de Fermat (1601–65) was a lawyer who did mathematics as a hobby and who published very little during his lifetime. Thus the exact date of his many profound and original discoveries is uncertain, and he did not during his life receive the credit he deserved. His deep contributions to the theory of numbers were mentioned in Chapter 2. He developed analytic geometry independently of Descartes who is usually regarded as its founder, and Fermat was also, with Blaise Pascal, a founder of the mathematical theory of probability. The introduction of powerful algebraic methods

Fig. 9.7

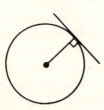
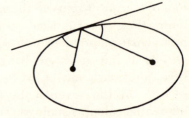

into geometry was itself one of the advances needed for the full development of the calculus.)

To find the slope of the tangent at say $x = 1$ to the curve $y = x^k$, Fermat used an argument equivalent to differentiation (Fig. 9.8). He regarded the direction of the tangent at P as given by the limiting position of the chord PP' when P' approaches P, so that the slope of the tangent is the limiting value of $P'Q/PQ$, i.e.

$$\lim_{x \to 1} \frac{x^k - 1}{x - 1}$$

which Fermat could evaluate as k. We see that in the determination of this limit Fermat had to deal with essentially the same mathematical problem as in his calculation of the area under the same curve. Was Fermat aware of the relation between differentiation and integration? He does not mention it, and at first the techniques of differentiation were developed quite separately from those of integration – they arose, after all, from problems that appeared to have no obvious relation to each other.

At some stage in the seventeenth century it was realised – we cannot name any single discoverer – that differentiation and integration were inverse mathematical processes; a realisation that was to play a fundamental part in the subsequent development of the calculus as a systematic discipline. This inverse relation involves the idea of the *indefinite integral*: if $f(x)$ is a given function and $F(x)$ is any function whose derivative $F'(x)$ equals $f(x)$, we call $F(x)$ an indefinite integral (or

Fig. 9.8

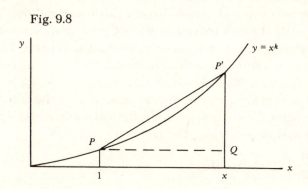

antiderivative) of $f(x)$ and write it $\int f(x)\,dx$ (it is not unique: if $F(x)$ is an indefinite integral of $f(x)$ so is $F(x)+c$, where c is any constant).

What has this notion to do with areas under curves? It is necessary to *show* that, if $f(x)$ has an indefinite integral $F(x)$, the area under the curve $y=f(x)$ between $x=a$ and $x=b$ is $F(b)-F(a)$ (with certain provisos regarding signs. This is of course the standard rule for evaluating 'definite integrals' $\int_a^b f(x)\,dx$ in terms of indefinite integrals). Newton gave such a proof for the curve $y=ax^{m/n}$, but several of his predecessors were undoubtedly aware of the idea. (All these proofs relied on 'area' as a geometrically plausible idea which needs no further definition.) If we now regard the 'upper limit' b as a variable quantity, the inverse relation between differentiation and integration can be expressed by the two equations

$$F(b)=\int_a^b f(x)\,dx + \text{constant}, \qquad F'(b)=f(b).$$

The approach to quadratures via the indefinite integral, adopted by Newton and Leibniz and their successors, elevates *differentiation* into the primary concept and makes *integration* a secondary idea. Since computation of derivatives is very much simpler than the laborious direct evaluation of areas (this was certainly true in the days before computers!) this formulation provided a highly convenient quick method for working out definite integrals of many simple functions – all those which were known to be derivatives of other functions – and thus it quickly converted the calculus from a difficult and esoteric discipline into a useful easy-to-handle mathematical tool. But the method of the antiderivative did not provide a *systematic* way of carrying out quadratures; quite simple functions like e^{-x^2} cannot be written as derivatives of other simple functions. It was only about 200 years later that a return was made, by Riemann and others, to the *direct* definition of the integral $\int_a^b f(x)\,dx$, in the Greek manner, as the limit of a sum without any reference to differentiation. The fact that

$$\frac{d}{db}\int_a^b f(x)\,dx = f(b)$$

then becomes a basic theorem in analysis; it is still known as the 'fundamental theorem of the calculus'. The more powerful nineteenth-century concept of the integral as a 'sum' rather than an antiderivative thus includes the earlier approach as a special case, and in the present age of computers it should be the natural way of thinking about integrals in practical as well as in theoretical terms. Unfortunately the teaching of elementary calculus in our schools is, even now, all too often still dominated by the thinking of the seventeenth century.

We return to Fermat and early notions of differentiation. The determination of maxima and minima, like the problem of tangents, suggested methods equivalent to finding the derivative of a function. Take the classical geometrical result that, of all rectangles with a given perimeter, the square has the greatest area. The following purely geometrical proof is given by Euclid (Fig. 9.9): suppose $A + C$ is a rectangle and $B + C$ a square of the

Fig. 9.9

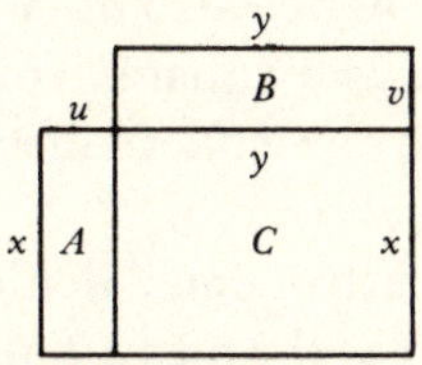

same perimeter. Since the perimeters are equal, $x + u + y = x + v + y$, so $u = v$. Since $B + C$ is a square, $y = v + x$, so $y > x$, hence the area of B (yv) is greater than the area of A $(xu = xv)$, and therefore the area of the square $B + C$ is greater than the area of the rectangle $A + C$. Fermat uses instead a (modern) analytical method: he notes that the problem amounts to finding the value of x for which the *area function* $J(x) = (a - x)x$ has its greatest value (Fig. 9.10). To do this Fermat exploited the idea, which

Fig. 9.10

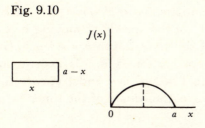

was not a new one, that near a maximum a function varies particularly slowly; thus $J(x)$ will change only very little when x changes by a small amount, so that we have a *stationary value* of the function. So, replacing x by $x - e$ where e is small, we form

$$J(x-e) = [a-(x-e)](x-e)$$

and put it equal to $J(x)$:

$$(a-x)x = (a-x+e)(x-e).$$

This equality should be more nearly true the closer e is to zero. Simplifying, we have

$$(a-x)x = (a-x)x - e(a-x) + ex - e^2$$

or

$$2ex - ea - e^2 = 0$$

or (dividing by e)

$$2x - a - e = 0.$$

Now setting $e = 0$ we have $x = a/2$ and hence also $a - x = a/2$; thus the rectangle with maximum area is a square. This procedure is of course entirely equivalent to our modern method of setting the first derivative $dJ(x)/dx$ equal to zero.

Even earlier, around 1610, the great astronomer Kepler had considered a similar problem, arising from the measurement of volumes of wine barrels. (He even published a book on the subject, the *Stereometria Doliorum*.) Kepler objected to his wine merchant's way of calculating the price of the wine; the measure of the price was the length l of a measuring rod which was inserted into the cylindrical barrel through a hole half-way up and made to rest against the top edge opposite (Fig. 9.11). Kepler realised that many different volumes could correspond to a given l (some very small!), and he worked out, for given l, the barrel height h_m for which the volume is a maximum. (*Exercise*: show that $h_m = 2l/\sqrt{3}$.)

The concept of differentiation arose also in a physical context in *kinematics*, the study of the speeds of moving bodies – a major preoccupation of seventeenth-century science. Galileo, Kepler's great contemporary, found in his experiments on bodies moving down inclined planes under gravity that the distance travelled varies as the square of the time, $x = at^2$. In trying to link this result with the behaviour of the speed, $v = dx/dt$, Galileo did not in fact proceed by differentiation; instead he tried various laws for the speed (first v proportional to x, later v proportional to t) and attempted to recover the distance/time law, by rather obscure reasoning, from the graph of speed against time (thus he was really trying to integrate the velocity function). A similar approach was used by Descartes (about 1618). Did Galileo and Descartes realise that the distances x were proportional to the *areas* under the velocity/time graph? We cannot be sure; a clear enunciation of the relation $x = \int_0^t v\,dt$ was given only about 40 years later, by Newton's teacher Isaac Barrow (see below). Certainly during this period it came to be more and more clearly accepted that functions and curves defined kinematically – i.e. the positions, orbits and speeds of particles as functions of the time – were mathematically indistinguishable from functions and curves defined in more general fashion, and that the time t was just a mathematical parameter equivalent to any other variable. Thus the approach to the calculus via mechanics became gradually fused with the approach via geometry.

We mention briefly some other major contributors to the early calculus before Newton and Leibniz:

Blaise Pascal (1623–62) was a highly original genius who contributed to many branches of mathematics. We have already

Fig. 9.11

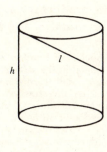

mentioned that he was a founder of the mathematical theory of probability and that he designed and built the earliest calculating machine. He made an intensive study of the properties of the cycloid, and he knew how to integrate simple functions such as x^n and $\sin x$. The writings of Pascal greatly influenced the young Leibniz.

Christiaan Huygens (1629–95), a wealthy Dutchman living in Paris, was distinguished as mathematician, physicist and astronomer. He is the creator of the wave theory of light. His book on pendulum clocks, the *Horologium Oscillatorum* (published in 1673), and his letters are rich in new results on properties of curves. Many of these were found only after Leibniz had already published his general method for tackling such problems. Huygens found it difficult to accept Leibniz's calculus, probably because of Huygens's insistence (unusual among mathematicians of the seventeenth century) on the high standards of rigour demanded by the Greek geometrical tradition of Archimedes.

John Wallis (1616–1703) was Savilian Professor of Geometry in the University of Oxford and helped to organise the Royal Society (founded 1660).† Wallis's *Arithmetica Infinitorum* (published in 1655) represents, together with Huygens's *Horologium*, the most highly developed form of infinitesimal calculus in the period before Newton and Leibniz. As the title shows Wallis wanted to demonstrate the power of the new 'arithmetic' (i.e. algebra), not the ancient geometry, and his bold methods in the treatment of infinite series and products gave him many new results. A typical formula obtained by Wallis is his famous infinite product for π. He derived this by writing $\frac{1}{4}\pi$ as the area of a quadrant of the unit circle $x^2 + y^2 = 1$, i.e. (in

---

† The Royal Society of London was one of the scientific academies which developed in the sixteenth and seventeenth centuries from discussion groups of learned men. The academies expressed the new spirit of free investigation, typifying 'this age drunk with the fullness of new knowledge, busy with the uprooting of superannuated superstitions . . .' (Ornstein). In this they contrasted with the universities which, founded in the Middle Ages, tended to maintain the medieval attitude of presenting knowledge in fixed forms. The earliest academies were Italian: Naples 1560, Rome (the 'Accademia dei Lincei') 1603.

modern notation) as the integral $\int_0^1 (1-x^2)^{1/2} \, dx$. The square root in the integrand caused trouble, as there was no binomial theorem for general non-integral powers. Wallis therefore evaluated $\int_0^1 (1-x^2)^n \, dx$ for $n = 0, 1, 2, \ldots$, and guessed the answer for $n = \frac{1}{2}$ by a complicated interpolation process.† This led him finally to his result

$$\frac{\pi}{2} = \frac{2 \times 2 \times 4 \times 4 \times 6 \times 6 \times 8 \times \cdots}{1 \times 3 \times 3 \times 5 \times 5 \times 7 \times 7 \times \cdots}.$$

James Gregory (1638–75) was a Scot who studied in Italy and who was in possession of large elements of the calculus by 1668. Unfortunately he used geometric rather than analytic methods which made his work difficult to follow. The infinite series

$$\tan^{-1} x = x - \frac{x^3}{3} + \frac{x^5}{5} - \frac{x^7}{7} + \cdots$$

is known as 'Gregory's series'; it was obtained by writing $\tan^{-1} x$ as an integral,

$$\int_0^x \frac{dy}{1+y^2} = \int_0^x (1 - y^2 + y^4 - y^6 + \cdots) \, dy,$$

and integrating the series term by term. Gregory knew the fundamental expansion known as the *Taylor series*:

$$f(a+x) = f(a) + xf'(a) + \frac{x^2}{2!} f''(a) + \cdots,$$

long before Brook Taylor published it in 1715.‡

Isaac Barrow (1630–77) was Newton's predecessor in the Lucasian chair at Cambridge (he resigned in 1669 and proposed Newton as his successor). Barrow's *Geometrical Lectures*

---

† In fact Wallis considered, more generally, the integral of $(1 - x^{2/\mu})^n$ for various integer values of both μ and n. For details see Edwards (1979).

‡ Not to mention Maclaurin: Colin Maclaurin's series

$$f(x) = f(0) + xf'(0) + \frac{x^2}{2!} f''(0) + \cdots,$$

which is only a special case of the Taylor series, was published in 1742. The naming of theorems is often a matter of historical accident rather than historical justice! The history of the Taylor series is actually very complicated; historians of mathematics claim that a special case was already known in India before 1550.

appeared in 1670 and were much concerned with tangent problems and quadratures. We have mentioned that Barrow saw clearly that the distance travelled in rectilinear motion is proportional to the area under the velocity/time graph. From his kinematical studies he must have been aware of the relation between the derivative regarded as the slope of a tangent and the integral regarded as an area. One of Barrow's results which involves this relation is the following: suppose two curves $y = f(x)$, $Y = F(x)$ are such that the ordinates Y are proportional to the areas $\int_c^x y \, dx'$, i.e. $aF(x) = \int_c^x f(x') \, dx'$, then the tangent at (x, Y) to $Y = F(x)$ cuts the x-axis at the point $x - T$, where T is given by $y/Y = a/T$. To obtain this theorem Barrow argued with small quantities in a manner similar to Fermat's; we would now obtain it at once by observing that the slope of the tangent is y, the derivative of Y. Barrow gives many results of similar type, but the *general* significance of the relation between integration and differentiation is not made clear by him, and his insistence on old-fashioned geometric language made his *Geometrical Lectures* difficult for others to follow.

The 1650s and 1660s were thus a period of rapid advance in the handling of a variety of infinite methods. Infinite series, infinite products and continued fractions were all in fashion. The publication of *Mercator's series* (1668)[†]:

$$\log(1+x) = \int_0^x \frac{dy}{1+y} = \int_0^x (1 - y + y^2 - y^3 + \cdots) \, dy$$

$$= x - \frac{x^2}{2} + \frac{x^3}{3} - \frac{x^4}{4} + \cdots$$

made a great impression; the realisation that a non-algebraic function like a logarithm could be represented in this way as a simple power series drew the attention of mathematicians to the use of infinite series as a general method for studying functions of all kinds. (Newton himself contributed the first enunciation of the binomial theorem for general non-integral powers.) Many

---

† Nicolaus Mercator (1620–87) must not be confused with the geographer Gerard Mercator (1512–94) who introduced 'Mercator's projection' in map-making.

integrations had been done by this time, differentiation was known and the relation between the two had been recognised; various techniques were known for relating one integral to another (thus Barrow had the rule for integration by 'change of variables'); even some problems equivalent to the solution of simple differential equations had been solved. The time was ripe for the creation of a general algorithm which could handle, in a single unified notation, all the fundamental operations of the infinitesimal calculus. This is what Newton and Leibniz achieved.

Newton and Leibniz were among the greatest minds of all time, and their creation of the calculus formed only a part of their many profound contributions to knowledge. There has been much (too much!) discussion about who should have the credit for being the first with the calculus; it is now generally agreed that the discoveries were made independently. In fact Newton's work (in 1665–6) antedated that of Leibniz (in 1673–6), but Leibniz was the first to publish, and his work exerted a much greater *immediate* influence on the mathematical thinking of the time.

Isaac Newton was born in 1642 (the year in which Galileo died) in the village of Woolsthorpe in Lincolnshire. He studied in Cambridge under Isaac Barrow and succeeded his teacher as Lucasian professor in 1669. Newton's most famous work is the *Principia* (the full title is *Philosophiae Naturalis Principia Mathematica*, published in 1687). In this unique work Newton establishes the laws of mechanics on an axiomatic basis and derives the laws of planetary motion from the universal inverse-square law of gravitation. The approach laid down in the *Principia* has become the model for all subsequent developments in physical science.

Newton's chief discoveries, including his calculus – which he called the 'method of fluxions' – were made during 1665 and 1666 when he had retired to his native village to escape from the plague in Cambridge. Rather surprisingly, the demonstrations in the *Principia* do not use the calculus but are based on 'old-fashioned' geometrical methods, presumably because

Newton considered these to be more logically satisfying. Throughout his life Newton was reluctant to publish his discoveries, and this makes the extent of his influence on his contemporaries difficult to assess. The *Method of Fluxions* was actually not published until 1736, after Newton's death.

Newton thought in mechanical terms: curves were generated by the continuous *motion* of a point. The coordinates (x, y) of a point on a plane curve are called 'fluents' (flowing quantities), their rates of change are 'fluxions', denoted by $(\dot{x}, \dot{y})$ (these are our modern derivatives dx/dt, dy/dt, with t as the time parameter; thus the fluxions are velocity components). The fluxion of $\dot{x}$ is $\ddot{x}$, and so on. The 'moment' of the fluxion $\dot{x}$ is the infinitesimal quantity $\dot{x}o$, where o is an 'infinitely small quantity'. Newton argues typically as follows: given, say, a plane curve $x^2 - axy - y^2 = 0$, substitute $x + \dot{x}o$ for x, $y + \dot{y}o$ for y, and so obtain

$$x^2 + 2x\dot{x}o + \dot{x}^2o^2 - axy - ax\dot{y}o - ay\dot{x}o$$
$$- a\dot{x}o\dot{y}o - y^2 - 2y\dot{y}o - \dot{y}^2o^2 = 0.$$

Now $x^2 - axy - y^2 = 0$; expunge this and divide the rest by o; there remains

$$2x\dot{x} + \dot{x}^2o - ax\dot{y} - ay\dot{x} - a\dot{x}\dot{y}o - 2y\dot{y} - \dot{y}^2o = 0.$$

'But whereas zero is supposed to be infinitely little, that it may represent the moments of quantities, the terms that are multiplied by it will be nothing in respect to the rest; I therefore reject them, and there remains

$$2x\dot{x} - ax\dot{y} - ay\dot{x} - 2y\dot{y} = 0.\text{'}$$

(This is the calculus result, x and y being differentiable functions of t.)

What kind of quantities are the os? Are they zeros? Or 'infinitesimals' (whatever that means)? Or finite numbers? Newton tried to explain their nature by a primitive notion of a limit, but his argument (from the *Principia*) is hardly clear:

'Those ultimate ratios with which quantities vanish are not truly the ratios of ultimate quantities, but limits toward which the ratios of quantities, decreasing without limit, do always converge, and to which they approach nearer than by any given difference, but never go beyond, nor in effect attain to, until the quantities have diminished in infinitum.'

Newton in practice knew well enough what he wanted to do with his calculus and was able to use it in the absence of clear definitions; but lesser mortals were more easily confused.

Gottfried Wilhelm Leibniz was born in Leipzig in 1646 and spent most of his life at the court of Hanover, in the service of the dukes (one of whom became King George I of England). He was the great universal genius of the seventeenth century, with interests in history, theology, linguistics, biology, geology, diplomacy and mathematics; he invented a computing machine, conceived the idea of a steam engine, studied Sanskrit and tried to promote the unity of Germany. Leibniz met Huygens in Paris in 1672 and took lessons in mathematics from him. He developed his calculus between 1673 and 1676 and published it between 1684 and 1686. Leibniz was as much philosopher as scientist and wanted to find a 'universal language' to describe all change (motion included), and beyond this a universal method for acquiring knowledge and for making new inventions. A modern reader may feel sceptical about such sweeping ambitions, but Leibniz's attitude led to important results: he laid the foundations for symbolic logic, and he was aware, more than any of his contemporaries, of the importance of a well-devised and easily handled mathematical *notation*. The symbolism he introduced for the calculus made it easy for others to understand and handle his methods, and his notation is in fact the one that has survived to the present day. Leibniz's first paper on the calculus contained our symbols dx, dy, the product rule $d(uv) = u\,dv + v\,du$ and the condition $dy = 0$ for extreme values; later he introduced the integration sign $\int$ (which is a long S, denoting 'summa'); and the names 'differential calculus' and 'integral calculus' are also due to him.†

The publication of Leibniz's calculus initiated a period of extremely fertile productivity. Two very able disciples who

---

† Leibniz's first suggestion for the integral calculus was 'calculus summatorius', later replaced by 'calculus integralis'. Modern analysis has re-adopted Leibniz's earlier suggestion.

eagerly took up Leibniz's methods were the brothers Jakob and Johann Bernoulli. Working together – and often in bitter rivalry – these two had by 1700 discovered most of the material in the present-day A-level calculus syllabus, together with portions of more advanced subjects such as the solution of many ordinary differential equations and results in the calculus of variations. In 1696 the first textbook on the calculus (the *Analyse des infiniment petits*) was published by the Marquis de l'Hospital; this was essentially a text written a few years earlier by the Marquis's teacher Johann Bernoulli. The Marquis is remembered today by 'L'Hospital's rule', given in this book, for finding $\lim_{x \to 0} f(x)/g(x)$ when f and g both tend to zero.

Leibniz's calculus was just as vague as Newton's about the logical foundations; he, also, could not say clearly whether the quantities dx, dy were to be regarded as finite or zero or as something in between.

Two further comments should be made.

(1) The lack of precise foundations for the new calculus provoked criticism. The best known came from Bishop Berkeley, the Irish idealist philosopher, who resented Newtonian science because it supported materialism, and who attacked the theory of fluxions in his *Analyst* (published in 1734). Berkeley was a lively debater: he derided infinitesimals as 'ghosts of departed quantities' and called Newton's arguments, in which o is sometimes taken as non-zero and sometimes as zero, a 'manifest sophism'. According to Berkeley, 'he who can digest a second or third fluxion, a second or third difference, need not, methinks, be squeamish about any point in divinity'. Although these and similar criticisms had justification, they were purely destructive and did not supply any better basis for the calculus. They did however underline the need for further work to be done on the foundations of the subject.

(2) There were prolonged disputes as to whether Newton or Leibniz deserved the priority for discovering the calculus, disputes which the followers of the two great men pursued with zeal and venom, and which were made disagreeable by accusations of plagiarism.

These criticisms and quarrels contributed to the generally feeble state of British mathematics in the eighteenth century, at a time when enormous mathematical advances were made in Europe with the aid of the calculus. No doubt other factors were also to blame for Britain's weakness, such as an over-emphasis on old-fashioned geometric concepts and a general lack of public regard for the importance of mathematical studies. An over-pious adherence to all the details of Newton's fluxional methods led to revolt in 1812 when the 'Analytical Society' was formed by young mathematicians in Cambridge to promote Leibniz's notation and to reform British mathematics generally. But it was a long time before the writings of the great continental analysts came to be fully understood in England (see Hardy 1949).

10

The function concept

The new calculus was developed with vigour in the eighteenth century, mainly on the Continent of Europe. The foremost name was Euler who was Swiss but spent most of his life in St Petersburg and Berlin; his mathematical output was immense. The calculus provided a powerful tool for developing Newton's mechanics and applying it to all sorts of physical systems. For this purpose people learned to handle *differential equations* with skill and a highly developed technique. Because of the success of the calculus in leading to physical theories which made sense, mathematicians did not worry too much about the fact that the rigorous foundation was lacking. It was a period of happy and bold experimentation in mathematics. But there was no lack of argument about the meaning and validity of the new developments.

We shall pick out for brief discussion a topic important in the creation of present-day analysis: early controversies surrounding the concept of a *function*. For Euler and his contemporaries functions were entities like e^x, $\log(1+x)$, $\sqrt{(1+x)}$; they could all be represented by a *formula*. Thus when faced with (for example) the expressions

$$y = x(x \leqslant 0), \qquad y = x^2(x > 0),$$

Euler would say that we have here *two* functions because we have two formulae. Alternatively, looking at the graph of y against x (Fig. 10.1), Euler might say that we have one function (since there is only one curve), but that it is 'discontinuous'. Nowadays we have a much more general view of the concept of a function. It is just a rule which assigns to each element of a set A a unique element in a set B. Thus for us the above example is a single function (which, according to modern definitions, is continuous and has a discontinuous derivative at $x = 0$); the fact that two different formulae are needed is an aspect of minor significance. (We learn this in analysis but sometimes forget about it in applied mathematics.) Note also that Euler's functions usually had the property, much used in the eighteenth-century calculus, that they could be expanded as infinite series in powers of x. For example:

$$e^x = 1 + x + \frac{x^2}{2!} + \cdots ,$$

$$\log(1+x) = x - \tfrac{1}{2}x^2 + \tfrac{1}{3}x^3 - \cdots ,$$

$$\sin x = x - \frac{x^3}{3!} + \frac{x^5}{5!} - \cdots .$$

Euler and his contemporaries were ingenious in manipulating infinite series. Usually they did not worry about convergence, and some of the results do not make any sense to us. Thus Euler somewhere argues as follows: since

$$\frac{1}{1-x} = 1 + x + x^2 + \cdots , \quad \text{one has} \quad \frac{x}{1-x} = x + x^2 + x^3 + \cdots$$

and

$$\frac{x}{x-1} = \frac{1}{1-(1/x)} = 1 + \frac{1}{x} + \frac{1}{x^2} + \cdots = -\frac{x}{1-x}.$$

So, adding, one obtains the expansion

$$\cdots + \frac{1}{x^2} + \frac{1}{x} + 1 + x + x^2 + \cdots = 0.$$

We would call this a *formal* result which is meaningless: since the first series converges only for $|x| < 1$ and the second only for $|x| > 1$, the two series cannot be added.

Fig. 10.1

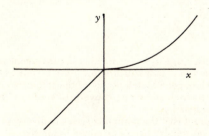

For us the *sum* of an infinite series is a *limit* and exists only when the limit exists.† Although eighteenth-century concepts of the sum of an infinite series were not precise, it should not be thought that questions of convergence were completely ignored. Mathematicians were well aware of the convergent or divergent nature of particular series: they knew for example that the 'harmonic series' $\sum_1^\infty 1/n$ diverges while $\sum_1^\infty 1/n^2$ converges.‡ They were particularly interested in the use of series to obtain good approximations in numerical calculations, and some important methods for evaluating sums of the form $\sum_{k=1}^n f(k)$ when n is large were first given by Euler. Although they often could not prove their results rigorously, the mathematicians of the period were guided by an excellent intuitive feel for the correct approach.

A particular problem solved by Euler was that of finding the sum of the convergent series

$$\sum_1^\infty \frac{1}{n^2} = \frac{1}{1^2} + \frac{1}{2^2} + \frac{1}{3^2} + \cdots,$$

a problem that had defeated Leibniz and Jakob Bernoulli. Euler not only obtained accurate numerical *estimates* for this sum, but he also evaluated the sum *exactly* by the following bold approach. He first considered the algebraic equation of degree n

$$(x - x_1)(x - x_2)(x - x_3) \cdots (x - x_n) = 0$$

with roots $x_1, x_2, \ldots, x_n$, where we are given that the constant term is equal to 1, so that

$$(-1)^n x_1 x_2 \cdots x_n = 1. \tag{1}$$

The coefficient of x in the equation is

$$(-1)^{n-1}(x_2 x_3 \cdots x_n + x_1 x_3 \cdots x_n + x_1 x_2 \cdots x_{n-1}),$$

and this, dividing by (1), is seen to be equal to

$$-\left(\frac{1}{x_1} + \frac{1}{x_2} + \cdots + \frac{1}{x_n}\right).$$

---

† We recall that a series $u_1 + u_2 + \cdots + u_n + \cdots$ is convergent with sum s when the sum of n terms $(u_1 + u_2 + \cdots + u_n)$ tends to the limit s as $n \to \infty$. More general definitions of the sum of an infinite series can be given which allow non-convergent series to be summed in a generalised sense.

‡ It seems that the proof that the harmonic series is divergent goes back to the medieval scholar Nicole Oresme (1323?–82).

Euler's idea was to apply this result to the equation $\sin x = 0$. Using the series for $\sin x$ he regarded this as an algebraic equation of *infinite* degree:

$$x - \frac{x^3}{3!} + \frac{x^5}{5!} - \cdots = 0,$$

or (dividing by x and putting $x^2 = w$)

$$1 - \frac{w}{3!} + \frac{w^2}{5!} - \cdots = 0. \tag{2}$$

The non-zero roots of $\sin x = 0$ are known to be the infinite set $x = \pm\pi, \pm 2\pi, \pm 3\pi, \ldots$, so we know that the roots of (2) are π^2, $(2\pi)^2$, $(3\pi)^2, \ldots$. Also the constant term is 1, and the coefficient of w is $-1/6$. Hence we have for the sum of the reciprocals of the roots

$$-\left(\frac{1}{\pi^2} + \frac{1}{(2\pi)^2} + \frac{1}{(3\pi)^2} + \cdots\right) = -\frac{1}{6},$$

or

$$\frac{1}{1^2} + \frac{1}{2^2} + \frac{1}{3^2} + \cdots = \frac{\pi^2}{6}.$$

This elegant formula is the correct result. Euler's derivation would not be accepted nowadays without a careful justification of the transition from finite n to infinite n, but it was a brilliant achievement in its time. Alternative derivations confirming the result were also given by Euler.

A particular physical problem much discussed in the eighteenth century contributed greatly to the formulation of the modern concept of a function. The problem is that of calculating the shape of a *vibrating string* (for example a violin string), fixed at its ends and undergoing small transverse oscillations. The mathematical task is to find the function $y(x, t)$ which specifies the transverse displacement of the string at a distance x along the string at time t (Fig. 10.2). y is thus a function of the

Fig. 10.2

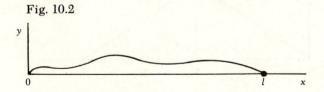

two variables x and t. If the ends of the string are at $x = 0$ and $x = l$, then, since these ends are fixed, y must satisfy the *boundary conditions*

$$y(0, t) = y(l, t) = 0 \quad \text{for all } t.$$

If the *initial* displacement of the string (at time $t = 0$) is given, by specifying some function $f(x)$, then y also satisfies the *initial condition* $y(x, 0) = f(x)$. Around 1747 d'Alembert and Euler solved the partial differential equation (the *wave equation*) satisfied by $y(x, t)$, and they showed that, with the specified initial and boundary conditions, the problem has a well-defined unique solution which can be expressed in the following elegant form. The wave equation, together with the boundary condition at $x = 0$, can be satisfied by writing y in the form

$$y(x, t) = F(ct + x) - F(ct - x), \tag{3}$$

where $F(u)$ is any 'function'. Physically the two expressions on the right-hand side represent *waves* travelling along the string to the left and to the right, where the constant c is the *wave velocity*. The function F is determined by the initial displacement of the string. We must have $f(x) = y(x, 0) = F(x) - F(-x)$; suppose we define $F(u)$ to be an *odd* function of u (so that $F(u) = -F(-u)$), then this gives us $F(u) = \frac{1}{2}f(u)$. For example, suppose the initial displacement of the string is a pure sine curve, with $f(x) = 2 \sin(\pi x/l)$, then the solution (3) is

$$\sin \frac{\pi}{l}(ct + x) - \sin \frac{\pi}{l}(ct - x) = 2 \sin \frac{\pi x}{l} \cos \frac{\pi ct}{l}. \tag{4}$$

Fig. 10.3

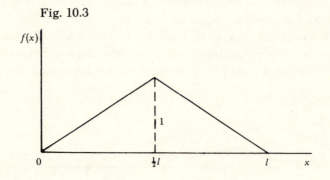

(Note that this expression also satisfies the boundary condition at $x = l$.) The second form of the solution shows that we have here a vibration with time dependence of the form $\cos 2\pi \nu t$, i.e. a *pure tone* with a single frequency $\nu = c/2l$. (This important special solution had been given earlier by Brook Taylor, around 1715.) To satisfy the end condition at $x = l$ in general we must require that $F(ct + l) = F(ct - l)$. This condition can be written $F(u) = F(u + 2l)$ for all u; thus $F(u)$ must be a *periodic function* of u with period $2l$. (This is certainly true of the function $\sin(\pi u/l)$, since $\sin(\pi u/l) = \sin(\pi/l)(u + 2l)$.)

Euler realised that the 'pure tone' solution is only a special case: for example, if we pull the string aside at its mid-point by a unit amount and let go (the case of a 'plucked string'), we have the initial shape illustrated in Fig. 10.3 and described mathematically by

$$f(x) = 2x/l \qquad (0 \leqslant x \leqslant \tfrac{1}{2}l),$$
$$= 2(1 - x/l) \quad (\tfrac{1}{2}l \leqslant x \leqslant l). \tag{5}$$

To what kind of function $F(u)$ does this initial condition lead, in the general solution (3)? Remember that $F(u)$ must be periodic with period $2l$, and that $f(u) = 2F(u)$ if $F(u)$ is an odd function of u. Thus we take $F(x) = \tfrac{1}{2}f(x)$ in the interval $0 \leqslant x \leqslant l$, and we *continue* it for other values of x as an odd function of x which has the required periodicity. We obtain the function illustrated in Fig. 10.4. With this choice of $F(x)$ Euler's solution $F(ct + x) - F(ct - x)$ satisfies all the conditions of the problem.

Fig. 10.4

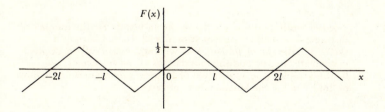

Daniel Bernoulli had quite a different way of tackling the same problem.† He used a more physical argument. It had been known since about 1700, from experimental work on vibrating strings, that *any* vibration could be regarded as made up of a superposition of a *fundamental tone* and *overtones* vibrating at frequencies which are multiples of the basic frequency. (The Pythagoreans had already, 2000 years earlier, connected the properties of whole numbers with music; they knew that when the lengths of strings are in the ratios of simple whole numbers the tones emitted are harmonious.) Mathematically the fundamental tone will be of the form of equation (4), and we must add to this all the overtones. Thus a general displacement $y(x, t)$ is on this view to be written as an infinite linear super-position of different modes of vibration as follows (the Ks being suitable amplitude coefficients):

$$y(x, t) = K_1 \sin \frac{\pi x}{l} \cos \frac{\pi ct}{l} + K_2 \sin \frac{2\pi x}{l} \cos \frac{2\pi ct}{l}$$

$$+ K_3 \sin \frac{3\pi x}{l} \cos \frac{3\pi ct}{l} + \cdots \tag{6}$$

All the terms in this series are zero at $x = 0$ and $x = l$ as required – but what about the initial shape $f(x)$? Put $t = 0$ in (6), then the cosines are all equal to 1, and so we must have

$$f(x) = K_1 \sin \frac{\pi x}{l} + K_2 \sin \frac{2\pi x}{l} + K_3 \sin \frac{3\pi x}{l} + \cdots \tag{7}$$

Does this make sense? More specifically, can a series of smooth sine functions possibly represent a function with a 'corner', such as the function (5) representing the initial displacement of a plucked string? The eighteenth-century mathematicians had a new and unfamiliar problem here, since the function (5) is not a simple function in Euler's sense, and the series (7) is not the

---

† The Bernoulli family holds the record in history for the number of distinguished mathematicians it produced. Daniel Bernoulli (1700–82), the son of Johann, was what we would call an 'applied mathematician'; he laid the foundations of the science of hydrodynamics (the application of Newton's mechanics to the flow of fluids) and of the kinetic theory of gases.

usual Taylor series expansion in powers of x. Euler's view was that Bernoulli's series (7) *cannot* represent the initial shape of the string in general, since a series of sines cannot 'add up' to a function with corners. His argument seemed convincing. After all, the series (7) is a single *formula* (even though it has an infinity of terms), and (5) is not; also each sine function is smooth, with no corners (we say that it has a continuous derivative) – the higher terms in (7) just oscillate faster (Fig. 10.5) – how can a series of such smooth oscillations possibly represent a function such as that in Fig. 10.4? Bernoulli was nevertheless firmly convinced that he had written down a general solution, and there was a lengthy controversy over just what kind of function can be represented by *trigonometric series* of the type (7). The argument went on throughout the eighteenth century, and several mathematicians (in particular Lagrange) came close to the answer, but the first man to give a clear resolution of the problem was Joseph Fourier, who lived from 1768 to 1830. He fully understood the situation but had no rigorous proofs for his results, and his ideas were regarded as so revolutionary that his first paper on the subject was rejected (in fact by Lagrange, in 1807). But Fourier was undaunted and finally published in 1822 his famous work *Théorie analytique de la chaleur* (where essentially the same problem is discussed in connection with heat flow). What was Fourier's insight; was Euler right or Bernoulli? Fourier realised that *both Euler's and Bernoulli's* solutions were correct, and that (surprising, but true) a function with 'corners' can indeed be represented by an infinite trigonometric series as in (7), now called a *Fourier*

Fig. 10.5

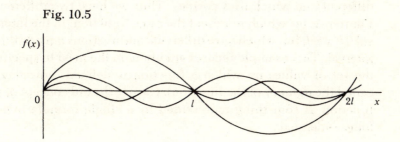

series.† Moreover, to represent $f(x)$ in (5) as the series (7), we must calculate the coefficients in accordance with the formula

$$K_n \doteq \frac{2}{l} \int_0^l f(x) \sin \frac{n\pi x}{l} \, dx. \tag{8}$$

This integral is easily evaluated for our particular $f(x)$ to give the result

$$K_n = 0 \quad \text{when } n \text{ is even,}$$

and

$$K_{2m+1} = (-1)^m \frac{8}{(2m+1)^2 \pi^2} \quad \text{for } m = 0, 1, 2, \ldots$$

With these coefficients the series (7) represents the function (5) in the interval $(0, l)$. What function does it represent outside the interval? It is clearly an odd function of x (since the sines are odd functions), and it has the period $2l$ (since each term has this period); so we have just the function sketched in Fig. 10.4, required by Euler's solution!

If instead we had continued the function (5) as an *even* function of x, we would have obtained the function sketched in Fig. 10.6. This can also be represented as a Fourier series but a

Fig. 10.6

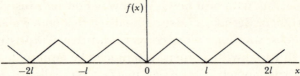

different one which uses cosines. Thus we have two different Fourier series which represent the same 'function' in the inter-val $0 \leq x \leq l$, but which have different continuations outside this interval. This example focuses attention on the need to specify the set of values on which a function is defined (nowadays called the *domain* of the function). Clearly the old concept of a function as something represented by a single formula is no longer adequate.

† In general a Fourier series will contain both sine and cosine terms.

Fourier went further, and claimed that one can represent not only functions with 'corners' (i.e. continuous functions with discontinuous derivatives), but also periodic functions which are themselves discontinuous, by trigonometric series. Take for example the function defined in $0 \leqslant x \leqslant l$ by

$$y = 1 \quad (0 \leqslant x \leqslant \tfrac{1}{2}l), \quad y = 0 \quad (\tfrac{1}{2}l < x \leqslant l),$$

shown in Fig. 10.7. Application of the formula (8) leads to the Fourier sine series

$$\frac{2}{\pi} \left(\sin \frac{\pi x}{l} + \sin \frac{2\pi x}{l} + \frac{1}{3} \sin \frac{3\pi x}{l} + \frac{1}{5} \sin \frac{5\pi x}{l} + \cdots \right), \qquad (9)$$

which represents the odd periodic function shown in Fig. 10.8.†
The claim that such a discontinuous function can be expanded as a Fourier series caused more controversy, involving a new and subtle point. Cauchy, the leading French mathematician of the early nineteenth century – one of the founders of rigorous analysis – claimed to have *proved* that any sum of a series of

Fig. 10.7

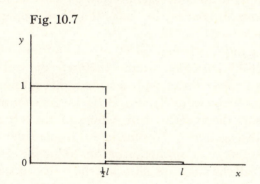

Fig. 10.8

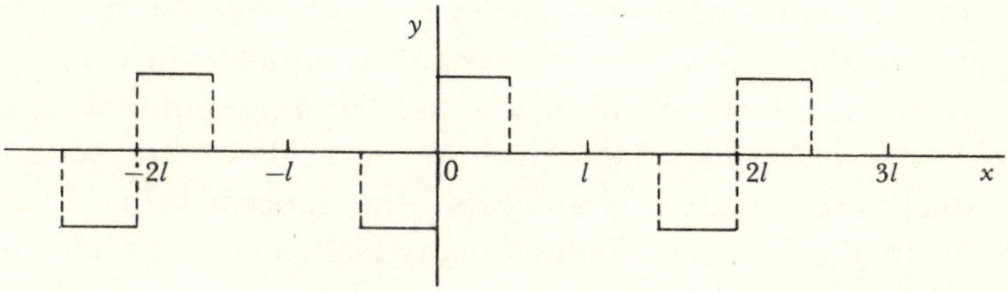

† The coefficient of the nth term is $(2/\pi n) (1 - \cos \tfrac{1}{2}n\pi)$.

continuous functions must itself always be continuous. If this were true, a Fourier series could not possibly represent a discontinuous step-function of the type shown in Fig. 10.8. Cauchy was wrong on this point, and Fourier's boldness was again justified; it is indeed possible for an infinite sum of continuous functions to have discontinuities (a remarkable result)! The need to settle this question led to the first careful study of the convergence properties of series of *functions of x*. This is a more difficult question than that of the convergence of series of numbers, and it was not fully cleared up until some time later. Several mathematicians contributed; the full theory was given around 1850 by Weierstrass who was the foremost architect of rigour in analysis. We have to say that, when we approach a point of discontinuity of $f(x)$, the convergence of the Fourier series is no longer *uniform* in x; which means (very roughly speaking) that the series converges more and more slowly the nearer x gets to the point of discontinuity. Cauchy's result does not apply to all convergent series, but only to those which are *uniformly convergent*, and thus the apparent contradiction is resolved.

The first satisfactory mathematical proofs of Fourier's main results were given by Dirichlet, around 1830. He showed for example that the Fourier series representing a discontinuous function converges to the value $\frac{1}{2}[f(x-0)+f(x+0)]$ at a point of discontinuity, i.e. to the average of the values on the left and the right of the discontinuity. To illustrate this, consider the Fourier sine series for the step-function of Fig. 10.8 at the origin $x = 0$. When $x = 0$ all the sines are zero, and the series adds up, not to $y = 1$, but to $\frac{1}{2}[1+(-1)] = 0$, in accordance with Dirichlet's theorem.

Fourier's work with its startling results helped to give impetus to the renewed emphasis in the nineteenth century on questions of rigour in mathematical proof and on the clarification of basic mathematical concepts. The central part of this story is the creation of analysis – the rigorous form of the infinitesimal calculus – to which many mathematicians contributed. It is beyond our scope to describe this, but we shall conclude the chapter by noting a few points of special interest.

Dirichlet (1805–59), who made many fundamental contributions to both pure and applied mathematics, gave as long ago as 1837 a general definition of a function which was close to our modern one. He suggested, as an example of a 'badly behaved' function $f(x)$, the function which has the value 1 whenever x is rational and 0 whenever x is irrational. This is a perfectly well-defined function but it is *everywhere* discontinuous. There can be no question of 'drawing the graph' of such a thing; it is far removed from Euler's concept of a function as something given by an explicit formula, with a smooth curve and a power series expansion.

The generalized view of the idea of a function made it essential to re-examine the concept of the *definite integral*. The old intuitive idea, deriving from the Greeks, of $\int_a^b f(x)\,dx$ as the 'area under the curve' is applicable without any difficulty to functions with 'corners' and discontinuous step-functions of the type we discussed in connection with Fourier series. We can always break up the region of integration into pieces if necessary, and evaluate the integral as the sum of separate areas, as indicated in Fig. 10.9. The rigorous formulation of the area concept is due to Riemann who made precise earlier work by Cauchy. It restored the definite integral as a primary concept of the calculus, no longer defined in terms of a mere antiderivative (compare our discussion on p. 114); as Fig. 10.9 indicates, the 'area' definition holds for functions which need not possess derivatives everywhere. In 1854 Riemann gave a strict analytical definition of a definite integral based on the old idea of breaking up the area into a large number N of small rectangular strips, taking the total area of these (a sum of N terms), and then

Fig. 10.9

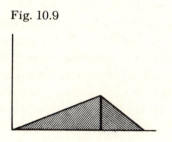
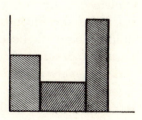

studying the limiting behaviour of such a sum as N tends to infinity and the widths of all the strips tend to zero. This allowed Riemann to define the integral for a wide class of functions and to state necessary and sufficient conditions for a function to be integrable. Riemann's work put the definite integral of the Newton–Leibniz calculus on a rigorous footing. But his definition could not be used for all the generalised functions of the new kind: thus for the completely discontinuous function introduced by Dirichlet the 'area under the curve' has no meaning, and Riemann's sum limit does not exist. If we want to define $\int_a^b f(x)\, dx$ for such functions, we need a more general definition of an integral. Many modern generalisations of Riemann's integral have been given, applicable to much wider classes of functions. A particularly important generalisation is that given by Lebesgue (about 1900): it requires a general (set-theoretic) definition of the length of an interval (called its *measure*) which allows us to say (for example) what 'fraction' of the length of the interval (0, 1) of the real axis is occupied by rational numbers. This is a subtle matter (we obviously cannot give the answer by measuring such lengths with a ruler); we shall return to it in the next chapter. A new branch of analysis called *measure theory* studies questions of this type and has given deep general insights into the concepts of function and integral. Although Dirichlet's function may seem an artificial invention, highly discontinuous functions frequently occur in applications of mathematics (see below), and measure theory is by no means only an abstract *jeu d'esprit*. It is needed for example to give a satisfactory mathematical formulation for the basic concepts of the *theory of probability*.

What about the notion of the derivative, and the problem of clarifying the exact nature of the 'infinitesimal quantities' (Newton's o, Leibniz's dx and dy) which had remained obscure since the seventeenth century? Definitions of a continuous function and of the derivative of a function were given by Cauchy in a series of influential textbooks (1820–30). Cauchy's concepts were essentially those used nowadays, although his formulations were not yet as precise as we would require today. His basic notion was that of a limit (50 years earlier d'Alembert had already insisted on this as the fundamental idea), and the derivative of $y = f(x)$ was defined as

$$f'(x) = \lim_{h \to 0} \frac{f(x+h) - f(x)}{h}.$$

This is just our modern expression, and Cauchy's attempt to define what is meant by a limit was also similar in spirit to the modern definition: 'When the successive values attributed to a variable approach indefinitely a fixed value so as to end by differing from it by as little as one wishes, this last is called the limit of all the others.' In this approach the mystery of the infinitesimals is entirely contained in the notion of the limit. The significant step forward was to regard an infinitesimal no longer as a *fixed* number, with all the difficulties of defining its ('infinitely small'?) magnitude, but as a *variable* number which can take values as small as one wishes. In this way it was possible to give a precise meaning to dy/dx, and there was no longer any need to worry about the nature of the quantities dy and dx as separate entities. In a modern calculus course one is taught very firmly that dy/dx is not a *ratio* but a *limit*, and that dy and dx have no separate meaning.† Has this solved the problem of the nature of the Newton–Leibniz infinitesimals, or has it merely side-stepped it? The reader is invited to form his own view. The formulation of the calculus in terms of limits is the one generally adopted and taught nowadays, but it has not satisfied all mathematicians, and there has always been a feeling that it should be possible to give a precise formulation of the calculus based directly on Newton and Leibniz's 'infinitesimally small' quantities as 'numbers' in their own right. This can indeed be done nowadays, and such a theory was worked out in detail about 20 years ago by A. Robinson who called the subject 'non-standard analysis'. It is based on an extension of the real

---

† Once $f'(x)$ has been determined, one can if one likes define differentials dy and dx as *finite* quantities which are such that their ratio equals $f'(x)$: thus we can write $dx = 1$, $dy = f'(x)$; but this of course adds nothing new. Physicists like to think in terms of finite small increments δx, δy whose ratio $\delta y / \delta x$ is *approximately* $f'(x)$; mathematicians generally prefer to avoid the use of finite differentials. Cauchy himself still tended to think of dy and dx as 'infinitely small' quantities; see Robinson (1966), ch. 10.

number system – the 'hyperreal numbers' – for which the Archimedean axiom (see Chapter 8) does not hold and which includes 'infinitely large' and 'infinitely small' numbers. An elementary 'non-standard' account of the calculus has been given by Keisler (1976).

Once satisfactory definitions had been given of continuity and differentiability, it began to be realised that a *continuous* function (whose curve has no breaks or jumps, so that it can be drawn 'without raising the pencil from the paper') is not necessarily also *differentiable* (i.e. it may not possess a gradient or tangent anywhere). It was certainly realised early on that a function such as that illustrated in Fig. 10.3, whose graph has a 'corner', will have no tangent at that point; but it was generally assumed that, apart from the occurrence of such isolated corners, a function which was continuous must also be differentiable. Various mathematicians in the nineteenth century realised that this was not necessarily so and gave examples of functions which were continuous everywhere but differentiable nowhere. It seems that the first example was given by Bolzano in 1834. (Bernhard Bolzano, 1781–1848, was a Czech scholar who found for himself many of the concepts of rigorous analysis well before others did so. As he worked in Prague, far from the chief centres of mathematics, his work was hardly noticed in his lifetime.) Later examples of continuous functions without tangents were given by Riemann and Weierstrass and attracted more attention. The peculiar behaviour of

Fig. 10.10

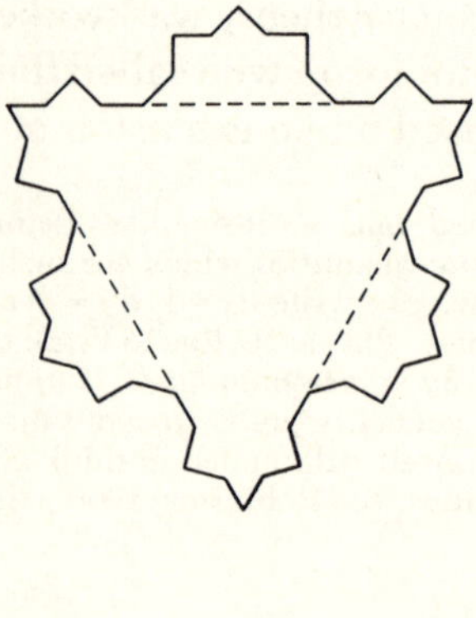

such functions cannot be fully illustrated by drawing a graph: roughly speaking, the 'graph' will *look* smooth, but close inspection will reveal that it is extremely 'crinkly', with a 'corner' or 'prickle' at every point. Such curves can be constructed by elementary methods; a simple example is the 'snowflake curve' suggested by von Koch in 1904. We start with an equilateral triangle and construct prickles by trisecting the sides and erecting further equilateral triangles on the middle portions (Fig. 10.10). This process of subdivision is to be continued indefinitely, so that ultimately there is a prickle at every point of the curve. Obviously many constructions along similar lines are possible.

Such creations may, again, strike the reader as mere mathematical curiosities, not likely to be of interest to the serious-minded mathematician or scientist. Many nineteenth-century mathematicians trained in the classical tradition felt this repugnance; thus Hermite wrote: 'I turn away in horror from this regrettable plague of continuous functions that do not have a derivative at even one point'; and there was an equal lack of interest on the part of physicists and applied mathematicians, used to dealing with projectiles and planets which travel smoothly along orbits according to the laws of Newtonian mechanics. But this attitude was quite misconceived: there are many examples in nature of highly irregular configurations for which continuous non-differentiable functions can provide a useful description. Imagine for example measuring a coastline, first along every headland and beach, then around every rock,

Fig. 10.11

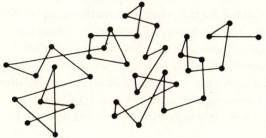

around every grain of sand on the shoreline, and so on. The irregular boundary of a cloud in the sky, and the turbulent dispersion of a blob of black ink in water, are two other examples, and the reader will be able to think of many more: it is reasonable to assert that irregular configurations are the rule and not the exception in nature. (Many examples are given by Mandelbrot (1977) who has coined the term 'fractals' to describe all such irregular shapes.) A characteristic feature of such configurations is that they grow more and more irregular the more closely we look at them: our image depends on the magnification employed and the method of measurement (when we represent the coastline on a map, the irregularity we see depends on the scale employed). The snowflake curve exhibits this property, but it is too regular in form to serve as a realistic model for naturally occurring irregularities. An important example of highly irregular paths in nature is provided by the *Brownian motion*: this refers to the tracks of small particles in a suspension which are suffering deflections caused by continual collisions with molecules which are themselves in irregular random motion (Fig. 10.11). Here the picture of the paths becomes more and more irregular the smaller the time interval at which successive positions are observed. We cannot in practice hope to have full information on the details of the path followed by any particle, and our theoretical description must make use of the concepts of the theory of probability. Thus the problem is treated mathematically as a 'random walk' in which we may assume (for example) that all paths between collisions are of equal length (which can be made infinitely small), but that all directions of motion after a collision are equally probable. The mathematical study of the paths traced out under such assumptions was initiated by the American mathematician N. Wiener (around 1920), and the theory of Brownian motion has become a major and active branch of the theory of probability.

Thus 'fractals' should not be regarded as pathological mathematical monsters, but they do have unusual mathematical properties. Consider for example the total *length* of Koch's snowflake curve: although the curve bounds a finite area, its length is multiplied by a factor $\frac{4}{3}$ at each of the subdivisions, so that after n steps the original length has increased by a factor $(\frac{4}{3})^n$, and this factor increases without limit as n tends to infinity; thus the length is clearly infinite! We are also forced to re-examine the intuitive idea of *dimension*. This question became acute when Peano in 1890 gave an example of a continuous non-differentiable curve which was so 'winding and twisting' that it passed through *every point* of a square area. Mathematicians had always regarded *curves* as one-dimensional configurations and *areas* (or *surfaces*) as two-dimensional (and the number of dimensions could be defined quite simply as the smallest number of parameters required to describe the figure). Peano's 'space-filling' curve seemed to remove the distinction between curves and surfaces; what dimension should be ascribed to it? The answer is: 'it depends how one defines dimension'; alternative definitions are possible and may give different answers in the case of irregular configurations. We briefly outline one possible approach, related to one suggested by the German mathematician Felix Hausdorff (in 1919). It applies to 'self-similar' figures, where we can reduce the scale of the figure in some ratio r (with $1/r$ equal to some integer), and obtain a reduced figure which is of the same form as the original one. Suppose that in this way we subdivide the original figure into N similar parts. In the case of a straight line of unit length we obviously obtain N segments each of length r, with $Nr = 1$; in the case of a unit square we obtain N squares each of area r^2, with $Nr^2 = 1$ (Fig. 10.12). A unit cube will give N cubes each of volume r^3, with $Nr^3 = 1$; in the general case of a D-dimensional figure we shall clearly expect a subdivision for which $Nr^D = 1$.

Fig. 10.12

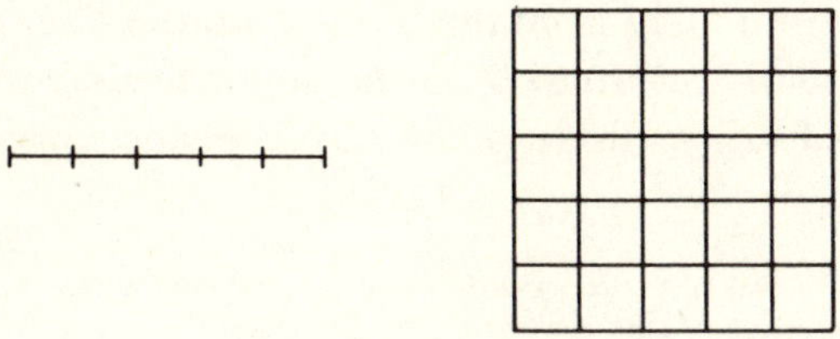

To solve this equation for D we take logarithms and find

$$\log N + D \log r = 0, \qquad \text{or } D = -\frac{\log N}{\log r} = \frac{\log N}{\log (1/r)}.$$

All this is simple enough, but note that, on this definition, D does not necessarily have to be an integer. An example of a shape for which D is non-integral is the snowflake curve, Fig. 10.10. By virtue of its construction this is a self-similar configuration, but a subdivision in the ratio $r = \frac{1}{3}$ now clearly gives us $N = 4$ similar parts! Thus in this case $D = \log 4/\log 3$, and so the dimension of the snowflake curve is a number which lies between 1 and 2. With other constructions other non-integral values of D can be obtained (see Mandelbrot 1977); while for Peano's space-filling curve it is found, as might be expected, that $D = 2$. But, as we have mentioned, other definitions of dimension can be given; and the general theory of the concept of dimension is a deep problem in topology which has not yet been fully resolved.

We note finally that space-filling curves also provide useful models of naturally occurring structures. Examples are 'branching networks' such as a river system, where we consider a main river together with all its tributaries, then the tributaries of the tributaries, and so on down to the very smallest side-streams; or a vascular system such as the complex intercommunicating set of vessels in the human lung. The mathematical model of such structures is a 'tree' like the one illustrated in Fig. 10.13, where we start with a 'trunk' which divides at one end into two branches, each of these branches dividing into two, and so on indefinitely. With such a network we can reach any point in the plane.† Suppose we regard the network as a model of a river system (all streams having zero width), and we follow the river bank continuously from the point A on the river's mouth until we eventually return to B on the opposite side: evidently we have traced out a single plane-filling Peano curve which

---

† There are complications (which we ignore here) when we consider the properties of the tree carefully: for example can we prevent its branches from intersecting themselves?

Fig. 10.13

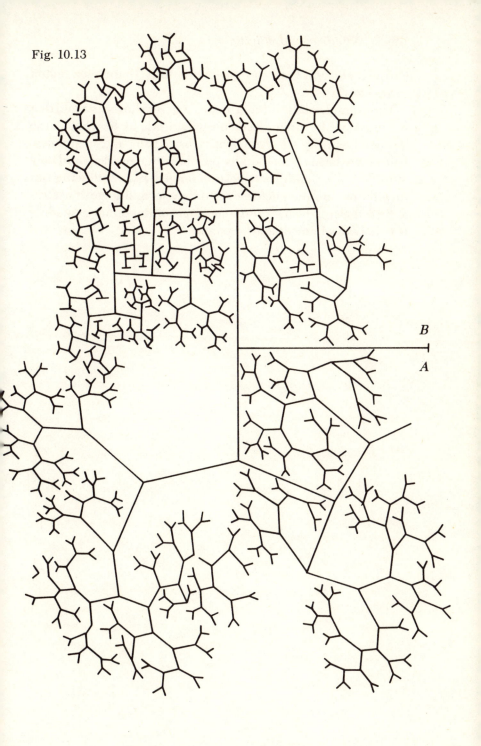

B

A

joins *A* and *B*. Our river network thus drains its region completely.

The example of these 'unorthodox' curves shows us again that we must not be prejudiced in our attitude as to what is the 'proper business' of mathematicians. Again and again new fields have been opened up by people with new ideas and new attitudes. We should not be discouraged from following our inspiration into such fields, even if they seem strange or useless at first: the significance and 'relevance' of important new ideas is not always immediately apparent.

11

Transfinite numbers

In this book we have been discussing the concepts of 'number' and 'infinity'. It will have been apparent to the reader that, as soon as one studies these concepts in any depth, they become very closely related: compare for example our discussion of real numbers in Chapter 3. In our last chapter we discuss the notion of 'infinite' (or 'transfinite') numbers. The modern theory – one of the most beautiful and important creations in mathematics – is mainly due to Georg Cantor (1846–1918).

The creators of analysis in the nineteenth century had insisted that the lack of clarity about 'infinity' (like that about infinitesimals) was to be removed by abandoning any attempt to treat infinity as a *number*. Instead they restricted the discussion to quantities which could become 'as large as one liked', which were 'potentially', not 'actually', infinite. In a calculus course one is discouraged from writing $1/0 = \infty$, since ∞ is not a number like 5 or $\pi/2$; but one may say that $1/x \to \infty$ as $x \to 0$, which means that $1/x$ can be made larger than *any* given (finite) number N by making x small enough; note that here the 'infinitesimally small' x and the 'infinitely large' $1/x$ appear together. This caution about ∞ is essential, because the standard rules of arithmetic (see Chapter 3) apply to finite numbers only; carelessness about this point leads to the familiar mathematical paradoxes which arise when we secretly 'divide by zero'. 'Potentially infinite' collections, that is to say, finite sets which can be made larger and larger without limit, had already been considered by Aristotle who distinguished them from 'actual', 'completed', infinite sets. From ancient times, of course, examples of 'actually' infinite sets had been familiar: the collection of *all* the positive integers, say; or all the *even* positive integers; or all positive fractions; or all the points on a line, all the points in a plane, and so on. If we are to do mathematics with such infinite sets we must find a way of comparing them, so that we can decide whether the 'size' of one set is equal to, or perhaps greater than, that of another. These are old questions which have been discussed throughout history, not only by mathematicians – scholastic philosophers in the Middle Ages speculated on the nature of such infinite collections as the number of angels that could balance on the point of a needle. Galileo, in his *Dialogue on Two New Sciences* (1638), also speculates on the subject (compare Stein 1976, ch. 18). Cantor was much influenced by earlier thinking on the subject. Following work by his friend Dedekind he showed (starting around 1873) that the attitude of Cauchy and Weierstrass in rejecting 'completed' infinite sets from mathematics was over-cautious, and that it was indeed possible to give clear and rigorous rules for calculating with such sets, provided one was willing to admit that these rules may differ from those for finite sets (and may, as we shall see, put strain on one's preconceived notions as to how sets 'ought to' behave).

Cantor's basic idea which makes it possible to compare infinite sets is extremely simple, and extremely powerful. How do we compare finite sets, for example a collection of m boys and n girls? Are there more boys or more girls? With finite sets we can just *count the numbers* in each set and compare them. With infinite sets elementary counting is not possible, since the counting process never ends. But we can do something else – something even more basic – which does not require us to count. We can start a dance in which each boy partners a girl and, when they have all taken their partners, we just see whether there are any *unpaired* boys left (then the number of boys is greater than the number of girls) or any unpaired girls (then the number of girls is greater than the number of boys) or, if *everybody is paired off* and no one left unpaired, then the number of boys is exactly *equal* to the number of girls. Note carefully that, to establish this equality, we do not actually need to know *how many* boys or girls there are in the set.

But this method also works for infinite sets! Let us try it out by comparing the set of *natural numbers* 1, 2, 3, . . . , with the set of *even integers* 2, 4, 6, ... (we consider only positive numbers but the argument easily extends to negative numbers). Can the members of these two sets be paired off, *with no member left unpaired*? The answer is, clearly, 'yes': we just have to associate 1 with 2, 2 with 4, 3 with 6, ..., and generally n with $2n$. Thus we must conclude that the 'number' of integers 1, 2, 3, ..., is *the same* as the number of even integers 2, 4, 6, ...! This number, which is clearly not finite, is our first *transfinite number*: it is denoted by $\aleph_0$ ($\aleph$ is the Hebrew letter 'aleph', so the number is called 'aleph zero'). It is not to be called 'infinity': that is too vague a concept.

The conclusion that our two sets have 'the same' number of elements is a straightforward deduction from our pairing principle, and yet it seems absurd. After all, the even integers do not include the elements 1, 3, 5, ... (technically, the even integers form a *proper subset* of the set of all the integers), so there are surely *fewer* of them than the numbers in the set of *all* the integers! Well – it all depends on what you mean by 'fewer'! The confusions and apparent paradoxes in this subject arise from the transfer of everyday language, acquired from experience with finite collections, to infinite sets where we must train ourselves to work strictly with the mathematical rules of the game even though they lead to surprising results. As it happens often in the history of mathematics, Cantor's fellow-mathematicians when presented with his bold and unorthodox ideas were reluctant to abandon traditional ways of thought and language, and there was much opposition (this no doubt contributed to Cantor's frequent states of depression; proper recognition came to him only towards the end of his life). By now these controversies are a part of history, and Cantor's arguments have long since been accepted as not only mathematically sound but also as highly significant for the development of mathematics.

The peculiar property of infinite sets which is illustrated by our pairing of all the integers with the even integers is that *an infinite set can be 'put into one-to-one correspondence' with a proper subset of itself*. This is a general property of infinite sets which is not possessed by any finite set (convince yourself of this!), and it can be used to give a formal definition of what we mean by an infinite set. Such a definition had in fact been proposed by Dedekind in 1872 and gave impetus to Cantor's work.

Now let us look at the number of elements in some other infinite sets. How about the set of all (positive) *rational numbers* a/b (a, b positive integers)? Are there 'more of them' than $\aleph_0$? One would surely think so.... Here we have a rather more subtle problem. Unlike the sets 1, 2, 3, ..., or 2, 4, 6, ..., the rationals cannot be arranged 'in order', such that any fraction a/b is followed by the 'next bigger' one; there is no 'next bigger' one. Recall (p. 32) the property of the rationals of being *dense*: between any two rational numbers there is an infinite number of other rationals.

Nevertheless, the rationals can also be paired off with the integers, so that their 'number' is also $\aleph_0$. Any set with this property is said to be *countable* or *denumerable*. The denumerability of the rationals was demonstrated by Cantor in 1873. It is necessary to devise a way of 'counting' the fractions a/b, such that any fraction a/b is uniquely associated with one (and only one) integer. This can in fact be done in many ways; any one of them will do. We may for example arrange all the fractions in a square array as follows, with all fractions having denominator 1 in the first row, all fractions having denominator 2 in the second row, and so on:†

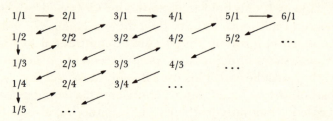

Now we can associate each occupant of the array uniquely with an integer (1, 2, 3, ...) by following the path indicated by the arrows. (Note that it is useless to try to number off by going

† We are here treating $\frac{1}{2}$ and $\frac{2}{4}$, etc., as separate fractions. This makes our argument simpler, but it is not necessary. The proof sketched here is not Cantor's original proof, but a simpler one that he gave later.

along the whole of the first row, then the second row, and so on – why?) In this way a/b (the fraction in column 'a' and row 'b' of the table) is assigned a definite integer, depending on a and b. The reader can work out the formula for this association as an exercise, but it is not needed for the purpose of our proof: just *how* the numbering is done is not important; what is important is *that* it can be done. Thus the set of rationals is denumerable! This result is actually a special case of a general theorem: suppose we have a denumerable collection of denumerable sets $S_1, S_2, S_3, \ldots$; then the union of these sets is also denumerable. In the above example S_1 is the set of rationals with denominator 1, S_2 the set of those with denominator 2, and so on. An extension of this type of argument can be used to show (see p. 154 below) that the set of all *algebraic numbers* is also denumerable.

You might by now begin to think that all infinite sets are denumerable. If this were indeed so the subject of the size of infinite sets would not be terribly interesting, as they would all be equivalent. Towards the end of 1873 Cantor found the crucial result which established different 'orders of infinity': he proved that the set of *real numbers* is not denumerable (or, equivalently: the set of *all points on the line* is not denumerable). The proof is very simple, and very ingenious.† The idea is to show that no labelling with integers can possibly be carried out which includes all the real numbers. It is in fact sufficient to consider the real numbers in some finite interval, say (0, 1), of the real axis (where the end points are excluded). If this set *is* denumerable, then we can label these real numbers with the integers, writing them as $a_1, a_2, a_3, \ldots$, and we then write each one as a *non-terminating* decimal as follows:

$$a_1 = 0.a_{11}a_{12}a_{13}\ldots,$$
$$a_2 = 0.a_{21}a_{22}a_{23}\ldots,$$
$$a_3 = 0\, a_{31}a_{32}a_{33}\ldots,$$

etc. (Note that any terminating decimal, for example 0.5, can always be written in this way by writing it as 0.4999...) Every real number has a unique decimal representation of this type

---

† Again, we give not Cantor's original proof, but a simpler one, discovered by Cantor in 1890.

(see p. 36). To show that any such list cannot possibly contain *all* the real numbers between 0 and 1 we now construct a real number between 0 and 1 which is not in the above list as follows: we look at the 'diagonal' digits $a_{11}, a_{22}, a_{33}, \ldots$, ($a_{nn}$ is the nth digit in the decimal representation of a_n). We then form digits $b_1, b_2, b_3, \ldots$, which are such that b_1 differs from a_{11}, b_2 differs from a_{22}, b_3 differs from a_{33}, and so on; for example we can take $b_n = 9$ if $a_{nn} \neq 9$, and $b_n = 1$ if $a_{nn} = 9$. Now we use the bs so defined to construct the real number

$$b = 0.b_1 b_2 b_3 \ldots b_n \ldots .$$

Then b differs from each a_i in our (denumerated) list! It can only be equal to an a_i if *each* digit in the decimal representation of b equals the corresponding digit in the decimal representation of a_i. But b cannot equal a_1 because $b_1 \neq a_{11}$; it cannot be a_2 because $b_2 \neq a_{22}$; and so on: it cannot be a_n because the nth digit in b differs from the nth digit in a_n. Thus we have shown that our list does not contain all the real numbers.

The transfinite number to be associated with the set of real numbers between 0 and 1 is thus not $\aleph_0$; it is called c (for 'continuum'). This gives us a second transfinite number which is *greater* than $\aleph_0$. Why can we say that it is greater? An infinite set A is *smaller* than a set B if the set A is in one-to-one correspondence with a subset of B but not with B itself. The rationals between 0 and 1 form a subset of the reals, so we see that $\aleph_0 < c$. Thus Cantor's notion of pairing can be used to give a perfectly well-defined meaning to the concepts of 'equal', 'greater' and 'less' for infinite sets (and these, moreover, are consistent with the usual meaning for finite collections).

There are other ways of demonstrating that the real numbers are not denumerable. A very instructive, more 'geometrical', approach is to think of the real numbers between 0 and 1 as points on the real line and to suppose again that they are denumerable, so that we can label them $a_1, a_2, a_3, \ldots$, and display them on the line (Fig. 11.1). Now *enclose* all these

Fig. 11.1

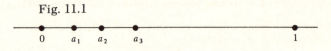

points in small intervals of the line as follows: an interval of length (say) $1/10$ is drawn containing the point a_1, an interval of length $1/10^2$ contains a_2, an interval of length $1/10^3$ contains a_3, and so on (these intervals may of course overlap, but this does not affect the argument). The *total length* of all these intervals, containing our points $a_1, a_2, a_3, \ldots$, is $1/10 + 1/10^2 + 1/10^3 + \cdots$, and the sum of this geometric series is

$$\frac{10^{-1}}{1 - 10^{-1}} = \frac{1}{9}.$$

Thus we have shown that any denumerable set of points can be enclosed in a set of intervals of total length only $\frac{1}{9}$, which indicates that such a set cannot cover the whole length of the line from 0 to 1. In fact, there is nothing special about the result $\frac{1}{9}$: we could have used, instead, intervals $\varepsilon/10,\ \varepsilon/10^2, \ldots$, with arbitrary ε, thus enclosing our denumerable set of points in a set of intervals of total length $\varepsilon/9$, and this length can be made *as small as we please* by taking ε small enough! This approach can be used to construct a well-defined way of measuring the 'length' of the interval $(0, 1)$ occupied by a denumerable set of points (such as the rationals); such a set is said to have the *measure zero*. It shows strikingly that the set of rational numbers is a smaller infinite set than the set of reals.

The result that the set of real numbers is 'larger' than the set of rationals shows, of course, that the set of real numbers must contain numbers other than the rationals: so Cantor's approach gives us a new proof, although an indirect one, that irrational numbers exist. There are many related interesting questions which we cannot discuss here; the subject of transfinite numbers has become a major branch of mathematics. Cantor's real breakthrough was to widen the whole scope of mathematics and of the idea of 'number' in particular; he created an entire 'transfinite arithmetic' with its own rules for calculating with transfinite numbers. What other transfinite numbers are there, beyond the two ($\aleph_0$ and c) we have encountered so far? That is a deep and difficult question which has not yet been fully answered (see below), but let us note one important point. The

numbers $\aleph_0$ and c are (transfinite) *cardinal numbers*; they have
to do with a process analogous to counting the members of a set
and are similar to 'one', 'two', 'three', ... In finite arithmetic we
also have *ordinal numbers* ('first', 'second', 'third', ...) which
tell us about the *order* of the elements in a set. In the finite case
we need not bother too much about the distinction between the
arithmetic of cardinal and the arithmetic of ordinal numbers;
there are no significant differences. In the case of infinite sets
this is no longer the case, and we have to study and define the
possibility of *ordering relations* very carefully for such sets.
This leads to a separate theory of *transfinite ordinal numbers*
which was also given by Cantor; its details are beyond our
scope. It turns out that the apparently simple notion of ordering
leads in the case of infinite sets to some of the very deepest
questions in modern mathematics. We should also stress that
the construction of number systems is by no means a finished
chapter in mathematics. A. Robinson's extension of the number
system which underlies his non-standard analysis was mentioned in Chapter 10, and a very interesting recent approach
is due to Conway (1976), whose very general construction
encompasses the real numbers, the transfinite cardinals and
ordinals and in addition many remarkable generalisations of
infinite and infinitesimal numbers.

Some questions of immediate interest in connection with the
set of real numbers are the following:

(1) What about the difference between algebraic and transcendental numbers? (Recall (p. 65) that algebraic numbers are
defined as roots of $P(x) = 0$, where $P(x)$ is a polynomial with
integer coefficients, and remember that Liouville had in 1844
constructed numbers which are not algebraic.) Now Cantor
showed that not only the rationals but the much more general set
of algebraic numbers forms a denumerable subset of the real
numbers. (To show this one proves that the set of all polynomials with integer coefficients is denumerable, and this is
done by pairing off this set with the rational numbers.) Since
the reals are not denumerable, we have here another proof
that transcendental (non-algebraic) numbers exist; and the
argument shows, furthermore, that it is the transcendental

numbers which give to the real number system the density which results in a cardinal number greater than $\aleph_0$. Transcendental numbers are not occasional curiosities: *all* numbers except those in a set of measure zero are transcendental! Unfortunately this type of existence proof does not allow us to construct any *examples* of the objects whose existence is proved; they are 'indirect', 'non-constructive' proofs. Such proofs, while perfectly logical, are in a sense not very satisfying, and attempts have been made from time to time to banish them from mathematics. But the cost is too high; it cannot be done without sacrificing large and essential aspects of mathematics.

(2) What about the cardinal number to be associated with *all* the reals, i.e. all the points on the whole infinite real line; is this greater than c? Another surprise: the cardinal of any segment of the real line is just c; it is the *density* of the points that matters, not the length of the interval. To show this we have to demonstrate a one-to-one correspondence between points of the two segments we wish to compare. This is illustrated in Fig. 11.2 for the comparison of the intervals $AB = (0, 1)$ and $AC = (0, \infty)$.

(3) An even stranger result is obtained when we ask about the number of points in a square (a *two-dimensional* set of points); surely *this* must have a cardinal number greater than c. That is certainly what Cantor believed at first, and he tried very hard to prove it, but in 1874 he found to his own amazement that he was wrong: the cardinal number is also c! (He wrote to Dedekind; 'I see it, but I don't believe it'.) The demonstration is simple enough: as always, we must establish a one-to-one correspondence, in this case between points (x, y) of the unit square (Fig. 11.3) and points on the line segment from 0 to 1. This can be done (apart from minor complications) by writing x

Fig. 11.2

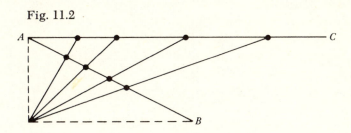

and y as decimals: $x = 0.a_1a_2a_3 \ldots$, $y = 0.b_1b_2b_3 \ldots$, and then associating with the point (x, y) of the square the unique point $z = 0.a_1b_1a_2b_2a_3b_3 \ldots$ of the line segment (whose decimal representation is constructed by mixing up the representations of x and y in the way indicated). Clearly we can show by a similar process that the cardinal number of the points in a *cube* is also c, and so on. The cardinal numbers of sets of points in spaces of arbitrary dimension are all equal; 'cardinality' is not the same as 'dimension'. This startling result underlines again, though in a different way from that discussed in the last chapter, the difficulties involved in giving a satisfactory definition of dimension.

After all this we may now begin to wonder whether there are in fact any cardinal numbers other than $\aleph_0$ and c. The answer is *yes*! Cantor showed that: *given any set A, we can always construct a set B with a greater cardinal number.* Thus we can go on constructing ever greater cardinal numbers, and there is no greatest one. The proof is very beautiful but, as we are dealing here with a very general theorem in set theory, the definitions and arguments are necessarily very abstract. Given A, the set B is defined to be the set whose elements are *all the subsets of the given set A* (including A itself and the empty set $\emptyset$). For example, if A is the finite set $\{1,2,3\}$, then B is the set whose elements are $\{1,2,3\}$, $\{1,2\}$, $\{1,3\}$, $(2,3)$, $\{1\}$, $\{2\}$, $\{3\}$ and $\emptyset$. Note that B contains $8 = 2^3$ elements. (*Exercise*: show that, if A contains N elements, where N is any positive integer, then B

Fig. 11.3

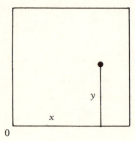

contains 2^N elements.) B is called the *power set* associated with A (we are not, of course, confining our arguments to finite sets).

We now show that there can be no one-to-one correspondence between the elements a of A and the elements of B (the subsets of A). Suppose there is such a pairing: $a \leftrightarrow S_a$, so that S_a *is the subset of A corresponding to the element a of A*. The subset S_a may or may not itself contain the element a to which S_a has been assigned. So the sets S_a are of two types: those which themselves do contain the element a (to which they are assigned), and those which do not. Now we construct a subset T of A which cannot be correlated with any element a! T *is the subset of A which consists of all those elements x of A such that S_x does not contain x.* This set differs from all the S_a above, i.e. T cannot be identified with any of the S_a. For, if S_a contains a, then T (from its definition) does not; and it cannot be an S_a which does not contain a: if S_a does not contain a, then T (from its definition) does! Hence T is not included in the above correspondence, and the proof is complete. It is easy to see that the cardinal number of B must be greater than that of A: there is a one-to-one correspondence between elements a of A and the subset of B which consists of all *one-element* subsets $\{a\}$ of A.

What happens when A and B are infinite sets? One remarkable relation is fairly easily obtained. Suppose A is the set of natural numbers, containing $\aleph_0$ elements. Then any infinite subset of A, consisting of numbers N_i such that $0 < N_1 < N_2 < N_3 < \cdots$, corresponds to a 'binary decimal'

$$\frac{1}{2^{N_1}} + \frac{1}{2^{N_2}} + \frac{1}{2^{N_3}} + \cdots,$$

and thus to some *real number* between 0 and 1. The totality of all such subsets gives the real number continuum, and thus we have the interesting equation $2^{\aleph_0} = c$ relating the transfinite cardinals $\aleph_0$ and c.

There are, however, disquieting aspects to Cantor's result that, given any set whatsoever, we can always find a bigger set. It leads us into logical difficulty. Suppose we contemplate the *set of all cardinal numbers*. Then we see that there can be no such thing, for, given this set, we can immediately construct a set with a *larger* cardinal, so that our original set cannot have contained *all* the cardinals! Many such logical paradoxes arise in set theory when we look at very general sets: they indicate that the 'naive' concept of a set, as simply any collection without restriction of any kind, is not after all so simple when it comes to infinite collections, and one must think very carefully about the 'rules of the game' in set theory if one wants to avoid contradictions. This realisation has let to an immense amount of work on the logical foundations of mathematics; it is by no means completed.

We note finally another curious point which has proved to be unexpectedly difficult. This is the question whether the cardinal number c of the real-number continuum is the 'next bigger' cardinal after $\aleph_0$. We have not assumed this (that is why we have not called this cardinal $\aleph_1$); in other words, we have left open the question whether there are infinite sets with cardinal numbers *between* $\aleph_0$ and c – or, what is the same thing, whether there are infinite sets of points on the real line which are not denumerable and which also cannot be put into one-to-one correspondence with the real numbers. This question arises naturally when one compares infinite sets, and it might seem at first sight that it should not be too difficult to settle. Cantor believed that there were no such intermediate cardinal numbers – he called this the *continuum hypothesis* – and he tried for many years to find a proof. He failed, and so has everyone else who has tried his hand. The deep-seated nature of the problem has been demonstrated by Kurt Gödel (in 1936) and Paul Cohen (in 1963). They have proved that the continuum hypothesis cannot be deduced from the standard axioms of set theory, but that, if it is adopted as a separate mathematical principle, then no contradictions will occur. These results are most remarkable. They mean that the continuum hypothesis is, in a deep sense, *unprovable*. Any decision about it involves consideration of the basic axioms to be adopted for set theory and thus for the whole of mathematics. We remain free to speculate about the 'right' form of these axioms, and whether our eventual choice will allow us to conclude that the continuum hypothesis is either true or false. These are questions about the very nature of mathematics: they remain open. The notion of infinity, so mysterious and tantalising since the days of Zeno, has not lost its power to intrigue us and to produce puzzles of deep and subtle complexity.

APPENDIX

Essay topics

As mentioned in the preface, this list is intended to help the student to pursue in greater depth something touched upon in the text, or suggested by it. A good essay should:

    (i) contain some discussion of mathematical ideas (i.e. it should not be just a list of dates, or unexplained problems);

  (ii) be interesting to the reader;

 (iii) be comprehensible to the reader (who may be presumed to have a little mathematical ability);

 (iv) give some indication that the writer understands the ideas involved;

  (v) be written essentially in the writer's own words;

 (vi) not complicate matters when a simple explanation is possible (thus it should not introduce unnecessary technical words).

The exact length of the essay is immaterial, but 3000–4000 words is recommended as a norm. The sources consulted should be listed at the end of the essay (the works listed in the bibliography will serve as a guide).

1 'The historical growth of a science does not necessarily pass through the stages in which we now develop it in our instruction.' Does the history of mathematics bear this out?

2 'In all the records of ancient civilisations there is evidence of some preoccupation with arithmetic over and above the needs of everyday life.'

3 'Oriental mathematics never seems to have been emancipated from the millennial influence of the problems in technology and administration, for the use of which it had been invented.'

4 'Already the pronounced tendency towards tediousness, which seems to be inherent in elementary mathematics, might plead for its late origin, since the creative mathematician would prefer to pay his attention to the interesting and beautiful problems' (Speiser). Describe some 'interesting and beautiful' mathematical problems of ancient origin, and their modern treatment.

5 'The eighteenth century had the misfortune to come after the seventeenth and before the nineteenth.' Discuss (in relation to mathematics).

6 Bertrand Russell claimed that it was the nineteenth century that discovered the nature of pure mathematics. What did he have in mind?

7 Mathematics in China and India.

8 The attitude to mathematics of Plato and Aristotle.

9 Euclid.

10 The Greeks' study of conic sections.

11 The mathematics of the Islamic period.

12 Mathematicians of the French Revolution.

13 The Bernoulli family.

14 Euler.

15 'Gauss is sometimes described as the last mathematician to know everything in his subject.'

16 Negative numbers.

17 Fractions: decimal, sexagesimal, and 'unit'.

18 The discovery of logarithms.

19 The history of the square root of minus one.

20 The solution of algebraic equations.

21 The number π.

22 Why are vectors so important in science and mathematics?

23 Squaring the circle.

24 'The method of exhaustion is a rigorous but sterile method.'

25 To what extent can the Greeks be said to have anticipated the 'infinitesimal calculus'?

26 'Seventeenth- and eighteenth-century mathematicians had little understanding of infinite series.' Discuss, with illustrations.

27 'Infinite processes were still carelessly handled in the eighteenth century and much of the work of the leading mathematicians of that period impresses us as wildly enthusiastic experimentation.' Discuss, with examples.

28 'Fermat, the true inventor of the differential calculus' (Laplace).

29 'Taking mathematics from the beginning of the world to the time of Newton, what he has done is much the better half' (Leibniz).

30 Did Newton and Leibniz 'invent' the calculus?

31 Joseph Fourier.

BIBLIOGRAPHY

The literature on the history of mathematics is immense. We give a selection of books and articles, at varying levels of difficulty, which we have found useful and which are recommended for further reading and deeper study. Books of general interest are listed first, followed by references related to particular chapters; some items additional to those mentioned in the text have been included, and some brief indications of scope and content have been given. Many further references will be found in the works listed here.

GENERAL WORKS
(i) Histories
E. T. Bell (1945) *The Development of Mathematics* (2nd edn) (McGraw-Hill, New York). (Chatty history of ideas.)

E. T. Bell (1937) *Men of Mathematics* (Gollancz, London). (Entertaining light reading, but as a history must be treated with caution.)

N. Bourbaki (1969) *Eléments d'histoire des mathématiques* (Hermann, Paris). (Collection of historical appendixes from the famous Bourbaki texts; highbrow).

C. B. Boyer (1968) *A History of Mathematics* (Wiley, New York). (Good American College text; many references.)

F. Cajori (1924) *A History of Mathematics* (Macmillan, New York). (Rather old but full of interesting items.)

F. Cajori (1928) *A History of Mathematical Notations*, Vol. 1: *Notations in Elementary Mathematics* (The Open Court Publishing Co., La Salle, Ill.) (Reprinted 1974).

P. Dedron & J. Itard (1978) *Mathematics and Mathematicians 1 and 2* (Open University Press, Milton Keynes). (Set book for Open University course.)

J. Dieudonné *et al.* (1978) *Abrégé d'histoire des mathématiques 1700–1900 I and II* (Hermann, Paris). (Authoritative 'digest' at advanced undergraduate standard.)

J. M. Dubbey (1970) *Development of Modern Mathematics* (Butterworths, London).

H. Eves (1969) *An Introduction to the History of Mathematics* (3rd edn) (Holt, Rinehart and Winston, New York). (Good for earlier history and elementary mathematics.)

J. E. Hofmann (1963) *Geschichte der Mathematik I, II and III* (Sammlung Göschen: De Gruyter, Berlin). (Extensive list of sources; indispensable for the serious historian.) (English translation, without sources, published as *The History of Mathematics to 1800* by Littlefield, Adams and Co., Totowa, N.J., 1967).

M. Kline (1972) *Mathematical Thought from Ancient to Modern Times* (Oxford University Press, New York). (Useful for reference.)

D. J. Struik (1954) *A Concise History of Mathematics* (Bell, London). (Masterly summary, quite highbrow. Emphasises social aspects.)

(ii) Ideas and concepts

E. T. Bell (1952) *Mathematics: Queen and Servant of Science* (Bell, London).

R. Courant & H. Robbins (1941) *What is Mathematics?* (Oxford University Press, London). (A superb survey.)

T. Dantzig (1947) *Number, the Language of Science* (Allen and Unwin, London). (A stimulating essay.)

H. Eves & C. V. Newsom (1965) *An Introduction to the Foundations and Fundamental Concepts of Mathematics* (Holt, Rinehart and Winston, New York).

H. B. Griffiths & P. J. Hilton (1970) *A Comprehensive Textbook of Classical Mathematics: A Contemporary Interpretation* (Van Nostrand, London). (Technical survey of 'modern mathematics', based on a course for school-teachers.)

T. S. Kuhn (1970) *The Structure of Scientific Revolutions* (University of Chicago Press). (A seminal work in the history of scientific ideas.)

I. Lakatos (1976) *Proofs and Refutations* (Cambridge University Press). (Profound and entertaining discussion of the development of mathematical ideas.)

G. Polya (1948) *How to Solve It* (Princeton University Press). (Shows how the mathematician sets about solving a problem.)

H. Rademacher & O. Toeplitz (1957) *The Enjoyment of Mathematics* (Princeton University Press). (Analysis of interesting problems for the non-specialist.)

W. W. Sawyer (1955) *Prelude to Mathematics* (Penguin Books, Harmondsworth), and

W. W. Sawyer (1970) *The Search for Pattern* (Penguin Books, Harmondsworth). (Good popular works.)

S. K. Stein (1976) *Mathematics, the Man-Made Universe* (3rd edn) (Freeman, San Francisco). (A selection of topics at a level similar to ours.)

S. J. Taylor (1970) *Exploring Mathematical Thought* (Ginn, London). (Concise introduction to important ideas and to mathematical notation.)

(iii) Source books and anthologies

H. Midonick (1965) *The Treasury of Mathematics* (Peter Owen, London).

J. R. Newman (1956) *The World of Mathematics*, vols. 1–4 (Simon and Schuster, New York).

D. J. Struik (1969) *A Source Book in Mathematics, 1200–1800* (Harvard University Press, Cambridge, Mass.).

(iv) **Journals**

Historia Mathematica (Academic Press, New York), and
Archive for History of Exact Sciences (Springer, New York). (Valuable
sources of articles on special topics.)

CHAPTER 1

J. M. Dubbey (1978) *The Mathematical Work of Charles Babbage*
(Cambridge University Press).

C. H. Edwards (1979) *The Historical Development of the Calculus*
(Springer, New York). (See ch. 6 for a fuller account of the introduction of
logarithms than is given here.)

H. H. Goldstine (1972) *The Computer from Pascal to von Neumann*
(Princeton University Press).

T. L. Heath (1921) *A History of Greek Mathematics*, vols 1 and 2
(Clarendon Press, Oxford). (The standard work.)

O. Neugebauer (1969) *The Exact Sciences in Antiquity* (Dover, New York).
(An account of ancient mathematics, by one of the leading interpreters.)

H. Rademacher & O. Toeplitz (1957) *The Enjoyment of Mathematics*
(Princeton University Press).

B. L. van der Waerden (1954) *Science Awakening* (Noordhoff, Groningen).
(Very readable account of ancient and Greek mathematics.)

C. Zaslavsky (1973) *Africa Counts* (Prindle, Weber and Schmidt, Boston,
Mass.) (African number systems.)

CHAPTER 2

H. Davenport (1970) *The Higher Arithmetic* (Hutchinson, London).
(Readable introduction to the theory of numbers; many useful
references.)

U. Dudley (1978) *Elementary Number Theory* (2nd edn) (Freeman, San
Francisco).

H. M. Edwards (1977) *Fermat's Last Theorem* (Springer, New York). (See
especially the first three chapters; contains much interesting history.)

T. Hall (transl. A. Froderberg) (1970) *Carl Friedrich Gauss* (MIT Press,
Cambridge, Mass.). (Short account of life and mathematics.)

M. E. Hellman (1979) The mathematics of public-key cryptography.
Scientific American **241** (no. 2), 130–9 (August 1979).

G. B. Kolata (1980) Testing for primes gets easier. *Science* **209**, 1503–4.

D. J. Newman (1980) Simple analytic proof of the prime number theorem.
The American Mathematical Monthly **87**, 693–6.

S. R. Ranganathan (1967) *Ramanujan, the Man and the Mathematician* (Asia
Publishing House, London).

E. J. Scourfield (1979) Perfect numbers and Mersenne primes. *Mathematical
Spectrum* **12**, 84–92.

CHAPTER 5

F. Cajori (1924) *A History of Mathematics* (Macmillan, New York).

CHAPTER 6

A. Baker (1975) *Transcendental Number Theory* (Cambridge University Press, London). (An advanced text.)

P. Beckmann (1971) *A History of* π (St Martin's Press, New York).

R. Courant & H. Robbins (1941) *What is Mathematics?* (Oxford University Press, London)

H. Davenport (1970) *The Higher Arithmetic* (Hutchinson, London).

O. Ore (1957) *Niels Henrik Abel* (University of Minnesota Press, Minneapolis).

I. Stewart (1973) *Galois Theory* (Chapman and Hall, London).

CHAPTER 7

M. J. Crowe (1967) *A History of Vector Analysis* (University of Notre Dame Press). (Non-technical history of vector analysis and its principal protagonists.)

R. W. Feldmann (1962) History of elementary matrix theory. *The Mathematics Teacher* **55**, 482–4, 589–90, 657–9.

W. R. Hamilton (1967) *The Mathematical Papers of Sir William Rowan Hamilton*, vol. 3: *Algebra* (ed. H. Halberstam & R. E. Ingram) (Cambridge University Press).

H. Kennedy (1979) James Mills Peirce and the cult of quaternions. *Historia Mathematica* **6**, 423–9. (Gives references to papers on the quaternion/vector controversy.)

P. M. Morse & H. Feshbach (1953) *Methods of Theoretical Physics*, part I, ch. 1 (McGraw-Hill, New York). (Spinors, quaternions and special relativity.)

L. Nový (1973) *Origins of Modern Algebra* (Academia, Prague). (Surveys developments in the first half of the nineteenth century.)

D. Quadling (1979) Q for quaternions. *Mathematical Gazette* **63**, 98–110. (Quaternions and rotations.)

CHAPTER 8

C. B. Boyer (1968) *A History of Mathematics* (Wiley, New York).

E. J. Dijksterhuis (1957) *Archimedes* (Humanities Press, New York).

O. Toeplitz (1963) *The Calculus – A Genetic Approach* (University of Chicago Press). (Historical introduction to the ideas of the calculus.)

CHAPTER 9

C. B. Boyer (1959) *History of the Calculus* (Dover, New York).

J. M. Dubbey (1978) *Development of Modern Mathematics* (Butterworths, London). (See chs. 2 and 3 for British mathematics 1800–30 and the Analytical Society.)

C. H. Edwards (1979) *The Historical Development of the Calculus* (Springer, New York). (Gives a fuller account of many topics treated here.)

G. H. Hardy (1949) *Divergent Series* (Clarendon Press, Oxford). (See pp. 18–20 for remarks on British analysis in the early nineteenth century.)

M. S. Mahoney (1973) *The Mathematical Career of Pierre de Fermat* (Princeton University Press).

CHAPTER 10

I. Grattan-Guinness (1972) *Joseph Fourier 1768–1830* (MIT Press, Cambridge, Mass.).

H. J. Keisler (1976) *Elementary Calculus* (Prindle, Weber and Schmidt, Boston, Mass.). (A 'non-standard' first course.)

B. B. Mandelbrot (1977) *Fractals* (Freeman, San Francisco). (Many examples of non-differentiable curves and other irregular configurations, with excellent illustrations.)

A. Robinson (1966) *Non-standard Analysis* (North-Holland, Amsterdam). (Highly technical, with a historical chapter.)

N. Ya. Vilenkin (1968) *Stories about Sets* (Academic Press, New York). (Entertaining account of the 'surprises' in set theory.)

CHAPTER 11

P. J. Cohen (1966) *Set Theory and the Continuum Hypothesis* (W. A. Benjamin, New York). (A technical but very clear account.)

J. H. Conway (1976) *On Numbers and Games* (Academic Press, London). (Highly technical.)

J. W. Dauben (1979) *Georg Cantor* (Harvard University Press, Cambridge, Mass.). (Full account of life, work and ideas.)

D. E. Knuth (1974) *Surreal Numbers* (Addison-Wesley, Reading, Mass.) (Entertaining popular introduction to Conway's system.)

S. K. Stein (1976) *Mathematics, the Man-Made Universe* (3rd edn) (Freeman, San Francisco).

INDEX